THE REFERENCE SHELF

Volume XVII

No.
4. Representative American Speeches: 1943-1944. A. C. Baird. $1.25.

No.
5. Lowering the Voting Age. J. E. Johnsen. $1.25.

Volume XVI

No.
1. Representative American Speeches: 1941-1942. A. C. Baird. $1.25.
2. Plans for a Postwar World. J. E. Johnsen. $1.25.
3. Independence for India. J. E. Johnsen. $1.25.

No.
6. Representative American Speeches: 1942-1943. A. C. Baird. $1.25.
7. Reconstituting the League of Nations. J. E. Johnsen. $1.25.

Volume XV

No.
1. Representative American Speeches: 1940-1941. A. C. Baird. $1.25.
2. Universal Military Service. R. E. Summers and H. B. Summers. $1.25.
3. Federal Regulation of Labor Unions. J. V. Garland. $1.25.

No.
6. Wages and Prices. R. E. Summers. $1.25.
7. The Closed Shop. J. E. Johnsen. $1.25.
9. Permanent Price Control Policy. J. E. Johnsen. $1.25.
10. A Federal Sales Tax. E. R. Nichols. $1.25.

Volume XIV

No.
1. Representative American Speeches: 1939-1940. A. C. Baird. $1.50.
2. Interstate Trade Barriers. J. E. Johnsen. $1.25.
6. Compulsory Military Training. J. E. Johnsen. $1.25.

No.
8. International Federation of Democracies. J. E. Johnsen. $1.25.
9. Debate Index. Supplement. J. E. Johnsen. 75c.

Volume XIII

No.
4. Europe: Versailles to Warsaw. R. S. Kain. $1.25.
5. Public Housing in America. M. B. Schnapper. $1.25.
6. United States Foreign Policy (Supplement) J. E. Johnsen. 75c.

No.
9. The National Labor Relations Act. Should It Be Amended? J. E. Johnsen. $1.25.
10. Trade Unions and the Anti-Trust Laws. J. E. Johnsen. $1.25.

THE REFERENCE SHELF

Vol. 22   No. 3

REPRESENTATIVE AMERICAN SPEECHES: 1949-1950

Edited, and with introductions,
by
A. CRAIG BAIRD
Department of Speech, State University of Iowa

THE H. W. WILSON COMPANY
NEW YORK   1950

641

PREFATORY NOTE

REPRESENTATIVE AMERICAN SPEECHES: 1949-1950 is the thirteenth in this annual series. Each volume contains some twenty-five "representative" speeches, delivered by Americans, or by others temporarily here (e.g. Madame Chiang Kai-shek, Winston Churchill). The thirteen volumes include 388 addresses by some 218 orators.

The speeches are grouped according to content, such as International Policies, Hydrogen Bomb, National Defense, Industry and Labor, Education. An alternate classification, based upon speech types of occasions, is also suggested, such as speeches of introduction, those of legislative bodies, executive statements, courtroom, pulpit, radio, luncheon or dinner gatherings, political conventions, professional meetings.

These divisions, whether based on content or on speech occasions, obviously overlap. A speech on foreign policy may also have to do with national defense or the theory of democratic government. A radio talk may be also a political address, one of introduction, farewell, or eulogy. The tentative classifications help students interested in contemporary problems or those concerned with speeches as models for original compositions.

This editor, as he has done in the previous volumes, disavows any assumption that these are the "best" speeches of the year, or that the combined group are the "best" of the decade. They are, he hopes, "representative" or "typical" of the kind and quality of the American public utterances of a given period. Most are "important" in that they deal with issues that have affected millions of Americans. Some of these speeches, especially those of outstanding national leaders in periods of crisis, have probably influenced the direction of recent American history.

The Introduction to each of these thirteen volumes expounds some phase of speech criticism. Together these partial treatments constitute a well-developed body of speech theory.

A brief introduction accompanies each speech. The background and immediate occasion, issues, ideas, structure, organization, language, audience adaptation, immediate results of the speaking are suggested. These comments, without pretense of completeness, aim to stimulate the student to further research on the speech. The assumption of this critic is that speech is for social adaptation; that it springs from immediate situations; and that the attitudes and trends of American life of 1949-50 are partly revealed through the speeches of this volume.

The biographical notes in the Appendix are of necessity much condensed. The investigator should explore fully the biography of each speaker, especially his intellectual background, his experiences, his personality, and previous speaking record. Such information may well help in the proper appreciation and evaluation of a given speech of 1949 or 1950.

The Table of Contents of each edition and the Cumulated Author Index at the end of this volume are further means of surveying issues and speakers of the period of 1937-1950. Since speakers are often included in successive years (e.g. President Truman since 1945), a review of his performances as reported in the earlier collections will be most helpful.

This volume, like the earlier ones, is a reference source for the study of contemporary American problems; a partial record of the history of recent months; a collection of material for courses in debate and extempore speaking; a series of speeches for the systematic study of contemporary American public address; and a series of examples of how to proceed with one's own speech composition. Each volume, then, in addition to its service as a library reference, is especially recommended to students of extempore speaking, communication, debate, social science, history, and general public speaking.

The editor here expresses his great debt to various speakers for their uniform courtesy in supplying authentic texts and in granting permission for publication. He is also grateful to publishers and organizations that have permitted reprinting of the texts. Specific acknowledgement is made in the footnotes accompanying the speeches.

A. CRAIG BAIRD

May 1, 1950

CONTENTS

INTRODUCTION

How Shall We Judge the Oral Language of a Speech?

How shall we judge the oral language or oral style of a speech?

Students of speechmaking have long agreed that the chief components of a speech include (1) thought, or ideas, (2) structure, or organization, (3) language or style, and (4) delivery. In previous Introductions to these annual collections I have discussed various aspects of rhetorical criticism.

The Introduction to the edition of 1948-1949, for example, includes a systematic series of suggestions concerning the criticism of ideas or thought as one of the basic elements of a speech. I propose here to summarize briefly the problem of language or style—the principles for its effective use, and the standards by which to judge its effectiveness in a given speech or speeches.

1. *The superior speaker is effective in his language usage.* His platform results may be due partly to his ideas, personality, delivery, rebuttal skill, anecdotal cleverness, or a combination of these and other factors. The more important contemporary speakers, however, including those in this volume, use language with uncommon readiness. To them words and phrases are no incidental factor in their speaking. John Foster Dulles, for example, uses much care in the composition of his speeches. He tries to state his ideas exactly. Outstanding speakers have been at home with word meanings. Webster, Phillips, Parker, Lincoln, Ingersoll, Grady, Bryan, Beveridge, Theodore Roosevelt, Wilson, and F. D. Roosevelt absorbed a good deal of the richness of the English vocabulary. Partly through their original and persuasive reflection of words and phrases, they produced powerful addresses.

2. *Language is closely related to the speaker's thought.* The thinking, we are told, is really not much wider than the thinker's vocabulary. One test of the breadth and depth of a given idea is the sharpness and completeness with which it has been form-

ulated in words. Although language is not identical with thought, the translation of mental activity into word symbols is "necessary for thinking and for communication." The words are thus an outward expression of these inner "thoughts."

3. *The speaker's language should correspond to his thought.* Obviously, your thoughts may pursue one highway; your words, another. Your inspired thoughts may soar; your language may remain below. Effective speaking, we assume, represents close identification of ideas and their expression. Sometimes, however, the wide gap is deliberate, as when a card-carrying Communist publicly rails against communism and eulogizes American democracy. Even when honest effort is made to translate ideas into equivalent language, the gulf may remain. Many meanings, as we know, attend a single word. Also each term has a different connotation to almost every hearer. Further, the limited vocabulary of a speaker may mean his failure to symbolize accurately his meanings. Nevertheless, good speaking demands that language move in the same channel with corresponding ideas. Only thus can a talker have much satisfaction in his utterances and only thus can his hearers be reasonably sure that they know what he is trying to say.

4. *Language should be for communication.* Speech aims at social control and social interaction. You are justified in talking only when you are attempting genuine communication. What are the factors of oral communication? They are (1) the initiation of an idea or ideas; (2) the formulation of the idea into symbolic equivalents—words; (3) the expression and interpretation of these word symbols through oral sounds and accompanying bodily activity; (4) the effective transmission by these visual-auditory means to an audience (one or more); (5) the appropriation by that audience of this communicated message and its reconstruction in their thinking; and (6) the completed response in belief, attitude, and action.

In such effective communication, language has a major role. Words must be no mere "blah-blah" of empty utterings. Nor must they be for mere showmanship. Rather the symbols must be selected and pronounced so as to aid in this clear broadcasting of ideas from speaker to recipient. Ideas as well as words should traverse the space and find recreation in the listener.

5. *The language should express effectively the speaker's purpose in communication.* What are the motives for communication? They are to inform; or to change belief; or to produce desired action; or to interest or entertain; or to impress and inspire; or to achieve any combination of these purposes. These aims, familiar to every student of speech, are also guiding principles for the selection and use of language. The necessity for information, for example, imposes on the vocabulary the requirement of absolute clarity; that of changing belief and conduct, or that of entertaining or impressing the auditor, calls for special skill in the selection of motivative (emotional and imaginative) language.

6. *The language should be closely adapted to the learning level, cultural background, experiences, beliefs and attitudes of the audience.* He who would address any group should be familiar with the personalities, cultural background, education, experiences, the beliefs and desires of these individuals. Such audience analysis will determine much of the speaker's vocabulary. Although the speechmaker will retain his usual habits of word selection, he will either talk only before audiences of which he is normally a part; or will either make satisfactory adjustments both in content and manner of expression, or will wisely remain silent.

The spoken language of each nationally prominent speaker has much in common with that of the others. Yet subtle differences appear as the discourse is directed to a specific audience. Note that in this volume the language employed in each case takes on somewhat the character of an audience on a specific occasion. Eisenhower at Columbia is lecturing to a Morningside Heights group; Judge Medina, in the courtroom in Foley Square, talks to the jury. President Truman, rising before five thousand Democratic diners, frames ideas so as to enlist the attention of that vast dinner party. So General Omar Bradley, Dean James McBurney, H. V. Kaltenborn, Philip Murray—each shapes his discourse to secure the maximum response from the special audience, for example, CIO unionists, speech teachers, Armed Services' Committee of the House of Representatives.

This principle does not mean that the specialist-lecturer on chemistry should abandon, before fellow chemists, his technical vocabulary. Neither does it imply that before a lay audience he should stick to his professional terms. Language, to be efficient, should be pitched to the understanding of the group, and we can judge the validity of that language only as we note its relation to the character of its hearers.

7. *The language should be accurate.* Accuracy is first of all a problem of absolute clearness. "Do I understand what the speaker is saying?" If he is wise, he will often insert repeated definitions. But beyond such clarity is a question of the reliability of the statements. Most platform orators (and lesser talkers) exaggerate in their phrasing. "The greatest crime of modern civilization is the growth of the welfare state," is ill defined (*welfare state* means what?), vague, and all-inclusive. "Since Frenchmen are defeatists, that nation should not share in America's military aid to Europe," an assertion frequently heard in early 1950, fails to qualify Frenchmen. Much of public speech, especially political persuasion, is filled with obvious exaggeration and sweeping generalizations. "All" and "every" are used when "many" and "some" would be more accurate. Words and phrases, then, should be free from these unqualified assertions that astute listeners will condemn as simply untrue or grossly overstated.

8. *The language should be concrete.* Words range from the most concrete, those that label simple objects, to the most abstract designations, such as "virtue" and "humanity." Although we need not limit our speaking vocabulary to the first few hundred words used most frequently by the general population, we should not by-pass the fact that auditors respond most readily to word symbols that suggest concrete situations and experiences. "James Jeffrey" is more meaningful and interesting than "a man." "Democracy" and other ideological political terms will also benefit if translated into more tangible equivalents.

For abstract terms, may well be substituted specific days, figures, instances, dialogues, direct quotations. Important speeches, including most of those in this volume, would be improved by a recasting for more concreteness.

9. *The language should be concise.* Herbert Spencer's argument for "economy of style"—that no more words should be used than are necessary—is to the point. Many radio talks and

debates in the House of Representatives are limited to five minutes. Not much excuse is there for long speeches elsewhere.

Conciseness is the opposite of garrulity and verbosity. Speech marathons have no justification. Compactness, nevertheless, does not imply a telegraphic style. The test of effective conciseness is, "Does the speaker say enough (but no more), in view of audience requirements, to establish his idea and the accompanying motivative responses?"

10. *The language should be varied and unhackneyed.* Audiences become bored with continual clichés. The good speaker who would keep his auditors awake and responsive will constantly prune from his style the worn out slogans, quotations, epithets, figures of speech, and threadbare words. The speeches of our day, in their effort to say things plainly, usually fall into conventionality of phrasing. The result is stylistic baldness, mediocrity, and dullness. The superior speakers are sensitive to fresh expression. Without being smartly journalistic, or obviously clever, the good talkers appeal through language that has marks of distinction from a million other speeches on the same theme.

11. *The language should be connotative as well as denotative.* The combinations of words should convey much meaning beyond the literal signification. Audiences are moved by emotion and imagination as well as by logic and fact, persuaded as well as convinced. The style, therefore, should be enlivened with analogies, similes, metaphors, personifications—forms that call up pictures and suggest much beyond the literal meanings. Here, as in other language usages, we are not implying that phrases and niceties of expression are for decorative purposes alone. The test is in the utility of language to realize the purpose of the discourse.

12. *Language should be oral.* The language should be that of talk rather than that of written literature. Platform speaking is heightened conversation. The language, like the delivery, should usually be direct, simple, lively, broken—as is good conversation. Pedantry and sentimentality are absent. Personal pronouns are frequent. The general movement is much more irregular than that of the written style. A certain rhetorical quality, repetition of phrases, balanced structure, asides, paren-

thetical interpolations, give the utterance a flavor and movement that set it off from the more orderly compositions that are chiefly designed for "permanence and beauty." Speech language is directly designed for a specific audience. The differences are those of degree rather than kind. Nevertheless these differences are well marked. Speakers, dealing with hearers, select materials and expression to that end. Word choice is controlled by the demands of an occasion. The choice will vary from audience to audience. "Essential marks of the oral style must, therefore, be determined in the light of the peculiar medium in which speech functions." [1]

13. *Effective sentence structure aids materially in securing the desired audience response.* Proper syntax as well as wise word selection is essential to effective oral style. Bad grammar and syntax are obvious blocks to satisfactory communication. Various sentence types have their function in informing and stimulating hearers. Short and long sentences, for example, both have their use in the process of defining, discriminating, emphasizing. Sentence choppiness gives thinness to the style and destroys rhythm. Periodic, loose, balanced structure, transitional and summarizing sentences properly phrased and incorporated in the text, contribute to clarity, interest, persuasiveness. Imperative, exclamatory, and interrogative types are natural modes of expressing aroused feeling. They suggest suitable conduct to the auditor, stimulate him to give answers (those desired by the questioner), and carry him along a logical emotional current.

Most speeches with rhetorical resourcefulness are more than a succession of declarative sentences. The stimulus of the audience and the orator's own platform purposes will inspire him to a variety of stylistic modes, including varied sentence structure, in keeping with the subject, the occasion, and the temper of the assembly.

14. *The larger units of the speech are to be composed with proper appreciation of the values of the speech structure.* Language and style are closely related to speech organization. Organic structure is an essential of every speech. The familiar units

---

[1] Thonssen, Lester and Baird, A. Craig. *Speech Criticism.* New York, Ronald . Press, 1948.   p427.

of introduction, body, and conclusion, with their subdivisions, are each to be developed with compositional skill. Unity, order, proportion, and interest govern also framing of these larger units, just as these principles help in the construction of phrases, clauses, and sentences.

Organization is an obvious mark of the good speech. To make that structure apparent and impressive is the problem of the speech composer. The introduction, for example, may or may not include personal reference, striking questions, reference to the occasion, statement of issues, quotation, or simple narrative, according to the subject, the speaker's goals, and the time, place, and other limitations of the occasion. So the main body and the conclusion will be constructed to secure stylistic appropriateness.

15. *The style is the man.* Language should be individual. Your words, if they really represent your thinking and ways of communication, will stamp your discourse as highly personal. Out of your background, education, emotional and intellectual attitudes will your language or style emerge. Your reserve, humor, informality, deductive or inductive appraisals of ideas, your tendencies to abstract thinking or to amplified illustration, your saturation in Biblical or other literature, all modify and illumine—or should—your methods of expression. Thus F. D. Roosevelt, Churchill, Hoover, Truman, Conant, Hancher, Sockman, Sheen have their style. More important than skill in using the machinery of correct English is the problem of retaining and developing individual habits of thought and expression that reveal the personality of the orator himself.

Text Authenticity and Completeness

Editors of speeches are always confronted with the problem, "Did the speaker write the speech which he delivers?" Ghost writers abound. Nevertheless it is hoped that the speeches here included were in general composed by those who gave them before audiences. Often "fact gatherers," consultants, and transscribers have contributed, but the personal quality of the document itself and other internal evidence support my assumption of originality of authorship.

A kindred problem is that of the completeness of the document. "Did the speaker say more than is reported in the text? Or did he say less (as in *Congressional Record* House or Senate debates printed in an Appendix)?" Wherever feasible, I have inserted the complete text. In Senate debates of several hours in length, for example, the Taft-Dulles debate; in court room speeches, as Judge Medina's two-hour instructions to the jury; in hearings before Senate or House Committees, for example, General Bradley's long testimony; in extended lectures, such as Dewey's four lectures at Princeton, and Eisenhower's at Columbia, I have been able to include only a part of the complete document. I can only hope that the reader of this volume will follow through, reading in the *Congressional Record*, or elsewhere, to appreciate fully the breadth and depth of the speaker's thinking.

INTERNATIONAL POLICIES

THE NORTH ATLANTIC PACT [1]

ROBERT A. TAFT, JOHN FOSTER DULLES [2]

Senator Robert A. Taft gave this Senate speech against the North Atlantic Treaty on July 11, 1949. The next day Senator John Foster Dulles replied. He had been appointed by Governor Thomas E. Dewey of New York to fill the vacancy caused by the resignation of Robert F. Wagner, and had been formally inducted into his Senate office on July 8th. To engage in a major speech within three days after entrance to the Senate was breaking with long-time precedent.

What were the specific issues in this historic debate? At Brussels, on March 17, 1948, Britain, France and the Benelux countries (Belgium, Netherlands, and Luxembourg) had signed an agreement for collective defense. Agitation for America's participation began immediately. On April 4, 1949, the foreign ministers of twelve countries, including Italy, Canada, Denmark, Norway, Portugal, and the United States, assembled in Washington, D.C., and signed a mutual defense pact of fourteen articles.

Article 3 pledged mutual aid to resist attack. Article 5 stated that "armed attack against one or more shall be considered attack against them all." In case of such attack, each was to "take such action as it deems necessary, including the use of armed force, to restore and maintain the security of the North Atlantic area."

On July 5 the Senate debate on the treaty began. Taft and others argued that (1) the treaty takes from Congress the war-making power and gives it to the President; (2) the treaty commits this country to arming the other members of the pact—the treaty and arms program are one; (3) an arms program of this kind will be a heavy drain financially; (4) it will certainly promote hostility and might lead to war with the Soviets.

Dulles, Vandenberg, and other supporters of the pact argued that (1) the instrument is one of concrete power—the only force sufficient to deter Soviet aggression; and (2) the arms program is not identical with the treaty.

Senator Taft's argument, like that of his other debates, was closely reasoned and expressed in comparatively unemotional language. He in-

[1] For the Taft speech, see *Congressional Record* (81st Congress, 2nd session) 95:9383, 9392, July 11, 1949 (daily edition); for that of Dulles, see 95:9492, 9502, July 12, 1949 (daily edition). A portion only of this extended debate is here reprinted.

[2] For biographical notes, see Appendix.

terpreted the document as a lawyer would. It meant to him a military alliance. He attempted to assess the results, financially, politically, and militarily, of the commitment.[3]

His debate speech was chiefly a refutation of the long series of arguments over the air and to the nation on this subject since April 1949. As he concluded, six of his fellow Republicans stood and applauded. The speech was one of Taft's strongest.

Senator Dulles, in his turn, accused Taft of raising "false and dangerous interpretations" of the proposed treaty. The Ohio Senator interrupted with many questions and replies. It was "one of the most heavily attended Senate debates in recent years." [4]

Like Taft, Dulles gave a scholarly analysis of the document, reviewed its history, and justified it as essential if war is to be averted. Taft accused Dulles of drawing "fine distinctions" and refusing to be candid about the obligations imposed by the treaty.

Taft's position, although logical, was held to be in contradiction to his own statements as given on February 20, 1949. His outspoken argument of July 11 was also regarded as a hard blow to the Vandenberg-Truman bipartisan foreign policy and as indicating a split in the Republican leadership. Taft's voting record on foreign policy would indicate that, as of this period, he was vacillating—"a Hamlet who cannot make up his mind." The strongest criticism of Taft was that he implied a retreat before Russian threats and a tendency, undesigned by him, to support "division and disarmament" of Western Europe.

On July 21st, the Senate, after rejecting reservation proposals, ratified the document, 82 to 13, thus with the two-thirds necessary majority. Two Democrats and eleven Republicans opposed—among them Taft, K. S. Wherry of Nebraska, E. C. Johnson of Colorado, G. H. Taylor of Idaho, W. N. Langer of North Dakota, W. E. Jenner of Indiana, R. E. Flanders of Vermont, and F. C. Donnell of Missouri.

For the first time in history, the nation was committed to the principle that its frontiers were in Europe.[5]

Later Congress ratified a bill, the Military Assistance Program (MAP), committing us during the first year to more than a billion dollars worth of equipment to increase the twelve nations' ability to resist Soviet aggression.

Taft is a mature debater rather than an orator. He speaks rapidly, sometimes tightens his voice, elevates the pitch unnecessarily, but convinces by his reasoning.[6]

Mr. Dulles, defeated in November 1949, by Herbert H. Lehman in the New York Senate campaign, prepares speeches with much care. Ob-

[3] See *Representative American Speeches: 1948-1949*, p 15-26.
[4] William S. White, in the New York *Times*, July 13, 1949.
[5] See *Representative American Speeches: 1948-1949*, p 15-26.
[6] For references to Taft's speeches in previous volumes of *Representative American Speeches*, consult the Cumulated Author Index at the end of this volume.

servers state that he spends many days in thought and in gathering material before he begins dictating to a secretary. He observes that he never repeats a speech. "He believes that there must be mental progression at all times and that each succeeding speech should represent an advance in thinking." [7]

His delivery and approach to an audience are those of the trained lawyer. "Seldom does he reply hastily to a new question," although he stood up very well under the sharp cross examination in the Senate on July 12th. His voice is well modulated. He uses few gestures, and is no impassioned orator.

MR. TAFT. Mr. President, I listened with great interest to the speech made today by the distinguished Senator from Iowa [Mr. Gillette]. I wish to assure the Senate that I have not consulted with the Senator from Iowa; but the arguments I shall make against the Atlantic Pact are very similar to the ones he made, and I agree thoroughly with the very effective argument and very effective speech he made on that subject. However, the same arguments have led me to the conclusion that I must vote against the pact, rather than for it, as he has announced he intends to do.

It is with great regret that I have come to my conclusion, but I have come to it because I think the pact carries with it an obligation to assist in arming, at our expense, the nations of western Europe, because with that obligation I believe it will promote war in the world rather than peace, and because I think that with the arms plan it is wholly contrary to the spirit of the obligations we assumed in the United Nations Charter. I would vote for the pact if a reservation were adopted denying any legal or moral obligation to provide arms. . . .

I have come reluctantly to the conclusion, therefore, that the arms program now presented to Congress must be considered an integral part of the Atlantic Treaty.

If that is the fact, we have a very different problem from the one which is urged upon us by the Committee on Foreign Relations, by its distinguished chairman, by the State Department, and by the distinguished Senator from Michigan.

[7] Statement from the headquarters of the Commission on a Just and Durable Peace, New York, 1950.

First. With the arms in the pact it is even more clear that the pact is a military alliance, a treaty by which one nation undertakes to arm half the world against the other half, and in which all the pact members agree to go to war if one is attacked. It cannot be described otherwise than a military alliance. Of course, it is not like some of the alliances in the past, although many of them, such as the Franco-British Alliance prior to World War I, were entirely defensive in character, or purported to be. Others were offensive and defensive alliances. I quite agree that the purpose of this alliance is not offensive, and that we have no offensive purpose in mind. But it is exactly like many defensive military alliances of the past.

Second. The pact standing by itself would clearly be a deterrent to war. If Russia knows that if it starts a war it will immediately find itself at war with the United States, it is much less likely to start a war. I see and believe in the full force of that argument. That is why I would favor the extension of the Monroe Doctrine to Europe. But if Russia sees itself ringed about gradually by so-called defensive arms, from Norway and Denmark to Turkey and Greece, it may form a different opinion. It may decide that the arming of western Europe, regardless of its present purpose, looks to an attack upon Russia. Its view may be unreasonable, and I think it is. But from the Russian standpoint it may not seem unreasonable. They may well decide that if war is the certain result, that war might better occur now rather than after the arming of Europe is completed. In 1941, Secretary Hull sent a message to Japan in the nature of an ultimatum which said, in effect, that if Japan did not withdraw from China, sooner or later they would face a war with the United States. The Japanese appear to have concluded that if ultimately there was to be such a war, it was to their interest to have it occur at once.

Third. The pact with the arms obligation, I believe, violates our obligations under the United Nations. The pact apparently is not made under articles 52 to 54 inclusive, because we do not propose to consult the Security Council as there contemplated, we do plan to take enforcement action without the authorization of the Security Council, and we do not plan to keep them fully informed. The pact must, therefore, be supported under article 51, which says:

Nothing in the present Charter shall impair the inherent right of individual or collective self-defense if an armed attack occurs against a member of the United Nations, until the Security Council has taken the measures necessary to maintain international peace and security. . . .

Fourth. The obligation to furnish arms is either a mere token obligation, or it is one of vast extent. I do not know enough about modern military equipment to make any estimate. I have heard that to provide sixty divisions, which is said to be the very minimum necessary and perhaps completely inadequate against Russian attack, would cost a total of $24 billion. We are entering on a new lend-lease. The history of these obligations has been that once begun, they cannot be easily brought to an end. Furthermore if the Russian threat justifies arms for all of western Europe, surely it justifies similar arms for Nationalist China, for Indochina, for India, and ultimately for Japan; and in the Near East for Iran, for Syria, and for Iraq. There is no limit to the burden of such a program, or its dangerous implications.

Fifth. The justification for the arms aid rests on the necessity of defense against Russia, but remember that once these arms are provided, they are completely within the control of the nation receiving them. They are subject to the orders of those who, at the time, control the government of the country. Those governors may be Communists or Fascists, they may be peace loving, or they may be aggressors. In furture years, these arms may be used against us instead of on our side. If Russia should choose to go to war within the next year or two, they might easily be captured by the Russians and turned against us. We would be playing a dangerous game if we encouraged every country in Europe to arm itself to the teeth. Modern arms are not toys.

Sixth. By approving this pact with the arms program, I believe we are committing ourselves to a particular course of action in war which may be unwise at the time when a war may actually develop. It is one thing to agree to go to war with

Russia if it attacks western Europe. It is another to send American ground troops to defend Norway or Denmark or Holland or Italy or even France and England. I cannot assert positively that we are committing ourselves to a particular type of war, but I am inclined to think that we are. Thus, General Bradley testified before the committee:

> Finally, after studied appraisal of the future security provisions for our country, the Joint Chiefs of Staff are in unanimous agreement that our strategy, in case we are attacked—

And that means if any member country is attacked, if we ratify this pact—

> must rely on sufficient integrated forces of land, sea, and air power to carry the war back to the aggressor, ultimately subjugating the sources of his military and industrial power. Plans for the common defense of the existing free world must provide for the security of western Europe without abandoning these countries to the terrors of another enemy occupation. Only upon that premise can nations closest to the frontiers be expected to stake their fortunes with ours in the common defense.

This appears to contemplate a land war with Russia on the continent of Europe. It appears to contemplate an invasion along the lines which Napoleon and Hitler found to be impossible. It asserts clearly that the nations which signed this pact expect us to send American troops to defend their frontiers.

If this is their expectation, I think we are promising something we cannot do, as I said earlier. I see no way in which we could defend Italy, for it is not even permitted to have an army of its own. The defense of Norway and Denmark would probably be impossible and, if we are bound to do it, may result in the loss of thousands of American lives. It may be that we should conduct a war on the Continent of Europe, even though it involves again the sending of millions of American boys to fight Russians who, on land, will outnumber them four to one. But I do not think we should commit ourselves at the present time to any such program or make any such promise to our allies. We may find, if war ever comes, that our part in the war should be conducted from the air alone. We may find that the occupation of an enemy country is vain and useless if the war can be won otherwise, by the destruction of all of their military potentials. We should not commit ourselves by the ratification of this pact to the military assistance program and the plan of campaign which has apparently been promised the members of the pact.

Seventh. Finally, Mr. President, it is becoming increasingly apparent that England, at least, intends to trade extensively with Russia, and inevitably the same thing will be true of other western European nations. They have provided airplane engines for Russia, heavy machinery and other equipment which can aid the Russians' war-making potential. The more we take off their shoulders the burden of providing for their own defense, the more free they will be to ship steel and heavy machinery to the east. As a matter of fact, trade between eastern and western Europe has prevailed for thousands of years, and it is going to go on, no matter what we say about it. Of course, the recent agreement between Russia and England is very clear evidence of that fact. We are providing extensive economic assistance. To a large extent, economic assistance and aid for arms will go into the same pot. I do not think that the American people at this time desire to increase the over-all aid we are giving to western Europe with its tremendous burden on the American taxpayer.

Mr. President, since I feel that this pact is inextricably linked with the arms program, and since I believe that, so linked, the program is a threat to the welfare of the people of the United States, I shall vote against the treaty.

I am quite willing to consider the providing of assistance to particular countries, at particular times, if such aid seems at that time a real deterrent to war, and on that principle I voted for aid to Greece and Turkey. But that is a very different thing from an obligation to build up the armed forces of eleven countries, and a commitment on the American taxpayer for twenty years to give continued aid under circumstances of which we have not the slightest conception today. It is a very different thing from arming half the world against the other half.

My conclusion has been reached with the greatest discomfort. When so many disagree with that conclusion, I must admit that

I may be completely wrong. I do not claim to be an expert in questions of foreign policy. I would like to be able to vote for a policy that will commit us to war if Russia attacks western Europe. I would be glad to join in an agreement to occupy Germany indefinitely to guard against a third attack from that quarter. I would waive my other objections to the Atlantic Pact if I did not feel that it was inextricably involved with the arms program. But I cannot escape the logic of the situation as I see it, and therefore I cannot vote for a treaty which, in my opinion, will do far more to bring about a third world war than it will ever do to maintain the peace of the world.

MR. DULLES. Mr. President, I am hesitant about speaking so soon. I feel that I am still wrapped in senatorial swaddling clothes rather than in a senatorial toga. But several Senators, both Republicans and Democrats, have been good enough to suggest that I should express myself about the North Atlantic Treaty before the debate closes. Those suggestions reflect the spirit of cordial reception which has welcomed me here, for which I am profoundly grateful, and by which I have been deeply moved. I say with all sincerity that I speak very humbly before Senators who, over the recent years, have dealt so wisely and constructively with the great problems of war and peace that have come before them.

During much of this period, and almost constantly since early in 1945, I have been in attendance at international conferences, seeking to establish a just and durable peace. The task has not been easy and there have been moments when another war was perilously near. But at last there has been evolved a strategy for peace in the west which I am confident will succeed if it is pushed vigorously to its full conclusion. The North Atlantic Treaty is one of the essential ingredients of that over-all strategy for peace. I shall give my understanding of the North Atlantic Pact from that viewpoint. . . .

There are some who hesitate to accept this commitment to organize the Atlantic community, because they believe it will require us to undertake a militaristic program for rearming the nations of western Europe. Of course, Mr. President, there is not a word in the North Atlantic Treaty that expresses any such obligation. The pending military-aid program does not even purport to be an implementation of the Atlantic Treaty, as the State Department's statement, read here yesterday by the Senator from Michigan [Mr. Vanderberg] made evident. Article 3 of the treaty does contemplate developing a collective capacity to resist armed attack and mutual aid in that respect, and Article 9 of the treaty provides for a council and for a defense committee which are to make recommendations regarding implementation of Article 3. What those recommendations will be, no one here can possibly know, for there is as yet no treaty, there is as yet no council, there is as yet no defense committee, and there are as yet no recommendations.

What we do know is that when the council exists and the defense committee exists, and when the recommendations are made, they will be only recommendations. That is specific in the treaty. When those recommendations are made, they will, I assume, be considered on their merits. If the recommendations seem to be advantageous, I assume we will accept them. If they appear to be disadvantageous, we are certainly free to reject them, and I assume and hope we shall reject them. Certainly the treaty gives no other nation or group of nations a blank check on the United States. That, it seems to me, is a preposterous and dangerous interpretation of the treaty, and I think it needs to be made perfectly clear that those who vote for the treaty totally reject that interpretation.

I find in the treaty no obligation, legal or moral, to vote for any armament program or for any item of any armament program unless it be meritorious in its own right.

Mr. President, the opponents of the treaty, in addition to assuming that it gives other parties a blank check on the United States, seem also to assume that the collective defense contemplated by the treaty will be more monumental and more militaristic than the total of twelve separate defenses. I confess that I have been surprised by that argument, for I myself have assumed precisely the contrary. I have supported the treaty because, in my opinion, it will make it possible to reduce the very heavy burden of military expenditure which our nation is now carrying.

I came to that conclusion because it seemed to me that the political commitment of the treaty, one for all and all for one, would itself greatly reduce the risk of war. No nation will be likely to assault the combined resources and facilities of twelve nations and the 350 million people who make up this Atlantic community. If the risk of war is reduced, the cost of insurance against that risk should be likewise reducible; and if the 350 million people each carries a fair share of the common defense, then surely that should be less burdensome to each than for each to attempt it alone. Instead of multiplying military establishments, the treaty should reduce them to diversifying and spreading the responsibility.

I am profoundly convinced that the North Atlantic Treaty, if it be ratified, will make it possible at long last to begin to realize the Atlantic Charter promise to lighten for peace-loving peoples the crushing load of armament. That is the way the treaty should work, once it gets into operation, and that is the way I believe the proponents of the treaty intend that it shall work. They do not intend or expect that the treaty shall work in the way its opponents propose. I think it is important to disabuse the other parties to the treaty of any illusion they might have come under as a result of hearing some features of the debate, that the United States Senate interprets the treaty as giving them a right to draw freely upon the United States for their own independent military establishments.

Mr. President, I have a feeling of regret that in all this debate we deal with it so much in a spirit that assumes that under the treaty we are to be the benefactor and others the beneficiaries. We are constantly talking about what we are going to do for others, but we have talked very little about what others are, through this treaty, going to do for us.

The prime minister of one of the gallant small countries of Europe recently said to me:

If we are attacked, it will be this time because we are your allies and friends; we are no longer an important target of ourselves.

That, Mr. President, is, I think, a fair estimate of the situation, and I think it is worth something to us that there are brave people close to danger who are willing, if need be, to absorb the first shock of devastating attack because they believe in the things in which we believe and want to show solidarity with us. Mr. President, I feel that it is not right to treat such people as mendicants.

Of course, it is never possible to know in advance that legislative authority such as is given for European economic recovery or for the common defense of the Atlantic community will, in fact, be used by the Executive to the best advantage and in the spirit intended by the Congress. I think we must frankly recognize, for example, that under the European recovery program there has been little progress in achieving in Europe a broad market and the reduction of currency and customs barriers which were the great goal.

Some, notably in England, want to limit international trade to a bilateral, governmental bartering of hard goods. That is properly a matter of deep concern to us, for it strikes at the heart of our anti-Communist strategy which depends on increased unity as the fountain for increased vigor.

Despite such setbacks, which are to be expected, and which, in my opinion, can be and must be overcome, the results to date under the European Recovery Act have fully justified the initial appropriations. Future appropriations remain subject to Congressional control and to the provision of the act that the continuity of American aid is dependent upon continuity of cooperation as between the European participants.

It is conceivable that, in the future, some of the parties to the North Atlantic Treaty might seek to pervert it by building up great military establishments and bringing about an armament race. If that happened it would, in my opinion, be a grievous distortion of the intent and purpose of the pact. But—and this is vital—that cannot occur under the treaty without our consent, and the Congress, through its control of appropriations, has that situation under its control.

In any great enterprise there are risks and possibilities of abuse. Such risks have to be taken to defeat the dynamism of Soviet communism. The greatest risk of all is the risk of doing nothing, for the dynamic always prevails against the static. When I say that, I do not say it as an apology for recklessness. Of course, it devolves upon us to seek scrupulously, painstakingly, to perfect and safeguard our programs before we act. The Committee on Foreign Relations has done a great task in this respect, and it has clarified some dangerous ambiguities that were found in the text. But in the end there comes a time for action, and that is where we now are.

Mr. President, no charter, no constitution, no treaty, can be judged merely by its words. Never was there an international instrument which expressed such lofty and noble sentiments as that which created the Holy Alliance. The Soviet constitution is replete with guaranties of human rights, freedom of speech and press, and of religious worship.

This North Atlantic Treaty purports to be an undertaking by the members of the Atlantic community to work together to safeguard free institutions, individual liberty, and the rule of law. Certainly that is a noble purpose. Already, even before its ratification, the treaty has brought new hope to our friends and new discomfiture to those who wish us ill.

Of course, I know that the North Atlantic Treaty has defects and that there are possibilities of abuse. It is not drafted precisely as I would have it. I know that it could be used as an instrument of militarism or to sabotage the United Nations. I have thought of all the horrid possibilities that have been suggested here—and then some. However, at this stage the decision must be made primarily as an act of faith—or lack of faith—in the American people. It is they who will determine whether this instrument is used for good or for evil. Because there are great possibilities of good, because the need is urgent, and because I have faith in the American people, I support the treaty.

All the world is watching to see what we do here. They have seen tension mount. Means of mass destruction are being feverishly developed, and there is conceded risk that mankind may be plunged into an awful abyss. Hundreds of millions, including our own people and peoples throughout the world, look to our nation as alone possessing the combination of material and moral power needed to lead humanity out of the present peril. That places upon us a great responsibility.

There are those, some deeply devoted to the cause of peace, who would swerve away from any line of effort that is cast in a military mold. But unfortunately no program will suffice unless it provides men with a sense of security as against the menace of those who exalt ways of violence and practice the use of terror.

The North Atlantic Treaty, as I said in the beginning, is not an isolated act. The union of our States was also a measure for common defense, but it was far more than that. Common defense is a part, a necessary part, of every organized community, but it is not the whole. Admiral Mahan said that the function of force in human affairs is to give moral ideas the opportunity to take root. I am confident that the North Atlantic Treaty will never be regarded as an all-sufficient end in itself. Rather, it can provide the opportunity for our spiritual faith to reassert itself in practices that will enlarge men's equal opportunity to develop, morally, intellectually, and materially. That is the core of our new program for peace. I am confident that the individual men and women who make up our citizenry understand that, and that they, with others, can be trusted to infuse into this treaty a spirit which will make it a living instrument for righteousness and peace.

STATE OF THE UNION [8]

HARRY S. TRUMAN [9]

President Harry S. Truman read his "State of the Union" address of six-thousand words before a joint session of the Senate and the House of Representatives, in the newly refurbished chamber of the House, at one o'clock, on January 4, 1950. Present were also the cabinet, ambassadors, ministers, and other distinguished guests. When the President walked down the aisle he received a rising ovation, and when Samuel Rayburn, Speaker of the House, introduced him.

The later frequent applause was obviously more partisan than general. His reference to the "ill considered tax reduction of the Eightieth Congress" brought forth good natured protests and laughter from the Republicans and loud cheers and applause from the Democrats.

The speech repeated the usual Truman New Deal and Fair Deal recommendations concerning taxes, business, agriculture, labor, social security, health, education, housing, military service, European Recovery program, and power resources.

The President was unusually optimistic. Some Republicans called the speech "sweetness and light" and described it as having a "hearts and flowers" refrain. Widely discussed, for example, was the section in which the President envisioned the year 2000 A.D. as a time when the American standards of living could be measured by an annual famliy income of some $12,000 ("about three times what it is today").

The Democrats, for example, Senator Herbert H. Lehman of New York, pronounced it a most able state document. The proposals for social welfare led Republicans to call the address a "soak-the-rich salestalk" (Senator William E. Jenner). Two hours after the address, the Republican Congressmen issued a statement (signed by 105 of 169) denouncing the document as not one concerning "the State of the Union," but "the State of Socialism." "Here and there," remarked the statement, "he bows politely to American love for its traditional institutions, its free markets, and its free men. In reality he is embracing black reaction in new gladrags." [10]

The President when he speaks "off the cuff" is much better than when he reads from a manuscript. His delivery in his routine reading is often monotonous. He occasionally lacks a lively sense of communication. When he becomes aroused on the platform, however, his vocal emphasis

[8] Text supplied by the White House.
[9] For biographical note, see Appendix.
[10] New York *Times*, January 5, 1950, p 11.

increases, and his audience orientation and response are much more effective. He makes the best impression as a popular speaker when he becomes vocally the "fighting" leader of millions of Democratic followers.[11]

Mr. President, Mr. Speaker, Members of the Congress: A year ago I reported to this Congress that the state of the Union was good. I am happy to be able to report to you today that the state of the Union continues to be good. Our Republic continues to increase in the enjoyment of freedom within its borders, and to offer strength and encouragement to all those who love freedom throughout the world.

During the past year we have made notable progress in strengthening the foundations of peace and freedom, abroad and at home.

We have taken important steps in securing the North Atlantic community against aggression. We have continued our successful support of European recovery. We have returned to our established policy of expanding international trade through reciprocal agreement. We have strengthened our support of the United Nations.

While great problems still confront us, the greatest danger has receded—the possibility which faced us three years ago that most of Europe and the Mediterranean area might collapse under totalitarian pressure. Today, the free peoples of the world have new vigor and new hope for the cause of peace.

In our domestic affairs, we have made notable advances toward broader opportunity and a better life for all our citizens.

We have met and reversed the first significant downturn in economic activity since the war. In accomplishing this, government programs for maintaining employment and purchasing power have been of tremendous benefit. As the result of these programs, and the wisdom and good judgment of our businessmen and workers, major readjustments have been made without widespread suffering.

During the past year, we have also made a good start in providing housing for low-income groups; we have raised minimum wages; we have gone forward with the development of

[11] For other Truman speeches and comment, consult the Cumulated Author Index.

our natural resources; we have given greater assurance of stability to the farmer; and we have improved the organization and efficiency of our government.

Today, by the grace of God, we stand a free and prosperous nation with greater possibilities for the future than any people have ever had before.

We are now, in this year of 1950, nearing the midpoint of the twentieth century.

The first half of this century will be known as the most turbulent and eventful period in recorded history. The swift pace of events promises to make the next fifty years decisive in the history of man on this planet.

The scientific and industrial revolution which began two centuries ago has, in the last fifty years, caught up the peoples of the globe in a common destiny. Two world-shattering wars have proved that no corner of the earth can be isolated from the affairs of mankind.

The human race has reached a turning point. Man has opened the secrets of nature and mastered new powers. If he uses them wisely, he can reach new heights of civilization. If he uses them foolishly, they may destroy him.

Man must create the moral and legal framework for the world which will insure that his new powers are used for good and not for evil. In shaping the outcome, the people of the United States will play a leading role.

Among all the great changes that have occurred in the last fifty years, none is more important than the change in the position of the United States in world affairs. Fifty years ago, we were a country devoted largely to our own internal affairs. Our industry was growing, and we had new interests in the Far East and in the Caribbean, but we were primarily concerned with the development of vast areas of our own continental territory.

Today, our population has doubled. Our national production has risen from about $50 billion, in terms of today's prices, to the staggering figure of $255 billion a year. We have a more productive economic system and a greater industrial potential than any other nation on the globe. Our standard of living is an inspiration for all other peoples. Even the slightest changes in our economic and social life have their effect on other countries all around the world.

Our tremendous strength has brought with it tremendous responsibilities. We have moved from the outer edge to the center of world affairs. Other nations look to us for a wise exercise of our economic and military strength, and for vigorous support of the ideals of representative government and a free society. We will not fail them.

Our objective in the world is peace. Our country has joined with others in the task of achieving peace. We know now that this is not an easy task, or a short one. But we are determined to see it through. Both of our great political parties are committed to working together—and I am sure they will continue to work together—to achieve this end. We are prepared to devote our energy and our resources to this task, because we know that our own security and the future of mankind are at stake.

Our success in working with other nations to achieve peace depends largely on what we do at home. We must preserve our national strength. Strength is not simply a matter of arms and force. It is a matter of economic growth, and social health, and vigorous institutions, public and private. We can achieve peace only if we maintain our productive energy, our democratic institutions, and our firm belief in individual freedom.

Our surest guide in the days that lie ahead will be the spirit in which this great Republic was founded. We must make our decisions in the conviction that all men are created equal, that they are equally entitled to life, liberty, and the pursuit of happiness, and that the duty of government is to serve these ends.

This country of ours has experienced many blessings, but none greater than its dedication to these principles. At every point in our history, these ideals have served to correct our failures and shortcomings, to spur us on to greater efforts, and to keep clearly before us the primary purpose of our existence as a nation. They have enshrined for us, as a principle of government, the moral imperative to do justice, and the divine command to men to love one another.

These principles give meaning to all that we do.

In foreign policy, they mean that we can never be tolerant of oppression or tyranny. They mean that we must throw our weight on the side of greater freedom and a better life for all peoples. These principles confirm us in carrying out the specific programs for peace which we have already begun.

We shall continue to give our wholehearted support to the United Nations. We believe that this organization can ultimately provide the framework of international law and morality without which mankind cannot survive. It has already set up new standards for the conduct of nations in the Declaration of Human Rights and the Convention on Genocide. It is moving ahead to give meaning to the concept of world brotherhood through a wide variety of cultural, economic, and technical activities.

The events of the past year again showed the value of the United Nations in bringing about the peaceful adjustment of tense international controversies. In Indonesia and in Palestine, the efforts of the United Nations have put a stop to bloodshed and paved the way to peaceful settlements.

We are working toward the time when the United Nations will control weapons of mass destruction and will have the forces to preserve international law and order. While the world remains unsettled, however, and as long as our own security and the security of the free world require, we will maintain a strong and well-balanced organization. The Selective Service System is an essential part of our defense plans, and it must be continued.

Under the principles of the United Nations Charter, we must continue to share in the common defense of free nations against aggression. At the last session, this Congress laid the basis for this joint effort. We now must put into effect the common defense plans that are being worked out.

We shall continue our efforts for world economic recovery, because world prosperity is the only sure foundation for permanent peace.

As an immediate means to this end, we must continue our support of the European Recovery Program. This program has achieved great success in the first two years of operation, but it has not yet been completed. If we were to stop this program now, or cripple it, just because it is succeeding, we should be doing exactly what the enemies of democracy want us to do. We should be just as foolish as a man who, for reasons of false economy, failed to put a roof on his house after building the foundation and the walls.

World prosperity also requires that we do all we can to expand world trade. As a major step in this direction, we should promptly join the International Trade Organization. The purpose of this organization, which the United States has been foremost in creating, is to establish a code of fair practice, and an international authority for adjusting differences in international commercial relations. It is an effort to prevent the kind of anarchy and irresponsibility in world trade which did so much to bring about the world depression in the 1930's.

An expanding world economy requires the improvement of living standards and the development of resources in areas where human poverty and misery now prevail. Without such improvement, the recovery of Europe and the future of our own economy will not be secure. I urge that the Congress adopt this legislation now before it to provide for increasing the flow of technical assistance and capital investment to underdeveloped regions.

It is more essential now than ever, if the ideals of freedom and representative government are to prevail in these areas, and particularly in the Far East, that their people experience, in their own lives, the benefits of scientific and economic advances. This program will require the movement of large amounts of capital from the industrial nations, and particularly from the United States, to productive uses in the underdeveloped areas of the world. Recent world events make prompt action imperative.

This program is in the interest of all peoples—and it has nothing in common with either the old imperialism of the last century or the new imperialism of the Communists.

Our aim for a peaceful, democratic world of free peoples will be achieved in the long run, not by force of arms, but by an appeal to the minds and hearts of men. If the peace policy of the democratic nations is to be successful, they must demonstrate that the benefits of their ways of life can be increased and extended to all nations and all races.

In the world today, we are confronted with the danger that the rising demand of people everywhere for freedom and a better life may be corrupted and betrayed by the false promises of Communism. In its ruthless struggle for power, Communism seizes upon our imperfections, and takes advantage of the delays and setbacks which the democratic nations experience in their effort to secure a better life for their citizens. This challenge to us is more than a military challenge. It is a challenge to the honesty of our profession of the democratic faith; it is a challenge to the efficiency and stability of our economic system; it is a challenge to our willingness to work with other peoples for world peace and world prosperity.

For my part, I welcome the challenge. I believe that our country, at this crucial point in world history, will meet that challenge successfully. I believe that, in co-operation with the other free nations of the world, we shall extend the full benefits of the democratic way of life to millions who do not now enjoy them, and preserve mankind from dictatorship and tyranny.

I believe that we shall succeed in our struggle for peace, because I have seen the success we have had in our own country in following the principles of freedom. Over the last fifty years, the ideals of liberty and equal opportunity to which our nation is dedicated have been increasingly realized in the lives of our people.

The ideal of equal opportunity no longer means simply the opportunity which a man has to advance beyond his fellows. Some of our citizens do achieve greater success than others as a reward for individual merit and effort, and this is as it should be. As the same time, our country must be more than a land of opportunity for a select few. It must be a land of opportunity for all of us. In such a land, all can grow and prosper together.

The simple truth that we can all go forward together is often questioned by selfish or shortsighted persons. It is strange that this is so, for this proposition is so clearly demonstrated by our national history. During the last fifty years, for example, our nation has grown enormously in material well-being. This growth has come about, not by concentrating the benefits of our progress in the hands of a few, but by increasing the wealth of the great body of our citizens.

In the last fifty years, the income of the average family has increased so greatly that its buying power has doubled. The average hours of work have declined from sixty to forty a week, while the hourly production of the average worker has tripled. Average wages, allowing for price changes, have increased from about 45 cents an hour to $1.40 an hour.

We have accomplished what to earlier ages of mankind would have been a miracle—we work shorter hours, we produce more, and we live better.

Increasing freedom from poverty and drudgery has given a fuller meaning to American life. Our people are better educated; we have more opportunities for travel and recreation and enjoyment of the arts. We enjoy more personal liberty in the United States today than ever before.

If we can continue in the spirit of cooperative adventure which has marked the recent years of our progress, we can expect further scientific advances, further increase in our standard of living, and a still wider enjoyment of democratic freedom.

No one, of course, can foretell the future exactly. However, if we assume that we shall grow as fast in the future as we have grown in the past, we can get a good idea of how much our country should grow over the next fifty years.

At present our total national production is $255 billion a year. Our working population and our output per worker are increasing. If our productive power continues to increase at the same rate as it has increased over the past fifty years, our total national production fifty years from now will be nearly four times as much as it is today. Allowing for the expected growth in population, this would mean that the real income of the average family in the year 2000 A. D. would be about three times what it is today.

These are estimates of what we can do in the future, but we can reach those heights only if we follow the right policies. We have learned by bitter experience that progress is not automatic—that wrong policies lead to depression and disaster. We cannot achieve these gains unless we have a stable economy and avoid the catastrophes of boom and bust that have set us back in the past.

These gains cannot be achieved unless our businessmen maintain their spirit of initiative and enterprise and operate in a competitive economy. They cannot be achieved unless our working men and women and their unions help to increase productivity and obtain for labor a fair share of the benefits of our economic system. They cannot be achieved unless we have a stable and prosperous agriculture. They cannot be achieved unless we conserve and develop our natural resources in the public interest.

Our system will not work unless our people are healthy, well educated and confident of the future. It will not work unless all citizens can participate fully in our national life.

In achieving these gains, the government has a special responsibility to help create and maintain the conditions which will permit the growth we know is possible. Foremost among these conditions is the need for a fair distribution of our increasing prosperity among all the great groups of our population who help to bring it about—labor, business, agriculture. . . .

As we move forward into the second half of the twentieth century, we must always bear in mind the central purpose of our national life. We do not seek material prosperity for ourselves because we love luxury; we do not aid other nations because we wish to increase our power. We have not devised programs for the security and well-being of our people because we are afraid or unwilling to take risks. This is not the meaning of our past history or our present course.

We work for a better life for all, so that all men may put to good use the great gifts with which they have been endowed by their Creator. We seek to establish those material conditions of life in which, without exception, men may live in dignity, perform useful work, serve their communities, and worship God as they see fit.

These may seem simple goals, but they are not little ones. They are worth a great deal more than all the empires and conquests of history. They are not to be achieved by military aggression or political fanaticism. They are to be achieved by humbler means—by hard work, by a spirit of self-restraint in our dealings with one another, and by a deep devotion to the principles of justice and equality.

It should make us truly thankful, as we look back to the beginnings of this country, that we have come so far along the road to a better life for all. It should make us humble to think, as we look ahead, how much farther we have to go to accomplish, at home and abroad, the objectives that were set out for us at the founding of this nation.

As we approach the halfway mark in the twentieth century, we should ask for continued strength and guidance from that Almighty Power who has placed before us such great opportunities for the good of mankind in the years to come.

A BASIS FOR RUSSIAN-AMERICAN PEACE [12]

DEAN G. ACHESON [13]

Secretary of State Dean Acheson gave this address at a conference on International Cooperation for World Economic Development, held at the University of California, Berkeley campus, on March 16, 1950.

Eight thousand "be-sweatered and be-jeaned" students packed the men's gymnasium for the occasion. "The Secretary spoke straight through, without interruption, in his best professional manner, and when he concluded, his audience applauded until he rose a second time and bowed and waved his appreciation." [14]

The speech, according to the State Department, was three months in drafting. The speaker outlined seven steps for ending the cold war between Russia and the Western democracies, for furnishing the basis of peace treaties, and for solving the problem of atomic controls.

Recent events had obviously caused a huge shift in our policy, especially as it related to the Orient. (1) China had fallen. (2) Russia had recognized the Ho Chi Minh Communist leadership in Viet Nam, Indochina, whereas this country had decided to support the Bao Dai French-backed force. (3) Our decision to build the H-bomb had led to a considerable national demand for this country to attempt to come to terms with Russia. (4) Secretary Acheson and his Department had been accused of having no positive or consistent policy with respect to Russia. Taft, McCarthy, and others had vigorously questioned Acheson's ability for his job. (5) Bipartisan direction of foreign policy had obviously broken down with the illness of Senator Vandenberg. (6) Associated with the State Department, Owen Lattimore, Philip Jessup, and others were under attack as "Communist sympathizers."

The Berkeley address was not so much a listing of agenda for any conference between the Soviets and Americans as it was a statement of the basic philosophies that separated the two powers. The speech set up the seven major issues that would have to be faced and settled before any twentieth century Pax Romana might be established.

American public opinion recognized the thorough analysis and statesmanship that underlay the California address. The explanation no doubt strengthened—for the time—the position of the State Department. The address had wide distribution in Western Europe and in the Far East. Nationalists were said to have engineered the distribution of thousands of copies among Chinese Communists.

[12] Text furnished by the Department of State.
[13] For biographical note, see Appendix.
[14] San Francisco *Examiner*, March 17, 1950.

As the cold war increased in violence, Secretary Acheson continued to address the Americans on Russo-American relations. Part of his speaking was directed toward defense of his Department staff against the charges that they were pro-Russian. Part was to denounce Russia for her continued acts of aggression. (1) In late April 1950, for example, Russia rejected an American protest against the alleged shooting down of an American unarmed naval airplane in the Baltic, and accused the United States of attempting to photograph military installations. (2) Russia demanded that the United States, Britain, and Yugoslavia withdraw their troops from Trieste and that under the Big Four an international regime be set up there. (3) Russia demanded again from Turkey the acknowledgment of special Russian rights in the control of the Dardanelles. (4) Communist-controlled Czechoslovakia closed down the United States Information Service and proceeded with further trials of Czechs accused of spying for the United States. Acheson, in one of his speeches of late April, called the Russian moves "saber rattling." Although the cold war was hardly expected to break immediately into a full scale conflict, the Russians were obviously stepping up their bitter opposition to the Marshall Plan, the Atlantic Pact, and the other programs for strengthening the non-Communist nations.[15]

I wish to make a report to you about the tensions between the United States and the Soviet Union.

Now, the right and obligation of the Secretary of State to speak to his fellow citizens, or to the representatives of other nations, about our foreign relations is not derived from any claim on his part to special knowledge or wisdom which makes him right and other people wrong. It is derived from the fact that our forefathers by free choice worked out and approved a Constitution. This Constitution, with the amendments and interpretations which have made it a living and growing thing, has survived to this day as an expression of the will of the entire people. A President is duly elected under this Constitution with a heavy and solemn responsibility to direct the foreign relations of the American people. The President has, in accordance with law and with the advice and consent of the Senate, appointed a man to serve as Secretary of State to assist him in the conduct of our foreign affairs. This right to speak on your behalf results directly from the constitutional processes by which the American people

[15] For further comment on Dean Acheson as a speaker, see *Representative American Speeches: 1948-1949*, p 15-26.

provide a government for themselves in an orderly, clear and democratic manner.

A little over thirty years ago there came into power in one of the great countries of the world a group of people who also claim the right to speak on your behalf. That claim was based not on any Constitutional procedure, or on any expression of the will of those whose representatives they professed to be. It was based on a claim which those men made to a monopoly of the knowledge of what was right and what was wrong for human beings. They further profess that their claim is based on a body of thought taken over in large part from the writings of a mid-nineteenth century German economist and theorist, Karl Marx.

I have no desire to debate here the errors of one version or another of what is today called "Marxism." But I think it must be recognized in the light of the experience of the last hundred years that many of the premises on which Marx based his thought have been belied by the known facts of what has actually happened in the decades since Marx made his studies. Marx's law of capitalist accumulation, his law as to the rate of profit, his prediction of the numerical decline of the middle classes, and of the increase of the class struggle: none of these calculations has been borne out by the experience of the societies of the West. Marx did not foresee the possibility of democratic solutions.

Furthermore, the body of doctrine now professed by the Moscow-controlled Communists is only tenuously identified with Marx's writings and is largely overlaid with Russian imperialism. We certainly cannot accept the thesis that such a doctrine can serve as the justification for the right of a small group of individuals to speak for the great masses of human beings who have never selected them as their spokesmen and whose own opinions they have never consulted.

Now for three decades this group of people, or their successors, has carried on as the rulers of that same great country. They have always, at the same time, maintained the pretense that they are the interpreters of the aspirations of peoples far beyond their borders. In the light of that professed philosophy they have conducted, as masters of the Russian state, a foreign policy which now is the center of the most difficult and troublesome problems of international affairs, problems designed to keep the peoples of the world in a state of deepest apprehension and doubt. In addition to this, they have operated within the limits of the Soviet state on the basis of a domestic policy founded, they say, on the same philosophy.

There are many points in this philosophy, and particularly in the way in which it has already been applied in practice in the Soviet Union and elsewhere, which are not only deeply repugnant to us, but raise questions involving the most basic conceptions of good and evil—questions involving the ultimate moral nature of man. There is no use in attempting to ignore or gloss over the profundity of this conflict of view.

The free society values the individual as an end in himself. It requires of him only that self-discipline and self-restraint which make the rights of each individual compatible with the rights of every other individual. Individual freedom, therefore, implies individual responsibility not to exercise freedom in ways inconsistent with the freedom of other individuals, and responsibility positively to make constructive use of freedom in the building of a just society.

In relations between nations, the prime reliance of the free society is on the strength and appeal of its principles, and it feels no compulsion sooner or later to bring all societies into conformity with it.

It does not fear, rather it welcomes, diversity and derives its strength from freedom of inquiry and tolerance even of antipathetic ideas.

We can see no moral compromise with the contrary theses of international communism: that the end justifies the means, that any and all methods are therefore permissible, and that the dignity of the human individual is of no importance as against the interest of the state.

To our minds, these principles mean, in their practical application, the arrogation to individual human leaders, with all their inevitable frailties and limitations, of powers and pretenses which most of us would be willing to concede only to the infinite wisdom and compassion of a Divine Being. They mean the police state, with all that that implies; a regimentation of the worker which is hardly distinguishable from slave labor; a loss to society of those things which appear to us to make life worth living; a denial of the fundamental truths embodied in all the great religions of the world.

Here is a moral issue of the clearest nature. It cannot be evaded. Let us make no mistake about it.

Yet it does not follow from this that the two systems, theirs and ours, cannot exist concurrently in this world. Good and evil can and do exist concurrently in the whole great realm of human life. They exist within every individual, within every nation, and within every human group. The struggle between good and evil cannot be confined to governments. That struggle will go on, as it always has, in the wider theater of the human spirit itself.

But it also does not follow from this coexistence of good and evil that the two systems, theirs and ours, will necessarily be able to exist concurrently. That will depend largely on them, for we ourselves do not find impossibility in the prospect of co-existence with the Soviet system.

However much we may sympathize with the Soviet citizens who for reasons bedded deep in history are obliged to live under it, we are not attempting to change the governmental or social structure of the Soviet Union. The Soviet regime, however, has devoted a major portion of its energies and resources to the attempt to impose its system on other peoples. In this attempt it has shown itself prepared to resort to any method or stratagem including subversion, threats and even military force.

Therefore, if the two systems are to coexist, some acceptable means must be found to free the world from the destructive tensions and anxieties of which it has been the victim in these past years and the continuance of which can hardly be in the interests of any people.

I wish, therefore, to speak to you about those points of greatest difference which must be identified and sooner or later reconciled if the two systems are to live together, if not with mutual respect, at least in reasonable security. What is it which the leaders of international communism could do to make such coexistence more tolerable to everyone?

There are a number of things they could do, which, while leaving much yet to do, would give the world new confidence in the possibility of peaceful change, in the principle and processes of peaceful settlement as an effective means of finding workable solutions in areas of disagreement.

Let us look first at the points where we and they are perhaps most closely in contact, and where the establishment of peace in its narrowest, most limited sense is dangerously impeded by the absence of common ground.

One: *Definition of Terms of Peace.*

It is now nearly five years since the end of hostilities, and the victorious allies have been unable to define the terms of peace with the defeated countries. This is a grave, a deeply disturbing fact. For our part, we do not intend nor wish, in fact we do not know how, to create satellites. Nor can we accept a settlement which would make Germany, Japan, or liberated Austria satellites of the Soviet Union. The experience in Hungary, Rumania, and Bulgaria has been one of bitter disappointment and shocking betrayal of the solemn pledges by the wartime allies. The Soviet leaders joined in the pledge at Tehran that they looked forward "with confidence to the day when all peoples of the world may live free lives, untouched by tyranny, and according to their varying desires and their own consciences." We can accept treaties of peace which would give reality to this pledge and to the interests of all in security.

With regard to Germany, unification under a government chosen in free elections under international observation is a basic element in an acceptable settlement. With that need recognized and with a will to define the terms of peace, a German treaty could be formulated which, while not pretending to solve all of the complex and bitter problems of the German situation, would, nevertheless, go far toward a relaxation of a set of major tensions.

With regard to Austria, that unhappy country is still under occupation because the Soviet leaders do not want a treaty. The political and economic independence of Austria is being sabotaged by the determination of the Soviets, camouflaged in technicalities, to maintain their forces and special interests in Eastern Austria.

With regard to Japan, we feel that the Soviet leaders could recognize the interest which nations other than the members of the Council of Foreign Ministers have in a Japanese peace treaty and could refrain from taking positions and insisting on procedures which block progress toward a treaty.

In the Far East generally, there are many points where the Soviet leaders could, if they chose, relax tensions. They could, for example, permit the United Nations' Commission in Korea to carry out its duties by allowing the Commission's entry into North Korea and by accepting its report as the basis for a peaceful settlement of that liberated country's problems. They could repatriate Japanese prisoners of war from Siberian camps. They could refrain from subverting the efforts of the newly independent states of Asia and their native leaders to solve their problems in their own way.

Two: *Use of Force.*

With regard to the whole group of countries which we are accustomed to think of as the Satellite area, the Soviet leaders could withdraw their military and police force and refrain from using the shadow of that force to keep in power persons or regimes which do not command the confidence of the respective peoples, freely expressed through orderly representative processes. In other words, they could elect to observe, in practice, the declaration to which they set their signatures at Yalta concerning liberated Europe.

In this connection we do not insist that these governments have any particular political or social complexion. What concerns us is that they should be truly independent national regimes, with a will of their own and with a decent foundation in popular feeling. We would like to feel, when we deal with these governments, that we are dealing with something representative of the national identity of the peoples in question. We cannot believe that such a situation would be really incompatible with the security of the Soviet Union.

This is a question of elementary good faith, and it is vital to a spirit of confidence that other treaties and other agreements will be honored. Nothing would so alter the international climate as the holding of elections in the satellite states in which the true will of the people could be expressed.

Three: *Obstruction in the United Nations.*

The Soviet leaders could drop their policy of obstruction in the United Nations and could instead act as if they believe the United Nations is, as Stalin himself has recently called it, a serious instrumentality for the maintenance of international peace and security. They are simply not acting that way now.

Their policy of walk-out and boycott is a policy that undermines the concept of majority decision. Indeed, they seem deliberately to entrench themselves in a minority position in the United Nations. This was illustrated last fall when they voted against the Essentials of Peace Resolution which solemnly restated and reaffirmed the principles and purposes of the United Nations Charter and which pointed to practical steps which members should take to support the peace.

A respect for the expressed will of the majority is as fundamental to international organization as it is to democracy. We know that a majority of the General Assembly has generally not agreed with the Soviet Union, whereas we ourselves have generally been on the majority side. There is nothing artificial about this situation. It has not been the result of any sleight of hand or pressures on our part. We do not have any satellites whose votes we control. The significant fact is that proposals which have commended themselves to a majority of the members of the United Nations have also commended themselves to us.

Let the Soviet Union put forward in the United Nations genuine proposals conducive to the work of peace, respectful of the real independence of other governments, and appreciative of the role which the United Nations could and should play in the preservation of world stability and the cooperation of nations. They will then doubtless have a majority with them. We will rejoice to see them in such a majority. We will be pleased to be a member of it ourselves.

Four: *Effective Control of Atomic Energy.*

The Soviet leaders could join us in seeking realistic and effective arrangements for the control of atomic weapons and the limitation of armaments in general. We know that it is not easy for them under their system to contemplate the functioning on their territory of an authority in which people would participate who are not of their political persuasion.

If we have not hesitated to urge that they as well as we accept this requirement it is because we believe that a spirit of genuine responsibility to mankind is widely present in this world. Many able administrators and scientists could be found to operate such an authority who would be only too happy, regardless of political complexion, to take an elevated and enlightened view of the immense responsibility which would rest upon them. There are men who would scorn to use their powers for the negative purpose of intrigue and destruction. We believe that an authority could be established which would not be controlled or subject to control by either ourselves or the Soviet Union.

Five: *Attempts at Undermining Established Governments.*

The Kremlin could refrain from using the Communist apparatus controlled by it throughout the world to attempt to overthrow, by subversive means, established governments with which the Soviet Government stands in an outward state of friendship and respect. In general, it could desist from, and could cooperate in efforts to prevent, indirect aggression across national frontiers —a mode of conduct which is inconsistent with the spirit and the letter of the United Nations Charter.

Six: *Proper Treatment of Diplomatic Representatives.*

The Soviet leaders could cooperate with us to the end that the official representatives of all countries are treated everywhere with decency and respect and that an atmosphere is created in which these representatives could function in a normal and helpful manner, conforming to the accepted codes of diplomacy.

The standards of conduct of our own representatives are known from more than a century and a half of American diplomatic experience. These standards are such that all countries which have accepted our representatives in a spirit of respect and confidence over periods of many decades have certainly remained none the worse for it. The independence of those countries has not been undermined; their peoples have not been corrupted; their economies have not been scathed by sabotage.

When we now find our representatives treated as criminals, when we see great official propaganda machines reiterating that they are sinister people and that contact with them is pregnant with danger—we cannot believe that such insinuations are advanced in good faith, and we cannot be blind to the obvious implications of such an attitude.

Seven: *Distortion of Motives of Others.*

In general, the Soviet leaders could refrain, I think, from systematically distorting to their own peoples the picture of the world outside their borders, and of our country, in particular.

We are not suggesting that they become propagandists for any country or system other than their own. But the Soviet leaders know, and the world knows with what genuine disappointment and concern the people of this country were brought to the realization that the wartime collaboration between the major allies was not to be the beginning of a happier and freer era in the association between the peoples of the Soviet Union and other peoples.

What are we now to conclude from the morbid fancies which their propaganda exudes of a capitalist encirclement, of a United States craftily and systematically plotting another world war? They know, and the world knows, how foreign is the concept of aggressive war to our philosophy and our political system. They know that we are not asking to be objects of any insincere and effusive demonstrations of sentimental friendship. But we feel that the Soviet leaders could at least permit access to the Soviet Union of persons and ideas from other countries so that other views might be presented to the Russian people.

These are some of the things which we feel that the Soviet leaders could do, which would permit the rational and peaceful development of the coexistence of their system and ours. They are not things that go to the depths of the moral conflict. They are not things that promise the Kingdom of Heaven. They have been formulated by us, not as moralists but as servants of government, anxious to get on with the practical problems that lie before us, and to get on with them in a manner consistent with mankind's deep longing for a respite from fear and uncertainty.

Nor have they been formulated as a one-sided bargain. A will to achieve binding, peaceful settlements would be required of all participants. All would have to produce unmistakable evidence of their good faith. All would have to accept agreements in the observance of which all nations could have real confidence.

The United States is ready, as it has been and always will be, to cooperate in genuine efforts to find peaceful settlements. Our attitude is not inflexible, our opinions are not frozen, our positions are not and will not be obstacles to peace. But it takes more than one to cooperate. If the Soviet Union could join in doing these things I have outlined, we could all face the future with greater security. We could look forward to more than the eventual reduction of some of the present tensions. We could anticipate a return to a more normal and relaxed diplomatic atmosphere, and to progress in the transaction of some of the international business which needs so urgently to be done.

I fear, however, that I must warn you not to raise your hopes. No one who has lived through these postwar years can be sanguine about reaching agreements in which reliance can be placed and which will be observed by the Soviet leaders in good faith. We must not, in our yearning for peace, allow ourselves to be betrayed by vague generalities or beguiling proffers of peace which are unsubstantiated by good faith solidly demonstrated in daily behavior. We are always ready to discuss, to negotiate, to agree, but we are understandably loath to play the role of international sucker. We will take the initiative in the future as we have in the past in seeking agreement whenever there is any indication that this course would be a fruitful one. What is required is genuine evidence in conduct, not just in words, of an intention to solve the immediate problems and remove the tensions which divide us. I see no evidence that the Soviet leaders will change their conduct until the progress of the free world convinces them that they cannot profit from a continuation of these tensions.

So our course of action in the world of hard reality which faces us is not one that is easily charted. It is not one which this nation can adopt without consideration of the needs and views of other free nations. It is one which requires all the devotion and resolve and wisdom that can be summoned up. We have had and continue to have the assistance and advice of distinguished leaders in all walks of life. We have the benefit of the great public discussion which has been proceeding in the democratic way, by free inquiry and free expression.

It is my purpose in talking with you to point a direction and to define the choices which confront us. We need to stand before the world with our own purpose and position clear.

We want peace, but not at any price. We are ready to negotiate, but not at the expense of rousing false hopes which would be dashed by new failures. We are equally determined to support all real efforts for peaceful settlements and to resist aggression.

The times call for a total diplomacy equal to the task of defense against Soviet expansion and to the task of building the kind of world in which our way of life can flourish. We must continue to press ahead with the building of a free world which is strong in its faith and in its material progress. The alternative is to allow the free nations to succumb one by one to the erosive and encroaching processes of Soviet expansion.

We must not slacken, rather we must reinvigorate, the kind of democratic efforts which are represented by the European Recovery Program, the North Atlantic and Rio Pacts, the Mutual Defense Assistance Program, the Point IV Program for developing the world's new workshops and assistance in creating the conditions necessary to a growing, many-sided exchange of the world's products.

We must champion an international order based on the United Nations and on the abiding principles of freedom and justice, or accept an international society increasingly torn by destructive rivalries.

We must recognize that our ability to achieve our purposes cannot rest alone on a desire for peace, but that it must be supported by the strength to meet whatever tasks Providence may have in store for us.

We must not make the mistake, in other words, of using Soviet conduct as a standard for our own. Our efforts cannot be merely reactions to the latest moves by the Kremlin. The bipartisan line of American foreign policy has been and must continue to be the constructive task of building, in cooperation with others, the kind of world in which freedom and justice can flourish. We must not be turned aside from this task by the diversionary thrusts of the Soviet Union. And if it is necessary, as it sometimes is, to deal with such a thrust or the threat of one, the effort should be understood as one which, though essential, is outside the main stream of our policy.

Progress is to be gained in the doing of the constructive tasks which give practical affirmation to the principles by which we live.

The success of our efforts rests finally on our faith in ourselves and in the values for which this Republic stands. We will need courage and steadfastness and the cool heads and steady nerves of a citizenry which has always faced the future "with malice toward none; with charity toward all; with firmness in the right, as God gives us to see the right."

WORLD PEACE: A BALANCE SHEET [16]

DWIGHT D. EISENHOWER [17]

President Dwight D. Eisenhower of Columbia University gave this lecture in McMillin Theater, at Columbia, on the evening of March 23, 1950. It was the first in a series of lectures under an endowment by Leo Silver, New Jersey industrialist, dedicated to the cause of international peace. The lectures were sponsored by the Columbia School of International Affairs. Part only of the one-hour lecture is here included.

The speech, in view of the speaker's background and of his relationship to the major problems of the "cold war" and national defense early in 1950, was highly significant.

The theme was peace—how to achieve and preserve it. As Eisenhower prepared the address, Dean Acheson and his staff of the State Department, Owen Lattimore and other "architects" of our Far Eastern policy were under strong attack by Senator McCarthy and other Republicans as "pro-Communist" in their thinking and perhaps actions. Eisenhower attempted to dissipate the foggy thinking and pessimism of the American people.

He was also concerned with the matter of the 1950-51 budget, then under consideration by Congress, for national defense. Should it be twelve, or thirteen, or fourteen billions? Was Congress too conservative in estimating the danger and too complacent in setting up powerful air, navy, and ground forces?

These issues were merely surface clues to the penetration attempted by Eisenhower as he discussed the age-old question: shall we assent to the philosophy of Christian pacifism? Or, at the other extreme, shall we measure might and estimate victory solely by the outward weapons more than by the inward resolution? Is there proper motive for any war? If so, what should be the nature of that justification?

Thus Eisenhower set up his postulates; cited graphic illustrations (Britain in 1940); defined the "peace" he would aim for, with its permanence, universality, and security; examined in detail the factors necessary for success—justice and freedom, international understanding, disarmament, and a "respected" United Nations.

The lecture has clarity and completeness of organization; refutational elements that skillfully blend with constructive propositions; concreteness of illustration; originality of phrasing, even occasional eloquence; quotable generalizations; and adaptation to his sophisticated audience.

[16] Permission for this reprint was given through the courtesy of President Eisenhower. The text was furnished by the President's Office, Columbia University.

[17] For biographical note, see Appendix.

The address ranks high among Eisenhower's public remarks of the period 1949-50. Others of his addresses that might well have been included in this volume were his New York *Herald Tribune* Forum address of October 25, 1949, in which he set forth his political beliefs, and his speech at the 193rd annual banquet of St. Andrew's Society of the State of New York, September 5, 1949, in which he attacked the kind of "security" that implied "slothful indolence and ease and stagnation."

President Eisenhower in 1950 was a platform leader of immense prestige, mental power, and superior speaking skill.

On behalf of Columbia University, I thank Mr. Leo Silver for the generous gift that will make the Gabriel Silver Lecture on Peace a recurring feature of the University calendar. His endowment will permit us at regular intervals to call on selected individuals for reports on peace. Perhaps there will be added new strength to the philosophical and social foundations of peace, and a stronger light thrown on the hazards within the international economy that endanger its permanence. Possibly there will be launched new attacks on inequities and injustices in which lurk some of the causes of war.

Mr. Silver has established a worthy memorial to his father and we are grateful that he has chosen Columbia University as its home. On my own behalf, I want to thank him for the honor paid me in his request that I deliver this inaugural of the series. Without his intervention, I should not be so presumptuous as to appear in this role before a distinguished gathering of Columbia faculty and graduate students because you are, in our country, part of the great body especially qualified to be the architects of world peace.

To you that classification may seem exaggeration beyond any warrant of fact. Quite the contrary. Any man who underestimates the importance of the American teacher in world affairs is misleading himself. Under our system, high governmental policy expresses the considered will of the people, and the will of the people, in the last analysis, is compounded out of the convictions, the idealisms, the purposes fostered in the classrooms of the nation's schools. What you teach is what the country does.

I come before you solely as a witness of things that have happened and of the impressions those have made upon me.

For some years, I was in the thick of war and reconstruction after war. A war that—despite all its terrors, its destruction, its cost—was, for the Allied Nations, a crusade in the best sense of an often misused word, a reconstruction after war that—despite its bickerings, its suppression of freedom in many places and its disheartening cynicism—has established in the political sphere at least a temporary—even if teetering—balance. These years and these experiences have served to ripen and enlarge my devotion to peace. I trust that they have also served to sharpen my powers of perception and judgment of the factors which seem always to balk man's efforts to close forever the doors of the Temple of Janus.

In discussing war and peace, we incline to paint one all black and the other all white. We like to repeat "There never was a good war, or a bad peace." But war often has provided the setting for comradeship and understanding and greatness of spirit —among nations, as well as men—beyond anything in quiet days; while peace may be marked by, or may even be the product of, chicanery, treachery and the temporary triumph of expediency over all spiritual values.

The pact of Munich was a more fell blow to humanity than the atomic bomb at Hiroshima. Suffocation of human freedom among a once free people, however quietly and peacefully accomplished, is more far-reaching in its implications and its effects on their future than the destruction of their homes, industrial centers and transportation facilities. Out of rubble heaps, willing hands can rebuild a better city; but out of freedom lost can stem only generations of hate and bitter struggle and brutal oppression.

Nor can we forget that, as Professor Lyman Bryson of Teachers College recently said: "There are even greater things in the world than peace." By greater things, he meant the ideals, the hopes and aspirations of humanity; those things of the soul and spirit which great men of history have valued far above peace and material wealth and even life itself.

Without these values, peace is an inhuman existence. Far better risk a war of possible annihilation than grasp a peace which would be the certain extinction of free man's ideas and ideals.

Clearly it was a choice between these two extremes that the British people were forced to make back in the dark summer of 1940. Whatever may be history's final judgment on the total war record of that nation, her people in that dire season of fear and foreboding proved themselves heroic and mighty in their spiritual greatness.

Twenty miles beyond their South coast, thinly manned by men—and women—armed with little more than their own courage, there was arrayed an invasion force of stupendous military might, hardened and flushed by sweeps from the Vistula to the Atlantic, from the Arctic to the Alps. Other members of the British Commonwealth of nations, though loyal, could do little to relieve the frightening crisis that suddenly faced the Mother Country.

In all Europe and Asia, from the Bay of Biscay far into the Pacific, men awaited the blow that would destroy the British. The multitude of millions that dwelled in those two continents—even those who lately were allies—had been corrupted into a conviction that material force was unfailingly greater than the spirit of free men.

Throughout most of the rest of the world, there seemed to be an appalling ignorance that the defeat of Britain would mean the eventual extinction of the freedom for ideas and ideals that her people had done so much to win and support for all mankind. So, in her hour of gravest trial she stood largely alone—another David to champion a righteous but apparently hopeless cause.

But the British spurned all offers of peace and their great leader asked for battle—on their beaches, in their towns, along the lanes of England. His faith was rewarded in the final and complete Allied victory of 1945.

Millions of Americans, who saw what the British endured—broken towns, years of austerity, staggering debts and near-destitution—must be witnesses all our lives to the greatness of spirit in that people. *Their decision* to fight on gave freedom a new lease on life and gave all free peoples more space in time to destroy a vicious dictator and regain an opportunity to work out an enduring peace.

Our memories are short indeed, or we have failed to read the lesson of that experience, if we in 1950 are fearful of the future and allow despair to paralyze our efforts to build a lasting peace.

By this allusion to the British record, I do not in any way belittle the wartime contributions of the other allies, including Russia; nor dull one whit the sharp fact that victory over the enemy could *not* have been accomplished without the giant strength of a united America. I dwell on the British role in 1940 and thereafter for two reasons. First, there is a tendency among us today to write off our friends in the Western nations because they are weak in numbers and weapons. Second, there is a parallel tendency to measure a possible enemy solely by the area he rules and the manpower he controls.

Many of us—even among professional soldiers—too easily accept as unfailingly true Napoleon's cynical statement: "God is on the side of the heaviest battalions." *Napoleon,* himself, lived and ruled and fought by that dictum—but his reign from coronation to final exile was shorter by months than even Hitler's; his fellow believer in the dominance of force.

Because there is one towering force in the world that often seems bent upon engulfing as much territory and as many people as it can, a great many surrender their hopes for peace as curtly as they write off our friends in Western Europe. Such pessimism invites disaster. Such an attitude, if it were founded on reason, would mean that the handful of men who dictate the policy of the Soviet system also dictate the fate of this globe. To any one ready to study the history of yesterday and the facts of today, that is a repugnant absurdity.

Granted that at any moment some one powerful nation could choose to follow a policy of world conquest by war. Nevertheless, the world has seen so many examples of this that, today, such a war would imply either an incredible stupidity, weakness, disunity and unreadiness on one side or a miscalculation equal to the insanity and moral guilt on the side of the predatory nation. Until war is eliminated from international relations, unprepared-ness for it is well nigh as criminal as war itself.

What then is the nature of the peace that we seek? What are the characteristics that distinguish it? These questions must be answered, if we are to know our objective, calculate our distance from it, decide on the measures necessary to its attainment.

Almost certainly, most men would agree that peace, to merit the name, should possess a reasonable assurance of permanence, should be the product of cooperation between all major nations, and should be secure against arbitrary violation by any power or group of powers. It is apparent, however, that we constantly use the word *"peace"* in two senses which differ sharply. One is the peace of our dreams—a peace founded in noble impulses, universally shared. It is always the ideal, the pole star that guides us on the proper path. The other peace is *something* of an armed truce; but today a half-loaf is better than none. By the improvisations, expediencies and agreements under which we strive to maintain a peace based as much upon force and power as upon concepts of justice and fair play, we hope to reach the point where this peace becomes the starting point of the *real* peace we seek.

But permanence, universality and security cannot be achieved *merely* by covenant or agreement. Treaties are too often scraps of paper; in our age the signal for two world wars was the callous repudiation of pacts and pledged word. There must be a universal urge to decency.

This fact compels the observation that they are thinking wishfully to pin their hopes of peace upon a single "high level" conference and a resulting paper that would bear the promise of governmental heads to observe all the rights of others. An agreement, though it should bear the seal and ribbon of every chancellery in the world, is worth no more than the confidence placed by each signer in the good faith and integrity of every other. We must sadly acknowledge that today such world-wide confidence does not exist.

By all means let us continue to confer—especially with the view and purpose of reaching the required level of mutual faith and confidence, or—as a substitute—of developing practical and mutually enforceable measures and reciprocal arrangements calculated to lessen the danger of war. But, equally, let us not delude ourselves that, in 1950, establishment of real peace is merely a matter of Very Important Personages signing papers or "talking tough" in Paris, Geneva, Washington or Tahiti.

It is obvious that an enduring world-wide and secure peace must be founded on justice, opportunity and freedom for all men of good will; be maintained in a climate of international understanding and cooperation; be free from militaristic menace; and be supported by an accepted and respected police power representing all nations. Critical factors in the problem of building such a peace are the needs of a human society comprised of individuals; and, further, the needs of a human society that is divided into independent nations, each sovereign within its own borders and competing with all others to promote the interests of its own citizens, often at the expense of others. There are two sides to the coin of peace, the individual and the national; if one is defective the coin is spurious.

On the side of the individual, peace requires an international society that is free from vicious provocations to strife among men. These are rooted in inequities so glaring that, to those who suffer them, they seem to make attractive any alternative. The gamble of war lures the desperate, for even overwhelming defeat can hardly worsen their state; while victory, if it gives the survivors any improvement, will be worth its cost in blood. It is possible, even probable, that hopelessness among a people can be a far more potent cause of war than greed. War—in such case—is a symptom, not the disease.

On the collective side of the coin, peace requires an international society liberated from the threat of aggression by neighbor on neighbor, a threat forever present when one or more nations are committed to the building or maintenance of gigantic military machines. No sane man will challenge, under present circumstances, the need for defensive strength designed to secure against internal or external attack the independence and sovereignty of a free state. But the continued existence of even one purely offensive force—a force for which there is no apparent need based in the logic of self-defense—denies enduring peace to the world. Those who have spawned such a force must either eventually destroy it by demobilization and find justification for the heavy cost already laid on their people; or use it, tacitly or actively, as a threat or as a weapon. There is no middle course.

Always it has been difficult to distinguish between offensive and defensive armaments. Advancing science has obliterated whatever qualitative differences that once existed; today even the atom bomb is included in defensive arsenals. But differences do exist—vital differences. They are found, partially, in the quantitative factor.

The world forms its own sound opinion of a nation's martial purposes, primarily by the size and combinations of armaments supported, and by their geographical disposition and estimated state of readiness. To be considered also is the record of the particular nation—the extent to which it observes the ordinary rules of decency, courtesy, fairness and frankness in dealing with others.

It is by such combinations of standards that we must today classify the world's armaments. For America, with whose professional security forces I have been intimately associated for almost forty years, I bear witness to peaceful intent. In all those years, I have never heard an officer of the Army, the Navy or the Air Force, or any responsible official of government, advocate, urge, discuss or even hint at the use of force by this country in the settlement of any actual or potential international problem.

And here it seems appropriate, in view of my insistent belief that the world must finally disarm or suffer catastrophic consequences, to assert my conviction that America has already disarmed to the extent—in some directions even beyond the extent—that I, with deep concern for her *present* safety, could possibly advise, until we have certain knowledge that all nations, in concerted action, are doing likewise.

I might state here also that the Baruch plan for the control of the atomic bomb was not only evidence of our peaceful intent, but was the most generous action ever made by any nation, equivalent in its field to the Marshall Plan.

Moreover, without American leadership in the search, the pursuit of a just and enduring peace is hopeless. Nowhere in the world—outside this land—is there the richness of resources, stamina and will needed to lead what at times may be a costly and exhausting effort. BUT leadership cannot be exercised by the weak. It demands strength—the strength of this great nation when its people are united in purpose, united in a common fundamental faith, united in their readiness to work for human freedom and peace; this spiritual and economic strength, in turn, must be reinforced in a still armed world by the physical strength necessary for the defense of ourselves and our friends.

Only by deliberate lies can the propagandist—foreign or domestic—stretch our arms program into more than the reasonable posture for defense that General Washington urged on his countrymen. And the heads of state everywhere, even the most suspicious and fearful, know that it is below even that level. Our processes are open to the inspection of all—we spend hardly a dollar or add a platoon to the military establishment without long and public debate.

Our twentieth century international record, the statistics of our military forces, and the open procedures of our political system—all provide proof of our peaceful purposes; they prove also that our support of programs, in which universal peace will be secure, is as honest as it is sturdy. . . .

I have spoken thus briefly of these two elements in world peace—disarmament and United Nations authority—because they are in a manner corollaries or sequels to the other two—justice, freedom, opportunity for all men of good will; and a climate of mutual understanding and cooperation among the nations. Progress is bound to come from slow, evolutionary processes rather than violent revolution in national and individual thinking.

But it is especially important that we do not fall prey to pessimism and defeatism. To describe the attitudes of many of us toward the current international scene, I give you the following quotation:

It is a gloomy moment in history. Not for many years, not in the lifetime of most men who read this paper has there been so much grave and deep apprehension; never has the future seemed so incalculable as at this time.

In France the political cauldron seethes and bubbles with uncertainty; Russia hangs as usual a cloud, dark and silent upon the horizon of Europe; while all the energies, resources and influences of the British Empire are sorely tried and are yet to be tried more sorely.

It is a solemn moment and no man can feel indifference—which happily no man pretends to feel—in the issue of events.

Of our own troubles no man can see the end.

That, ladies and gentlemen, though so vividly descriptive of today, appeared in *Harper's Weekly*, Saturday, October 10, 1857. Possibly we are wrong when we fearfully conclude that for the first time in history the governments regard each other with fear and suspicion.

What, actually, is the outlook for today? In my opinion, far better than most of us normally judge; the world of 1950 is a far brighter and better place than the world of 1850. Starvation is no longer endemic among many millions on every continent—China is the one tragic exception. Illiteracy has vastly diminished in the masses of almost every nation. In the west at least, there is a new and increased appreciation of spiritual values. Even Russia, despite its all-powerful police and purges, is for the average Russian a vast improvement compared to the Russia of 1850.

As to those countries outside the Curtain, I doubt that we can point to any era or any decade when there was as much intelligent comprehension of each other's purposes as now characterizes their relationships. And in the broader scope, the United Nations, however halting its progress may be, however much its sessions are torn by the jeers and vetoes from one sector, is a visible and working entity—substantial evidence of developing hopes and purposes, an earnest of better things to come.

All of us have come a long way in the past century; none of us should despair when we think of what our situation was, and our prospects, as recently as the summer of 1940. What then can be done now—by this University, by the United States, by the free peoples—to further the cause of peace?

The University, since its removal to Morningside Heights, has become an international center whose graduates can be found on every continent and whose influence has been a leaven for physical progress, intellectual fellowship and spiritual growth among all peoples. The purpose of this University, without over-simplification, can be epitomized in one phrase—the good of humanity.

We hope to build here on the campus a Nutrition Center in which the world's scientists will find concentrated all the knowledge, the tools, the facilities that will enable them to devise better, more productive and more effective techniques for the use of physical resources and the satisfaction of man's physical needs. We already have—and in every recent term we have further amplified—an Institute of International Affairs where we hope the political and social leaders of the world will find concentrated the materials, the information, the masses of data that will enable them to adjust the stresses and needs of one area to the strains and surpluses of another.

We hope to establish here a Chair for Peace, possibly an Institute. The purpose will be to study war as a tragic social phenomenon—its origins, its conduct, its impact, and particularly its disastrous consequences upon man's spiritual, intellectual and material progress. All this we should study in a scholarly atmosphere, free from emotional bias and the daily crises of public life. No American university, I am told, has ever undertaken this comprehensive task. For me, there is something almost shocking in the realization that, though many millions have been voluntarily donated for research in cancer of the individual body, nothing similar has been done with respect to the most malignant cancer of the world body—war.

We are presently engaged in a study of the Conservation of Human Resources—restricted, as of now, to the United States—but which will be of immeasurable benefit to all the world in furthering the dignity of man as a human being. Another hope is to conduct an exhaustive study into the ways and means of applying to every man's good, in today's intricate economy, *all* the resources of America, in such way as to maintain and enlarge every freedom that the individual has enjoyed under our system. There are other projects, under way or under discussion, that will take their places beside or even in front of these. Each of them will help Columbia University a little better to fulfill its purpose —the peace, freedom and good of America, and, therefore, of humanity.

As citizens of the United States, you and I—and all Americans in every corner of our land—must be forever mindful that the heritage of America and the strength of America are expressed in three fundamental principles: First, that individual freedom

is our most precious possession; second, that all our freedoms
are a single bundle, all must be secure if any is to be preserved;
third, that freedom to compete and readiness to cooperate make
our system the most productive on earth. Only within the framework of these principles can we hope to continue the growth that
has marked our history. Only thus can our millions reach the
fullness of intellectual, moral and physical welfare that is justly
ours—and avoid any risk of submission to the all-powerful state.
Moreover, only thus can the world have any hope of reaching the
millennium of world peace—for without the example of strength,
prosperity and progress in a free America, there is nothing to
inspire men to victory in today's struggle between freedom and
totalitarianism.

As friends of free people everywhere in the world, we can by
our own example—our conduct in every crisis, real or counterfeit;
our resistance to propaganda and passion; our readiness to seek
adjustment and compromise of difference—we can by our own
example ceaselessly expand understanding among the nations.
We must never forget that international friendship is achieved
through rumors ignored, propaganda challenged and exposed;
through patient loyalty to those who have proved themselves
worthy of it; through help freely given, where help is needed
and merited. In this sense there is no great, no humble among
us. In rights and in opportunity, in loyalty and in responsibility
to ideals, we are and must remain equal. Peace is more the
product of our day-to-day living than of a spectacular program,
intermittently executed.

The best foreign policy is to live our daily lives in honesty,
decency and integrity; at home, making our own land a more
fitting habitation for free men; and, abroad, joining with those
of like mind and heart, to make of the world a place where all
men can dwell in peace. Neither palsied by fear nor duped by
dreams but strong in the rightness of our purpose, we can then
place our case and cause before the bar of world opinion—
history's final arbiter between nations.

PEACE IN THE ATOMIC ERA [18]

ALBERT EINSTEIN [19]

Dr. Albert Einstein, in his first public statement since the decision to proceed with the hydrogen bomb, contributed to this first weekly television program, conducted by Mrs. Franklin D. Roosevelt, on Sunday, February 12, 1950. The telecast was seen (and heard) at four o'clock, Eastern Standard Time, over the Eastern and Midwestern networks of the National Broadcasting Company. The program originated in the Colonial Room of the Park Sheraton Hotel, New York. Dr. Einstein's remarks were recorded on a sound film at Princeton on the previous Friday, and inserted in the New York broadcast.

In the telecast Mrs. Roosevelt poured tea for the talking guests, Senator Brien McMahon (Connecticut), chairman of the Joint Congressional Committee on Atomic Energy; David Lilienthal, former chairman of the Commission; Dr. J. Robert Oppenheim, director of the Institute for Advanced Study of Princeton; Dr. Detev W. Bronk, president of Johns Hopkins University; Dr. Hans A. Bethe, Cornell University physicist; Harry Winne, vice president of the General Electric Company; and Allan Kline, president of the American Farm Bureau Federation.

The topic was atomic energy—whether it had gotten out of hand; whether it could now be controlled; whether its important peacetime benefits could be realized.

Critics of television and radio concluded that the topic was too broad for this thirty-minute treatment, and that too many speaking guests were "present." Each participant had at most a few minutes. Lilienthal, for example, exhibited a piece of uranium but had no time to expound its possible significance to society. The camera direction also was questioned. Each around the tea table "was too fleetingly seen and heard."

Dr. Einstein was given somewhat more time than the others. "We saw the great scientist with his wonderful, aged, inquiring face, wearing a tieless shirt and a sweater jacket, and we heard him speak quietly and with an almost dispassionate sadness, of the possible destruction of this planet." [20]

Einstein's analysis of the problem of how to secure peace was theoretical. Listeners and observers of his telecast asked, "How can we do away with the mutual fear and distrust as he proposed?" "What evi-

[18] Permission for this reprint given through the courtesy of Dr. Einstein and of the National Broadcasting Company. For text see also the New York *Times*, February 13, 1950.

[19] For biographical note, see Appendix.

[20] *New Yorker*. 26:88-89. February 25, 1950. "Television, Mrs. Roosevelt's Tea Party." Philip Hamburger.

dence did Einstein have that the Soviet Union and her satellite states would cooperate in the 'supranational body'?" "What hope is there to set up a supranational judicial and executive body after the preceding five years of experience with Soviet diplomatic 'road blocking'?"

The student, reviewing this speech, should examine in detail the scope and limitations of television as a medium for presenting current issues.

I am grateful to you for the opportunity to express my conviction in this most important political question.

The idea of achieving security through national armament is, at the present state of military technique, a disastrous illusion. On the part of the U. S. A. this illusion has been particularly fostered by the fact that this country succeeded first in producing an atomic bomb. The belief seemed to prevail that in the end it were possible to achieve decisive military superiority. In this way, any potential opponent would be intimidated, and security, so ardently desired by all of us, brought to us and all of humanity. The maxim which we have been following during these last five years has been, in short: Security through superior military power, whatever the cost.

This mechanistic, technical-military psychological attitude had inevitable consequences. Every single act in foreign policy is governed exclusively by one view point. How do we have to act in order to achieve utmost superiority over the opponent in case of war? Establishing military bases at all possible strategically important points on the globe. Arming and economic strengthening of potential allies. Within the country! Concentration of tremendous financial power in the hands of the military, militarization of the youth, close supervision of the loyalty of the citizens, in particular, of the civil servants by a police force growing more conspicuous every day. Intimidation of people of independent political thinking. Indoctrination of the public by radio, press, school. Growing restriction of the range of public information under the pressure of military secrecy.

The armament race between the U.S.A. and the USSR, originally supposed to be a preventive measure, assumes hysterical character. On both sides, the means to mass destruction are perfected with feverish haste—behind the respective walls of secrecy. The H-Bomb appears on the public horizon as a probably attainable goal. Its accelerated development has been solemnly proclaimed by the President. If successful, radioactive poisoning of the atmosphere and hence annihilation of any life on earth has been brought within the range of technical possibilities. The ghostlike character of this development lies in its apparently compulsory trend. Every step appears as the unavoidable consequence of the preceding one. In the end, there beckons more and more clearly general annihilation.

Is there any way out of this impasse created by man himself? All of us, and particularly those who are responsible for the attitude of the U. S. and the U.S.S.R., should realize that we may have vanquished an external enemy, but have been incapable of getting rid of the mentality created by the war. It is impossible to achieve peace as long as every single action is taken with a possible future conflict in view. The leading point of view of all political action should therefore be: What can we do to bring about a peaceful coexistence and even loyal cooperation of the nations. The first problem is to do away with mutual fear and distrust. Solemn renunciation of violence (not only with respect to means of mass destruction) is undoubtedly necessary. Such renunciation, however, can only be effective if at the same time a supra-national judicial and executive body is set up empowered to decide questions of immediate concern to the security of the nations. Even a declaration of the nations to collaborate loyally in the realization of such a "restricted world government" would considerably reduce the imminent danger of war.

In the last analysis, every kind of peaceful cooperation among men is primarily based on mutual trust and only secondly on institutions such as courts of justice and police. This holds for nations as well as for individuals. And the basis of trust is loyal give and take.

What about international control? Well, it may be of secondary use as a police measure. But it may be wise not to overestimate its importance. The times of Prohibition come to mind and give one pause.

NATIONAL DEFENSE

LONG RANGE MILITARY POLICY [1]

OMAR N. BRADLEY [2]

General Omar N. Bradley, chairman of the Joint Chiefs of Staff, gave this testimony before the House Armed Service Committee, Washington, D.C., on Wednesday, October 19, 1949. The Congressional inquiry was concerned with the bitter dispute between this country's military authorities about the strategic purposes, size, and character of the defense organization.

For the previous two weeks the Navy had stated its case, highlighted by Admiral Louis E. Denfield's criticism of alleged discrimination against the Navy in the unification of the armed services. He stated that the Navy did not object to such effort at unity, but strongly protested against the curtailing of naval aviation and the cutting down of the Marine Corps. He accused Secretary of Defense Johnson of taking "arbitrary action."

Air Secretary W. Stuart Symington, replying on October 18, stated that the Navy's testimony had been "false" and "untrue" and that the national security had been imperiled by the revealing of the "technical and operating details of our newest and latest equipment." Thus was the issued joined of Navy versus Army and Air Forces.

General Bradley denounced as "fancy Dans" the Navy officers who complained against the defense policies. He told the House committee that the Navy's attitude was "seriously wrong about our military establishment" and singled out Admiral Denfield for special criticism. General Vandenberg, head of the Air Force, offered similar criticism of the Navy.

The issues were mainly (1) What kind of unified armed defense should this nation have? (2) Should the policies of one branch of the service be overridden or vetoed by another branch? (3) What over-all military strategy should be followed in case of war?

The Navy specifically objected to the staff decision to build up the Air Force's B-36 bomber, armed with the atomic bomb, and to cut naval aviation.

[1] Text furnished by the Joint Chiefs of Staff, Pentagon Building, Washington, D.C.

[2] For biographical note, see Appendix.

General Bradley read his fifteen thousand word statement rapidly. He rarely raised his rather high-pitched voice. "Now and again there was a slight sharpening in his nasal drawl." [3]

The General stated that he had written the entire document himself, but that he was of course "helped by several aides."

His argument was a direct refutation of three principal charges given by the Navy: (1) The basic concept of our defense is wrong in that our plans for the execution of war are jeopardizing our national security; (2) the offensive power of the Navy is being destroyed; and (3) the Secretary of Defense and Joint Chiefs of Staff are underestimating the Navy's role. The student will study the methods by which Bradley attempted to refute each charge. The reply to the first of these three charges is included in this volume. In their public arguments and statements before Congressional groups, Bradley and the other military men often had to generalize without supplying the concrete but highly confidential evidence.

In this statement General Bradley frequently relied on his personal authority for proof.

The Committee adjourned on October 21. It announced that it would present its solution of the issues and recommendations to the second session of the Eighty-first Congress.

As this volume went to the publisher (May 1950), Congress was struggling with the size and distribution of the defense budget. The issues raised by Admiral Denfield and handled by General Bradley were thus being partly answered by the decisions concerning Congressional military appropriations.

Although General Bradley has had little speech training, he has had wide experience in speaking, including his service as instructor in the ROTC program at South Dakota State College immediately after World War I; his four years as instructor in mathematics at West Point, 1920-24; his instructorship in tactics and weapons at the Infantry School, 1929-1933; and his second four-year assignment at West Point as instructor in tactics, and later as plans and training officer, 1934-38. His later military career in North Africa and Europe, and his administration of the Veterans Administration, 1945-47, all involved continual speaking before military training groups, congressional committees, and many civilian audiences.[4]

Mr. Chairman, and Members of the Committee: My frequent appearances before this Committee have always been a pleasure. It would be so in this instance, if I were not adverse to public discussion of matters which might compromise our national de-

[3] New York *Times*, October 20, 1949.
[4] For this information the editor is indebted to Colonel Willis G. Matthews, Aide to General Bradley (letter of April 10, 1950).

fense. While I regret the circumstances which compel me to discuss the controversial subjects before your Committee, since they have already been discussed publicly, I welcome the opportunity to present my views.

Mr. Chairman, the testimony you have heard so far, and the remarks I am about to make emphasize war, and our war-making effort. I would like to express my gratitude to you for introducing into the record of this investigation last Thursday the article in the *Saturday Evening Post,* which I had the pleasure of writing with Mr. Beverly Smith, entitled, "This way lies peace." For in that article, I tried to emphasize the importance of a steadfast and determined effort on the part of the American people for peace. It is my sincere belief that "we [Americans] and our friends of the free world must combine our military potential and our peaceful intent in a strategy for peace—[which will ultimately make] us more secure than any strategy ever designed for war." . . .

Let's first discuss the basic concept of our defense planning. As far as I am able, without violating security, I want to discuss our plans and preparations for the execution of a war, if it is thrust upon us. As I have indicated, our basic concept for defense includes protection of the United States, and this continent, in case we are attacked. It provides for early retaliation from bases which we hope to have ready at all times.

This concept includes a decision that we shall have to be ready to seize other bases that we may need, and hold those bases against enemy attack, so that we may attack the enemy country at shorter ranges, and at the same time, deny to him bases close to this country from which he could attack us.

Ultimately, however, we will have to carry the war back to the enemy by all means at our disposal. I am convinced that this will include strategic air bombardment, and large-scale land operations.

I also believe that after the initial phases are over, there will be little need for any campaign similar to the Pacific "island hopping" that took place during the last war. And as I will develop later on in my discussion, I also predict that large-scale amphibious operations, such as those in Sicily and Normandy, will never occur again.

In addition to the concept I have just outlined, we must go back to the realization that the first prize for any aggressor in the world today is Europe, with its industrial potential and its market for goods. The American people realize this and have affirmed, in economic aid and by political tie, that we are still interested in Western Europe, which we have twice defended. Through the North Atlantic Treaty and with the Mutual Defense Assistance Act of 1949, we have indicated that our continent is linked with theirs in peace and for collective defense.

The basic defense principle of the North Atlantic Treaty, and of the mutual defense assistance program is that each nation shall contribute those things which it can best provide in the collective security plan. And in our own strategic plans, our part in this collective international security must be given its proper perspective.

Finally, our basic concept has never for a moment overlooked the primary consideration of protecting the continental United States, its coastal waters, and the key bases for this task.

At the same time, your planners have realistically assumed that the American people would never be content to sit down in confinement to this continent and suffer a long war of attrition, carried on by intercontinental bombing, and intercontinental missiles. We have realized that if we are ever attacked, our plans must include the tenacious holding of our frontiers in Europe, and the eventual defeat of the aggressor's land army.

This discussion is all too brief. There are many detailed considerations within the basic strategic concept that must be carried out. But I cannot see any jeopardy to our national security in this strategy.

Finally, if the military continues to effect more economies in defense measures, keeping constantly aware of the drain on our economy, there will be little danger of economic collapse, and our over-all risk will be less and less.

I would like to end the discussion of this accusation right here. However, in the testimony presented to the Committee, and related to this conception that our national security has been made insecure, are some specific points that I would like to deny.

First, that strategic bombing is wrong from a military standpoint, and from a moral standpoint, and that the Secretary of

Defense and the Joint Chiefs of Staff have permitted an unwarranted emphasis on strategic bombing for the best interests of national security. As a means of conducting war, I define strategic bombing as violent airborne attacks on the war-making capacity or potential of an enemy nation. I do not advocate a wanton destruction of cities or people, but it is obvious that workers live near factories, and that if you bomb the factories, you may bomb the people. From a military standpoint, any damage you can inflict on the war-making potential of a nation, and any great injury you can inflict upon the morale of that nation contributes to the victory. It has been proved that strategic bombing has such effect when properly applied. . . .

They have charged that the performance characteristics of the B-36 bomber in the eyes of the Navy make it an unsatisfactory weapon. In other words, that technically the B-36 airplane is no good for the mission of the Air Force. Without going into the technical details, I will only state that, in my opinion, it is the best bomber available for production that is capable of carrying out certain required missions in the case of emergency. I believe this opinion is substantiated by the comparative statistics as previously presented to the JCS by the Air Force on the various types of bombers available when they made their selection of the B-36 to fulfill the strategic bombing role they have been assigned.

I would also like to point out that the Joint Chiefs of Staff joined in the unanimous ratification of the Air Force investment in the B-36 last February. This ratification was not made under duress of any kind. And I raise the question, if it has become so disastrous to national security now, why did the Navy concur eight months ago?

The Navy has also made great moment of the fact that the B-36 is not the best plane for strategic bombardment, and that intercontinental bombing as such is an impracticable idea. May I point out that no member of the military establishment has said that better types won't be used when they are available, nor has any responsible individual indicated that there has been any cessation on the part of the Air Force in developing a better, faster, and longer-range bomber as soon as possible.

Meanwhile, I assure you that if war comes, we will make every effort to use bases as close as possible to the enemy for maximum effect and minimum expense of lives and material. The closer the range, the higher the speed for the run over enemy territory.

But I personally would hate to face the American people after abandoning any program for intercontinental bombing if we found ourselves suddenly devoid of bases, except for those on this continent, and we had to sit here and take it in the United States, with no means of reprisal. A long-range bomber can always be effective at shorter ranges, but a limited-range bomber is of little value beyond its distance.

The Air Force has facts and conclusions upon which they have based their judgment and belief that are at variance with some of the information presented to you by Navy personnel. However, to answer assertion with assertion would not only carry on this hearing indefinitely, it would serve no useful purpose. This is especially true when all of the services and their leaders are agreed that this weapon can best be tested by the Weapons Evaluation Group.

I would like to point out, in all fairness, that one service, the Navy, has taken this opportunity to publicly disparage a weapon—the B-36—that the Air Force, the service responsible, has chosen to perform an assigned mission. This is in direct contradiction to the Navy's own idea presented so forcefully and frequently to the public, that each service should be allowed to develop and have the weapons it feels it needs for the mission it is assigned.

Before concluding that the B-36 is unsatisfactory for the mission assigned to the Air Force, may I respectfully suggest that you await the results of the Evaluation Group report. This attack on the B-36 as a weapon included two other insinuations which I do not believe are valid charges. One was the implication *that from the B-36, our Air Force bombardiers cannot hit a target from high altitudes.*

Yet they admit that no Navy pilot has flown a B-36, nor have they participated in any tests with this bomber. On the other hand, our Air Force bombardiers have assured us that this aircraft can perform effectively under all conditions of weather, by night or day, and can deliver striking blows against their targets. These Air Force men, who will have to face the risk of the great losses that the Navy predicts, are perfectly willing to stake their reputations and their lives on their performance. Again may I suggest that you do not reach a decision on the accuracy of high level bombardment without consulting the men who are charged with doing it.

And too, *the testimony implies that the Russians—our only possible opponents for many years to come—have the capability of causing intolerable losses on any bomber engaged in mission where the Russians have adequate defenses.* They base this allegation on the creditable performance of one of the Navy's fighter-interceptor aircraft, the Banshee. However, we do not know whether or not the Russians have a "Banshee." At the same time, I might point out that the Navy is anxious to have a "flush-deck carrier" so that they can use even larger planes with longer ranges from their floating air bases. It seems to me that these larger planes would be subject to the same attack which Navy witnesses have visualized against the B-36.

This discussion of the Banshee and the B-36 does not convince me that the Russians have the capability attributed to them. It indicates only that the permanent contest between offensive and defensive weapons includes airplanes. Regardless of the planes used, I expect that some will be shot down. The number lost will be dependent upon many factors, but the fact that you may suffer *some* losses doesn't mean that you cannot still accomplish your mission.

And I must admit that I find some comfort in the fact that we have a long-range bomber that can fly from any base in the world and attack targets in the range of four thousand miles, and return home. We have accomplished a tie-up of enemy men and planes, and many millions of dollars in their radar equipment and fighter-interceptor equipment, as they look around a global circumference for any approaching attacks.

Again, I respectfully suggest that we heed the estimate of *what the enemy might do,* rather than the statistical reports of what our own Navy can perform.

Related to this entire discussion of strategic bombing is the ridiculous assertion *that the atomic bomb is effective on only a small area,* insinuating that we Americans have misplaced our confidence and our dollars in this weapon.

I believe that the insinuation that the atomic bomb is relatively ineffective as a weapon of war is refuted by every test that has been made. Contrary to many of the statements made before your Committee, the Navy case in these matters has been presented to the Joint Chiefs of Staff, and among other things, it has been the Navy's continuous argument that they should be permitted to use the atomic bomb, both strategically and tactically. If it is really so ineffective as some would have you believe, I wonder why the Navy is so anxious to use it.

And without clouding the issue, I would like to add one more relevant point on the atomic bomb. It is no secret the tests at Bikini and Eniwetok revealed that the Navy afloat is one of the most profitable targets for an enemy with an atomic bomb, and that its effect on ships is lasting. Even without sinking them, it promises to deny our use of them for many, many months after the onslaught. This, I know, contributes to the Navy's worries and indicates to some of their thinking members that surface fleets en masse might be a thing of the past.

Admiral Blandy also pointed out in his testimony, rightfully, that naval air protected the amphibious landing at Okinawa, and inferred that the success of this battle is largely dependent upon that arm, the Navy. Undoubtedly, without Navy support, any amphibious operation is impossible. However, by appraising the power of the atomic bomb, I am wondering whether we shall ever have another large-scale amphibious operation. Frankly, the atomic bomb, properly delivered, almost precludes such a possibility. I know that I, personally, hope that I shall never be called upon to participate in another amphibious operation like the one in Normandy.

If I may digress for a moment from my consideration of the atomic bomb, I would like to point out to those who hold that a tremendous Marine Corps is essential for future amphibious operations, and that naval air must be correspondingly large, that I have participated in the largest two amphibious assaults ever made in history. In neither case were any Marines present. And in neither case were any Navy carriers used.

The A-bomb is the most powerful destructive weapon known today. Personally, I hope it can be outlawed as a weapon by the adequate international control our government has recommended. But until that has been achieved, I shall not discredit its effect, nor shall I shortsightedly limit its role to purely strategic use.

As a believer in humanity I deplore its use, and as a soldier, I respect it.

And as an American citizen, I believe that we should be prepared to use its full psychological and military effect toward preventing war, and if we are attacked, toward winning it. The careless detractions of the power of this weapon have done national security no good, and may have done our collective security, in these precarious times, untold harm. Frankly, for the good of our nation, I wish that such testimony, belittling one of our great deterrents to war, had never been given.

I consider this first major charge, namely, *that the basic concept of our defense planning is wrong, and that our plans and preparations for the execution of a war are jeopardizing our national security,* the most serious detraction brought forth in this investigation.

FREEDOM AND MILITARY SECURITY [5]

W. STUART SYMINGTON [6]

W. Stuart Symington, Secretary of the Air Force, gave this address before the graduating class at Baylor University, Waco, Texas, at 9:30 A.M. (Central Standard Time) on Wednesday, February 1, 1950. The occasion was part of the University's 105 Anniversary ceremonies. The speaker received an honorary degree.

Mr. Symington, during 1946-47, had been Assistant Secretary of War, and Secretary of the Air Force in National Defense in 1947-50. He had steadily advocated a big air force, one that would comprise "seventy groups," as recommended in the Thomas K. Finletter Report of January 1, 1948. Mr. Symington made many speeches in support of vast air strength. He and Secretary of Defense Louis F. Johnson clashed sharply on the issue.

The issue specifically was whether by about 1953 the Air Force should be prepared to wage a sustained campaign, or whether it should be merely powerful enough to repel air attack from Russia. Upon analysis of air power as measured by "air frame weight," it became obvious that the Truman-Johnson force would be far inferior to that argued for by Symington and Finletter. General Eisenhower's proposed "air weight" was somewhat greater than Truman's and considerably less than that of the Symington Finletter formula. Were we to prepare for total war? Or were we to support a military machine that would be capable only of defensive action?

The Baylor speech was a comprehensive justification of a proposed national defense budget of thirteen or fourteen billion dollars, and was timed to shake national complacency concerning military power. Symington would enlist national support for the huge military budget, especially the Air Force portion.

Note the essence of Symington's logic and his appeal through an extended analogy or comparison of conditions in 1938 with those in 1950. (1) Russia in 1950 is heavily armed. (2) The threat to our security is great. (3) We are likely to be relatively in the same position as England was in 1938-39, except that there will be no America to come to our rescue. (4) Therefore, we must arm heavily—whatever the cost and however huge the unbalanced budget.

[5] Text supplied by the Department of Defense, Office of Public Information, Washington, D.C. Permission for this reprinting given through the courtesy of Secretary W. Stuart Symington.

[6] For biographical note, see Appendix.

This obvious logic was set forth in sharp, interesting, layman's language. The persuasion was carefully managed—though no doubt naturally developed in the speech composition and without mechanical contrivance.

On March 30, 1950, the President, at Key West, Florida, announced that Mr. Symington would resign and would be made chairman of the National Security Resources Board. His successor was to be Mr. Finletter. The change was widely interpreted as a victory for Secretary of Defense Johnson—and a more moderate air arm.

Symington as speaker, although not eloquent, talks with ease and communicative directness. His absorption in his theme of adequate national defense gave his public appearances of 1949-50 much persuasive cogency and intellectual drive.

For some years now I have been a member of your national defense structure, America's team of land, sea and air; and certain observations might be of interest to you today in connection with problems incident to the future security of the United States.

In his recent message to Congress on the State of the Union, our great President outlined the position and responsibilities of our country at this turn of the mid-century. In that challenging address he said in part:

The human race has reached a turning point. Man has opened the secrets of nature and mastered new powers. If he uses them wisely, he can reach new heights of civilization. If he uses them foolishly, they may destroy him.

In the world today we are confronted with the danger that the rising demand of people everywhere for freedom and a better life may be corrupted and betrayed by the false promises of communism.

While the world remains unsettled . . . and as long as our own security and the security of the free world require, we will maintain a strong and well-balanced defense organization.

It is common knowledge that the source of the unsettled conditions to which our Commander in Chief referred is the threat of communistic aggression. Four years ago World War II ended. In 1922, four years after the close of World War I, the major powers were able to sit around the conference table in Washington, in a conciliatory atmosphere, and arrive at an agreement for the reduction of armaments. This they accomplished because no major power threatened the peace..

Ever since the end of the last war, however, America has become increasingly aware there can be no true peace while there is this threat of Communist aggression.

Indeed we may have already lived so long in this postwar cold-war atmosphere that unrest and instability are now being taken for granted, and therefore disregarded. If so, that is a very serious matter, because such lack of interest might result in loss of our freedom.

Such disregard may be natural for normal, healthy, peace-loving people. In this air-atomic age, however, it is dangerous, because the cause for this unrest—Communist aggression—is a threat not only to the preservation of the peace, but also to our existence as a nation.

Never in the history of the United States has it been more important to recognize the truth about the world we live in; to recognize that truth, and then to follow the proper course necessary for America's preservation, no matter what the sacrifices required.

As our President said, "We know now that this is not an easy task or a short one." Professor Arnold Toynbee, famed historian, recently predicted that these sacrifices might be required for the next fifty years. Toynbee assumed, of course, there would be no successful world conquest by the Communists.

Some twelve and a half years ago, in the summer of 1937, I went to the seat of a great world empire, a gay and busy city. It was the end of the London season. There were the usual number of parties. Some of the wealthy were watching their horses race; others were taking off for the continent. With the exception of very few men, always and primarily Winston Churchill, foreign affairs were viewed with but normal apprehension. Many were sympathetic with Hitler. There was fear of Communist Russia, and fear of the growth of communism in the French army, which was considered the greatest army in the world. As against these two fears, many favored Hitler's Germany as providing a balance of power and a bulwark state.

Douglas Reed of the London *Times* sounded consistent warnings from his post in Berlin. Churchill pleaded with the good people of his country, in epochal speeches which later composed a famous book, *While England Slept.*

Appeasement, however, was the order of the day. World trade, and the stock dividends from it, were important. Some were trying to "buy" security through appeasement—as if any nation can ever "buy" security through compromise with evil.

Fourteen months later came Munich. Some countries, particularly Czechoslovakia, felt they had been sold down the river. By then, however, there was no alternative, because the wolf had taken off his sheep's clothing. Hitler and his gangsters had revealed their true intent, and neither England, nor any other democracy, had adequate armament with which to trade against the war now sure to come.

In all free countries men stirred uneasily. They realized that soon they might be called upon to fight and die. They asked one another: How did we ever get into this position so soon after having won before?

How did they? That is the point of such critical importance to us today.

Less than four years later I again visited London, in early 1941. We sneaked up the coast of Portugal by air, praying for bad weather, hoping to avoid Hitler's dominant Focke-Wulf long-range bombers, as they returned over the Atlantic from their attacks on Allied shipping.

Times had changed in London. Nobody took off for the continent of Europe except in battle planes, because the Nazis controlled that continent, just twenty miles away. Horses were being eaten instead of raced, and most of the entertainment was deep in the shelter of basements, comparatively safe from the bombs raining down overhead.

One of Britain's greatest battleships, the "Hood," had been sunk. Worse to them, a large island, Crete, had just been conquered from the air.

The British people stood up with indomitable courage. Their leaders knew, nevertheless, that all which stood between them and slavery was the potential production wealth and manpower of the United States.

At this point let me ask you—in case our country in turn is caught with its defense guard down, what nation has the strength to stand behind us as we stood behind England?

At present the people on this earth are, in effect, split into two main political groups. One group is headed by an aggressive dictatorship, ruling some 285 million people directly, plus many millions indirectly through puppet, or satellite, regimes. This central Communist dictatorship has reiterated many times, to its own people and to the rest of the world, that it is conducting the modern equivalent of a holy war against all non-believers.

In every issue of Communist dogma, under the title "Problems of Leninism," published over the signature of Stalin, appears this basic Communist tenet:

We are living not merely in a state, but in a system of states; and it is inconceivable that the Soviet Republic should continue for a long period side by side with imperialistic states. Ultimately one or the other must conquer. Meanwhile, a number of terrible clashes between the Soviet Republic and the bourgeois states will be inevitable. . .

The above statement of Communist policy has been reiterated many times, and as recently as after the close of World War II in 1945.

Furthermore, Communist leaders denounce all spiritual faiths, dictating as a substitute the cynical and materialistic doctrine of communism. As we all know, but sometimes are prone to forget, the Communist does not believe in God. That is part of the foundation of his philosophy. He has always fought to destroy religion.

The leaders of Russia have not only constantly reiterated their goal of world domination; they have also predicted the doom of all other political systems, especially capitalism. They inflamed all Communists against all non-Communists, wherever the latter may be. They have sealed off their own people behind an Iron Curtain, while taking advantage of free access in other countries to create constant distress and confusion from within.

Theirs has been a ceaseless campaign of aggression; ideological, political and economic; and wherever expedient, that campaign has been supported by guns and marching men.

In the middle thirties it was important to know what the people of France and England and Holland and Denmark and Belgium and Norway were doing. It was far more important, however, to know what the Nazis were doing. Were they really rearming? Did they really believe their marching slogan, "Today we rule Germany, tomorrow the world"?

I believe that in these United States, at this mid-century mark, the most important question for all of us today is, What are the Russians doing? Not what we are doing in the way of rearming, at some slight expense to our standard of living, but what are those other people doing—those people who say they cannot live in the same world with our way of life? What is their weapons program, and why?

Surely we Americans do not want to be caught at any future time the way the democracies were caught by Hitler in the thirties.

This we know. Those who reiterate America must be destroyed, now have: (1) A ground army greater in numbers than the combined armies of the United States and its allies; (2) An air force whose strength in nearly all categories is now the largest in the world and growing relatively larger month by month; (3) The world's largest submarine fleet; and an intensive submarine development and construction program.

It is our belief that if any democracy attempted to maintain in peacetime a comparable regular armed force, the free economy of that democracy would be wrecked. In Communist countries, however, the will of the rulers, and not the economy of the nation, is the controlling factor. People under a dictatorship do not know when great streams of national wealth, which could be used to raise their standard of living, are diverted instead to further the aggressive ambitions of their rulers

The Communist government dictators have no problems of money, because all money is owned by the state. The coin of the realm is the order of the dictator. Nor have these bosses any problem of labor, because they have millions of slaves, captive prisoners from other countries as well as their own political slaves. From our standpoint, every citizen of their state is but a slave to the handful of rulers at the top.

All men in such positions of dictatorial power, uncontrolled by the checks and balances of representative government, disdainful of the dignity and rights of the individual, and dedicated to the belief that the end justifies the means, are, and always will be, a threat to the freedom-loving peoples of the world.

Here are three facts which every American should know, because this is the world in which we live: (1) Behind the iron curtain there has been an atomic explosion. (2) Behind that curtain is the air equipment capable of delivering a surprise atomic attack against any part of the United States. (3) We have no sure defense against such an attack.

The bleak picture is that today we have a group of dictators dedicated to destroy our way of life. They are capable now of unleashing, without warning, the world's largest ground army, air force and undersea fleet. The gravity of this situation is multiplied many times by our knowledge of achievements being made by Russian scientists in the field of atomic energy.

I ask you, if these leaders want peace, why are they building their armed strength to such staggering proportions?

Today America holds the position of world economic, moral, intellectual, and in some respects, material leadership, in a struggle as bitter and fundamental as that in the Middle Ages between Islam and Christianity. In that ancient conflict the battleground was religious belief. It is with difficulty that we now understand the intensity of feelings which led to those holy wars. Many feel those dedicated to communism are, in effect, now waging a new religious war, with the dialectic materialism of communism the basis of a godless faith.

In the past the United States has been relatively safe, because our allies have given us the time necessary to build our defense against attack. Then we were at relatively safe distances from our enemies. That is no longer true. Distance is no longer any protection from the long arm and smashing fist of modern military air power. In this air-atomic age the oceans and polar wastes are not barriers against attack. Remember Russian soil is but five minutes flying time from the American soil of Alaska; and but a few hours away from our great cities. Waco is but an eighteen-hour flight from Moscow for the bombers we know Russia is now producing in quantity.

Based on these facts, are there any who would question the importance of this country maintaining as much military strength as will provide what George Washington called a "respectable posture of defense"? Would any of us like to forfeit either (1) the capacity to defend ourselves as best possible against sudden atomic air attack, or (2) the strategic air capacity necessary for instant effective retaliation against those who would make a surprise move against this country?

America is reconciled to the necessity for a peacetime defense program greater than ever required in the past. We must remain steadfast and alert until that day—God hasten it—when we can have complete assurance that any power or combination of powers which threaten peace will abandon their aggressive schemes and participate effectively in the community of nations to advance, and not destroy, civilization.

History teaches that mere races for armed might do not prevent wars. History also teaches, however, that weakness invites aggression.

Our patience in seeking peaceful solutions must not be interpreted as weakness. Rather it constitutes evidence of our own lack of aggressive designs, a manifestation of our sincere hope that as one member of a world organization, we may help to realize the aspirations of mankind for a permanent and responsible peace.

It is a basic dilemma of our time that those who menace our way of life may force arms expenditures of a magnitude that could cripple our economy and thus imperil our free institutions. I submit, however, that those who are critical of this administration for not bringing the national budget into balance may be guilty of ignoring the grim realities of the world in which we live.

I share the businessman's traditional dislike for deficits and am not unaware of the desires of the American taxpayer to have his burden made lighter. But under the circumstances of today, I am convinced that no loyal and informed American would knowingly consent to dangerous concessions in our security program in order to achieve some otherwise desirable fiscal objective. The risks involved are too great—the stakes too high, for any such false economies.

The arithmetic of the distribution of your tax dollars and mine establishes that during the current and coming fiscal year one third of that dollar, or 33c, is being allocated to the Army, Navy and Air Force. This figure does not include foreign aid, part of our payment for security, which averages 14c.

Those who say they would destroy the United States are thus forcing us to spend heavily from our resources, not only for our national defense but also for the rehabilitation and strengthening of our allies. They hope to force us into economic collapse.

This danger is always present—consequently efficiency and quality assume transcendent importance in all our preparations; and selectivity in the building of our defense structure grows increasingly vital to our solvency.

If it is more important to balance the budget than to guarantee our security, it would be a relatively simple matter for our President to do so by recommending still further reductions in appropriations for national defense.

Based on the facts presented to you above, however, I ask again, is there any American who wants to see our defense budget reduced further?

We have made the mistake more than once. Let us consider what a single mistake of this kind cost us in money alone—not to mention hundreds of thousands of American lives.

In 1913, at the start of the First World War, the national debt was a little over a billion dollars. That war heavily taxed our resources; and a few years later we went through the greatest depression of them all.

A new President came in. He helped those people who wanted work but couldn't find a job. He did so because he believed that human dignity was better for the nation than poverty and want.

At the time we started, somewhat leisurely, rearming for the Second World War, the national debt was around $40 billion. Today this debt is about $257 billion. Could there ever be clearer proof of the cost of unpreparedness?

If reports received from behind the iron curtain are correct, in a short time Russia will be at its strongest position in armaments; and under their present program that position will increase steadily year by year. So, I say today that further reduction in our payment for national security is unthinkable.

Our able and conscientious Secretary of Defense, Louis Johnson, is doing everything possible to promote true unification of the services which will guarantee the taxpayer maximum security at minimum cost. He is doing a fine job. But, it was Mr. Johnson himself who said recently that our "watchword should be military security first, economy second."

Both he and our President were front-line fighters in one war waged to preserve our way of life. They know that peace can be lost—but they know also, and you know, that the current price to America of losing any modern war is slavery.

I remind you that there is little, if any, peace in the world today. We don't have peace just because the guns are silent. Tragically, we do have "fronts" where the shooting could begin at any time; and no one knows when or where!

The history of Texas is the history of a battle for independence. May you in this great state, and in all our other states, remember the cost of such battles. When those who want to represent us in the halls of our government consistently close their request for votes with the stressing of two words—peace and prosperity—let us remember the long rows of those who have passed on to us another heritage, and who believed that we in turn would pass that heritage on to our children, and our children's children. Let us ask our statesmen to add a third word to the appeal of "peace" and "prosperity." From Sam Houston to Sam Rayburn one word is engraved on the heart of every Texan, every true American. That word is freedom.

NATIONAL DEFENSE [7]

LOUIS A. JOHNSON [8]

Mr. Louis Johnson, Secretary of Defense, gave this address before the Overseas Press Club of America, at the Waldorf-Astoria Hotel, New York, on Friday evening, March 3, 1950.

The problems which Secretary Johnson dealt with included: (1) Has our program to develop postwar military and political strength among our allies against Russia been successful? (2) Is our program of developing national defense with respect to the Navy, Air Force and Army and military equipment sufficient to meet all emergencies? (3) Is our political and military policy as it relates to China and Southeastern Asia a satisfactory one?

The student of this speech should weigh its statements and its evident persuasive techniques against the contemporary facts and subsequent developments. Critics, alarmed at the expansion of Soviet Russia and her satellites, especially the Communist victory in China and threat of further territorial inroads, condemned the Johnson speech as filled with confident and unwarranted generalizations. Some of the wide adverse criticism offered against Johnson at this time stemmed from the responsibilities piled upon him during the year 1949. He was required to enforce the unification of military services; to cut the combined budget (Congress and the people so demanded), and to determine what share each branch of service should have of that budget. The opponents of Johnson were charging that the armed might of Soviet Russia was much greater than that of the United States and its allies. This disparity, it was held, was due to the sharp cut of our defense budget from some $22 billion to $15 billion, with some $13 billion recommended for the coming fiscal year. This last-named figure, the critics charged, would not give us the minimum necessary defense in any sudden war. It was in this atmosphere of indictment and against such charges that Johnson spoke. He would reassure, mollify, and, if possible, further establish for the press and American opinion his personal leadership and that of his administrative colleagues.

The speaker, forceful on his feet, ready in extempore debate or discussion, always communicative, has had much earlier speech experience. He was president of the class of 1912 at the University of Virginia; president of the Johnson Literary Society, a debating club; winner of the intercollegiate oratorical contest of the University of Virginia in 1911;

[7] Text furnished by the Department of National Defense, Office of Public Information.

[8] For biographical note, see Appendix.

represented the University of Virginia at the Southern Intercollegiate Division contest in 1911 at the University of Alabama; and was elected to membership in Delta Sigma Rho. His later career in law, the Army, his national presidency of the American Legion, and his various government posts all called for continual speaking and contributed to his maturing as a highly capable public speaker.

A year ago today I became to the members of the Overseas Press Club, and to reporters everywhere, a commodity, an intangible commodity that you newspapermen dignify under the name "news." I became "news" on that day when President Truman announced at his press conference that he would nominate me for Secretary of Defense.

On practically every one of the 365 days that have passed since that day, some reporter, some editorial writer, some columnist, some commentator, or some cartoonist has found some opportunity to express himself on the Department of Defense. Tonight the tables are reversed. You are giving me the chance to express myself on the American press.

Let me say at the outset that I share with the American people a profound respect for our press and for your right to report and interpret news as you see it. That is your right—your freedom. Under "press" I include the radio, the pictures, television, and all other media of expression that report news and influence public opinion. On the whole, you have been eminently fair to me. True, you may not always have looked at the news as it appeared to me, and there have been times when I wondered whether both of us were looking at the same thing. Such differences are inherent to our democratic process.

Well, tonight I am a reporter myself—by command of your own President, Frank Kelley.

When Mr. Kelley came to the Pentagon to invite me to speak tonight I asked him what he would like to have me talk about.

"Why not report?" he asked, "Why not report where we stand, what problems lie ahead? Why not?"

Well, you asked for it, so for tonight, at least, I am a reporter —a reporter among reporters and their friends of the Overseas Press Club of America.

Let me open my report in the form of a lead paragraph. If I tried to sum up in a few words the answers to the questions, where do we stand, what problems lie ahead, I might perhaps put it in this way:

Off to a slow start and almost left standing at the post, the United States is now making substantial gains toward the achievement of its goal of peace through strength. America's condition is sound and is getting stronger. In Europe, the situation is improving. In Asia, it bears watching.

Now let us spell out this summary in greater detail.

Let's go back to V-J Day. The United States and her Allies had just won a terrific life-and-death struggle. Our margin of victory was so pronounced, and the possible rise of a contender to challenge our position was so remote that we planned to rest on our gains and relax. Our armed forces, we demobilized. Our war production machine, we shifted in gear to meet peace requirements. To friend and foe, we extended in all sincerity a warm heart and a firm hand. We poured out billions to hasten their economic recovery and strengthen their political stability. Our most precious military secrets, acquired by us through sweat and at tremendous cost, we stood ready to convert to the service of peace. Never in the history of mankind did a people manifest a more noble spirit of good will to all. Never was there a finer demonstration of altruism by a nation toward all of civilization.

We had every reason to be proud of our demonstration of good will to all mankind and our readiness to support it by action. Some of our erstwhile friends, however, even though they benefited most from our help when they most desperately needed it, chose to scorn our nation. They laughed at our losses, mocked at our gains, and deliberately did everything in their power to impugn our honorable motives. Wherever we came to help, they intervened to hinder. While we marched toward peace, they threw up road blocks and tossed around vetoes. At first we were patient. But realizing the state of such an international environment, we finally reacted in characteristic American fashion. We did something about it.

In succession, we created the Truman Doctrine and the Marshall Plan. We set up the Economic Cooperation Administration. We signed with eleven other nations the North Atlantic Pact. We embarked on a Mutual Defense Assistance Program with our friends under the North Atlantic Pact. In the challenge of the Berlin Airlift we showed that the American stamina, courage, and resourcefulness are forces still to be conjured with. We have strengthened our ramparts. We are carrying out the mandate of the Congress and the President backed by the will of the American people to unify our forces. We are determined to be strong and through strength to maintain peace for ourselves and for all the world.

We would have preferred to spend our money and our energies differently. There is no human gain developing hydrogen bombs or stockpiling the atomic variety for destruction when an equal amount of energy in a similar effort toward production for peace could make life so much more secure and happy for ourselves and for everybody else. Unfortunately, we have no alternative at the moment but to be prepared.

Where do we stand? Farther ahead than ever in our peacetime history. We are alert to the dangers of our times. We are girding our loins accordingly. We are getting into condition. We are removing waste. We are eliminating fancy trimmings. We are converting fat to muscle. We are releasing civilians and men in uniform whose jobs do not contribute directly to national defense. By getting rid of what we no longer need for national defense, we get that much more money with which to meet our pressing requirements in men and munitions. We are taking officers away from desks and assigning them to the field for combat training. We are approaching the problem of reserves realistically, and are setting up a strong nucleus capable of orderly, rapid expansion in an emergency. We are getting more defense value out of every appropriated dollar than ever before. We are getting deliveries on weapons and equipment. We are ordering the manufacture of items now which will keep us up to date.

We may not have all the bombs, or all the planes, or all the submarines, or all the carriers, or all the tanks, or all the guns to carry on a war today; and we never will have enough to satisfy everybody concerned with national defense. The jaws of Mars are traditionally wide open and his appetite is insatiable.

We are tailoring our defense to fit today's situation. We face danger from one source. And we are determined to make ourselves strong in the most effective ways to thwart his aggressive intentions and capabilities.

I can say to you tonight, that the Air Force today is in its best state of combat readiness since the war.

Secretary Symington and General Vandenberg, the latter having only recently returned from an extensive tour of foreign stations, advise me that the esprit of officers and men is high. General Vandenberg states the combat readiness of the Air Force units he inspected was unexcelled at any time since the demobilization at the end of the war.

As for the United States Navy, let me repeat what Admiral Forrest P. Sherman, Chief of Naval Operations, has just put in a special message to all Navy personnel:

Navy Department is exerting every effort to translate available appropriations into maximum fighting strength and mobilization potential. Savings made are generally available for increasing the state of readiness of authorized forces. Economics already effected have permitted increasing previously planned fleet strength by one large carrier and one cruiser, to provide additional equipment for antisubmarine warfare, and to augment general readiness. Planned economies are an important contributing factor in retaining two additional Marine battalions.

And as for the Army, this is what General J. Lawton Collins, Chief of Staff, said to a New Orleans audience only a few days ago:

We have units that are ready to move right now in case of aggression; we have the best men in the Army today that we have ever had in peacetime and, although we have a number of critical equipment problems yet to solve, I can assure you that our troops, with the equipment that they have, would give a good account of themselves if we were attacked.

The recent reduction of our occupation commitments has enabled us to concentrate more of our efforts upon strengthening the combat units which form the hard core of our fighting force. We are giving our divisions and other combat units more officers and men, some items of better weapons and equipment, and improved training under field conditions.

Let me add for the benefit especially of all Army men that our success in converting fat into muscle enables us to allot to the Army approximately $150 million for new postwar models in tanks and anti-aircraft equipment, and for the modernization of other existing weapons.

In the meantime, the dread of being caught with inadequate supplies is real, and it rises to torment all of us responsible for the production and distribution of munitions. I know what it is myself. I sympathize with it. I experienced it as an infantry officer on the western front in the First World War when it looked as though my outfit would run out of rations or ammunition. And then again, between 1937 and 1940, when I was the Assistant Secretary of War responsible for current procurement and industrial mobilization, the dread of shortages gave me constant concern. I had many sleepless nights worrying about the acute need for bombers and fighters for the growing Army Air Force, which was my special concern. I understood the struggle of the Chief of Ordnance, the Quartermaster General, and the heads of other departments for larger shares of the national defense pie.

I have that same concern today, and I understand the worries of the Secretaries of the Army, the Navy, and the Air Force. I am sure, too, that the President of the United States understands them. He, too, had sleepless nights on the Western Front in 1918 worrying about food and ammunition for the artillerymen of his beloved Battery "D". When I now stand before him to plead for a larger share of the national budget to meet the defense needs, I know he understands. He wishes, and so do all of us, that we could meet all of the demand of our armed forces.

If we did, we would certainly feel a lot happier about our ability to hasten an enemy's defeat. But, unfortunately, if we gave our Army, our Navy, and our Air Force all the equipment that they felt they needed, our budget would have to be greatly increased; and there is a limit to expenditures beyond which we dare not go without destroying the very free American system which enables us to have the strength with which to maintain peace.

Hence, to keep adequately prepared, we must always be alert to the intentions and the capabilities of a possible foe, and a most convenient yardstick in gauging this is a comparison of relative strengths. How many long-range bombers do we have? How many does he have? How many submarines do we have? How many does he? What can ours do? What can his do? How many divisions do we have? How many does he? And what are the relative capabilities of the respective tanks?

Comparisons such as these are very important, but there are other factors in the measurement of a nation's ability to wage war successfully, and they, too, must be considered. What of the relative capabilities of mass production, of industrial know-how, of national morale, and of potential allies and their capabilities? When all these factors are considered and added to the defense programs now under way, it must make an aggressor hesitate to start an attack, if he is at all prudent.

The forces we already have in being, plus what our potential allies are developing, should tend to discourage aggressive action. For the security and the peace of the world look not only to American manpower, American industry, and American weapons, but also to the formidable British Navy and the Royal Air Force. They count also on a French Army and a French Marine now growing in strength. They count on the potential of all of our partners under the North Atlantic Pact who, with their own efforts plus our aid, are arming for the defense of our common ideal.

We took calculated risks in aiding Europe when it looked as though the spread of communism could not be halted. Our investment is now paying off. The hunger, the disorder, and the frustration in which communism is fostered no longer prevail. There is a new hope and a new confidence.

The situation is more encouraging than at any time since V-J Day. While there is no warrant for complacency yet it is an occasion for some satisfaction. We have held communism at bay in Western Europe. We have gained partners in Europe to help maintain a free world.

While Russia has been making satellites, we have been adding partners, and there is the big difference between their ways and ours. It has always been our attitude to support the rights of states, large and small, to determine for themselves, without external pressure, how they wish to be governed. It is the doctrine of the inalienable rights of the individual stated so forcefully in our own Declaration of Independence applied to peoples. It is the inalienable right of peoples to enjoy security, freedom and a decent standard of living. These are rights we recognize. We will not be pushed around, and we do not like to see others pushed around.

Woodrow Wilson had this in mind when he proposed that "No nation should seek to extend its policy over any other nation or people, but that every people should be left free to determine its own policy, its own way of development, unlimited, un-threatened, unafraid, the little along with the great and powerful."

Franklin D. Roosevelt reiterated it when he insisted that "The rights of every nation, large or small, must be respected and guarded as jealously as are the rights of every individual within our own Republic."

Finally, President Truman implemented this ideal into action when he declared: "I believe that we must assist free peoples to work out their own destinies in their own way."

We have not always lived up to our own ideals, but beginning with the administration of Franklin D. Roosevelt we have consistently adhered to them. This doctrine of the equality of states and the recognition of their legitimate national aspirations has been approved whole heartedly by the American people and is now basic to the policy that guides us in our present relation-ship with other peoples. It is especially important that we keep these principles in mind when we look at the present situation in Asia.

In Asia we are confronted with formidable dynamic move-ments of human forces. First is the old Russian imperialist design under a new red cloak. It would control the strategic areas of North Asia and penetrate into every part of South Asia. The attempt at domination of Asia by any one country, if successful, would be a most serious threat to our security.

Second is the awakening of the national consciousness of millions of people in the Orient now determined to govern them-selves. All of Southeast Asia is alive with national hopes and aspirations. It is a spirit that we as Americans should certainly understand. It is our example of 1776 and our Declaration of Independence which so greatly inspire this movement. Much depends on these new nations of Asia, their peoples, and their governments. They will have difficulty in standing alone, and require the help of friends just as we did in our early days to set us on our course.

The chief obstacle to our efforts to help is the spread of communism. In and of itself, communism is foreign to the progressive minds emerging in the Orient. These public leaders who chafed under the yokes of foreign exploitation and helped cast it off would hardly substitute the more loathsome saddle of the Soviet. Unfortunately, these peoples face misery and want. They lack experience in self-government. What may be but a momentary success may leave a permanent mark on their national pattern; and the spread of Communist powers in China is an example of the dangers inherent in the situation.

Faced with the full implications of these movements, we are following these general principles. We are trying to maintain a quarantine of Soviet communism wherever we feel that our efforts have a reasonable chance of success. We are judiciously applying our resources to help build a healthy, strong community of free Indo-Pacific nations founded on equality and friendship. We are developing the security and the well-being of Japan, the Ryukyus, and the Philippines. Our specific actions will depend upon time and circumstances.

Our specific actions in the future as in the past, will involve certain risks, calculated risks, that a strong, reasonable and confident people dare take and must take in a dangerous age. Risks will be taken only when the promise for the success of the venture is more than reasonably good. We do not promise the unattainable.

We do not and cannot promise, for instance, full immunity to all of America against atomic attack. There is a risk to living in the middle of the twentieth century instead of an earlier age which all of us must share. It is a risk that every community must take in an atomic age. We must reconcile ourselves to the fact that in case of war, some atomic raids might penetrate our cordon of defense, no matter how strong we make it. Some enemy pilot with the zeal and the fanaticism of a Kamikaze might get through our net on a one-way suicide mission, and the

United States might get hurt. No amount of money appropriated for national defense can prevent this possibility. We are spending $13 billion a year, and that is a terrific outlay. If we put all that money in air defense to the exclusion of all other forces needed for victory, we still could not guarantee against the possibilities of bombs falling on an American city. No one could honestly guarantee against the possibility of a suicide pilot eluding our air defense even if we spent twice or three times that amount, or even $50 billion a year.

This is what we can do and will do: We can build a strong air defense. We can make enemy raids costly—so costly that the attrition rate will destroy so many of his bombers that he will find himself unable to continue his attack. We can make retribution so deadly that he will wish he had never started. These will be the objectives of our defensive system. These are the goals of our present plans.

There are risks in these plans. Each is the risk of a prudent and energetic people whose economy is sound, whose courage is firm, and who faces the future unafraid; a people dedicated to peace and justice who today see no surer way to realize their ideals than through strength. Peace through strength is the goal of our defense program. To its achievement, I pledge you the full support of the unified national defense team.

And that, Gentlemen of the Press, is my story—my report to you.

HYDROGEN BOMB

THE HYDROGEN BOMB AND INTERNATIONAL GOVERNMENT [1]

Harold C. Urey [2]

Professor Harold C. Urey, of the University of Chicago Institute for Nuclear Studies, gave this address at the annual Roosevelt Day Dinner, at the Waldorf-Astoria Hotel, New York City, on January 27, 1950. The speech was broadcast by Columbia Broadcasting Company at 11:15 to 11:30 P.M. (EST). The dinner, one of eighteen throughout the country, was sponsored by the Americans for Democratic Action, to commemorate President Franklin D. Roosevelt's birthday anniversary, January 30.

Paul A. Porter, former Price Administrator, was toastmaster. Senator Frank P. Graham, of North Carolina, also spoke. A sketch, written by Marc Connelly and Howard Lindsay, recreating historic broadcasts of Roosevelt's White House career, was given.

Dr. Urey was the "first atomic scientist to speak out publicly about the hydrogen bomb." [3] His prestige as winner of the Nobel Prize in chemistry for his discovery of heavy hydrogen, and as key member of the atomic development program, gave immense prestige to his remarks.

On January 31, 1950, President Truman announced that this country would proceed with the making of the hydrogen bomb. General debate and discussion followed in the Senate and over the national networks.

Dr. Urey, widely experienced as a speaker, is unusually effective before popular, as well as scientific audiences. On December 29, 1949, for example, he participated with much speaking ability in a panel discussion on "the philosophy of speech in a democratic society," at a general session of the 1949 Convention of the Speech Association of America, at Chicago. He is an able extemporizer. [4]

I am happy to be addressing the members and friends of Americans for Democratic Action especially on the occasion of your Second Annual Roosevelt Day. The courage and daring of

[1] Text supplied by the Americans for Democratic Action. Permission for this reprint through the courtesy of Dr. Urey.

[2] For biographical note, see Appendix.

[3] William L. Laurence. New York *Times*. January 28, 1950.

[4] For further comment on Dr. Urey, see *Representative American Speeches*, 1945-46, p95-108.

Franklin D. Roosevelt made possible the long gamble that led to the development of atomic power. It is appropriate then, on this occasion, to discuss further developments in this field. I trust as well that these views of mine will be helpful to the ADA when it considers this whole question at its April convention in Washington.

Recently a very great service has been done for the people of the United States by Senator Johnson [Democrat of Colorado]. Quite unwittingly, and I believe unwillingly, he has brought to the attention of the people of the United States a problem which should have been considered by them a very long time ago, but because of the unwillingness of the United States officials to take the people into their confidence had not previously been brought before us. Most of the facts in regard to this have appeared occasionally in the newspapers, but most people have believed that the discussions were on a par with a great deal of the hysteria in regard to atomic bombs. I refer to the so-called hydrogen bomb. The Alsop brothers are my authority for the statement that this problem was considered in 1945 by President Truman, and on the advice of two prominent scientists it was decided that no development of this weapon should be made. I was not aware that such a decision had been made, and I think few people in the United States were aware of it.

These decisions in regard to the hydrogen bomb have been made in an almost unbelievable atmosphere. These people who decided we should not develop it believed that the USSR could not get the ordinary atomic bomb in less than ten or fifteen years. Time has proved them incorrect on this point. Moreover, due to some curious prejudice which I think I understand, the advisers to the United States government have not wished to follow certain lines of development in regard to this problem. No such prejudice exists among the Canadians, British, French and presumably the USSR, and this has put the United States in a very unfavorable position relative to what might have been, even though we decided not to build the bomb. I cannot be more specific without disclosing technical information, which it is not my intention to do at all. The result of this is a situation highly dangerous to the United States, in fact, we may have already lost the armaments race.

The question before us is this: Should the hydrogen bomb be built? First of all, it has been publicly reported for several years that such bombs would have a capacity of the order of one thousand times the capacity of the atomic bomb which has been developed in the past. It has been reported that if such bombs were dropped off the Pacific Coast of the United States the prevailing winds would carry the radioactivity over this country and would result in the extinction of all forms of life. I cannot vouch for the accuracy of this statement, but the effects of the radioactivity would certainly be far greater than those so dramatically exhibited at the Bikini Baker-Day bomb test. It is unnecessary to emphasize the great undesirability of such bombs in the world. I think it is something we all hope very much cannot in the nature of things be done. I personally hope very much that the bombs will not explode, no matter how much effort is put into the project. However, nature does not behave in the way I should like at times, and so there is no use in engaging in wishful thinking. I think we should assume that the bomb can be built.

The Alsop brothers say that the cost would be two to four billion dollars for the development of these bombs. This I doubt seriously. I am not connected with this project in any way, but it is difficult to see how the development itself should cost more than a hundred million dollars exclusive of the cost of materials. It would of course involve a considerable scientific and engineering talent, which I would much prefer to see employed on peacetime developments.

But let us turn to what the situation is in the world today. I think we should not be complacent in regard to what other countries can do in this respect, as many people were in connection with the development of the ordinary atomic bomb. To be specific, let us assume that the USSR is developing this bomb; and suppose that she should get it first. Then it seems to me that there is nothing in the temperament of the present negotiations between east and west that would lead us to believe that the rulers of the USSR would not reason approximately as follows:

It is true that the bomb is exceedingly dangerous, and we would not wish to produce so much radioactivity in the world as to endanger ourselves and the people of Russia, but the explosion of a few of these bombs will win us the world. Therefore we will build these bombs and issue ultimata to the western countries, and the millenium of communism will be with us immediately. After this the universal government of the USSR will abolish all stocks of bombs and no more will ever be made in the world.

This is a very good argument. In fact, I doubt if any bombs would need to be exploded. The atomic bomb is a very important weapon of war, but hardly decisive, as everybody has emphasized from the beginning. But I wonder if the hydrogen bomb would not be decisive, so that ultimata would be accepted and it would be unnecessary to deliver the bombs. This seems to me to be the situation.

In view of such a situation the United States can decide to intentionally lose the armaments race, which is what our decisions to date have amounted to. Suppose instead of deciding this, we decide we will build the hydrogen bomb. Suppose that we get the hydrogen bomb first. Then what do we do? Do we merely wait until the USSR also has it and we have a stalemate? It is quite out of character for the democracies to deliver ultimata with the philosophy I have ascribed to the Russian government. This is one of the things which I cannot answer, and which I merely put before you. Suppose we develop the hydrogen bomb, and suppose we get it first. Then what do we do next?

Suppose that two countries have the hydrogen bomb. Is it not believable that sooner or later an incident may occur which would make these bombs be used? This is a question again which I cannot answer definitely. I would say, however, that the probability that a war will start is increased if two groups each believe that they can win the war. This is true regardless of weapons and their magnitude. It is very difficult to get an exact balance of power. This is what we know in physical sciences as a situation of unstable equilibrium; one like balancing an egg on its end. The slightest push topples the egg in one direction or another. I have maintained, and many of my friends have maintained, that the only constructive way to solve the present situation is by adopting the Atlantic Union Resolution now in the Senate and House of the Congress of the United States, looking forward to a federal union of the democratic countries. Only in this way will we be able to maintain an overpowering political, commercial, military and ideological strength relative to the east. Only in this way do we have an enormous unbalance of power, so that perhaps the one side does not attempt to start a war because they recognize that they cannot win, and the other side does not need to start a war because the weaker side cannot attack. If this organization were perfected in the next few years there would be no question about the strength of the west, and this, regardless of the existence of any type of bombs in the world, might lead to a peaceful solution of the problem.

My own conclusion in regard to this problem is, first, I am very unhappy to conclude that the hydrogen bomb should be developed and built. I do not think we should intentionally lose the armaments race; to do this will be to lose our liberties, and with Patrick Henry, I value my liberties more than I do my life. It is important that the spirit of independence and liberty should continue to exist in the world. It is much more important that this spirit continue to exist than that I or you or any group should continue this mortal existence for a few years more. Second, there is no constructive solution to the world's problems except eventually a world government capable of establishing law over the entire surface of the earth. It is necessary to take whatever steps we possibly can in that direction, and to take them as rapidly as possible—any steps of any kind whatever that move in this direction, including the United Nations, all of the international organizations sponsored by the UN, the establishment of an Atlantic Union over the democratic countries of the world which understand each other from the standpoint of political institutions, general philosophy of life, and religions, and the extension of any such organization to as much of the rest of the world as possible and in as short a time as possible. May I emphasize, this is the only constructive direction in which to work in connection with the whole problem.

I wish to say in conclusion that I am much indebted to Senator Johnson for having dramatized this situation so that you and I can discuss it intelligently. Now, if he or someone else will only do the same thing for peacetime uses of atomic energy I shall be very grateful indeed. In fact, if we would only forget secrecy and regard it as the wholly unimportant subject that it is, progress in all lines of scientific activity of benefit to the United States and to the world would be enormously increased.

HOW CAN WE SECURE PEACE IN A
HYDROGEN BOMB WORLD? [5]

GEORGE V. DENNY, JR., SENATOR BRIEN MCMAHON,
AND H. V. KALTENBORN [6]

Senator Brien McMahon, chairman of the Joint Congressional Committee on Atomic Energy, and H. V. Kaltenborn, "dean of American commentators," participated on Thursday evening, February 14, 1950, in one of the regular Town Hall debates. The program which originated in the Town Hall, New York, was released over the network of the American Broadcasting Company, and was telecast.

These Town Hall programs, given continuously since May 30, 1935, have several million listeners each week. Crucial issues are frankly debated or discussed. The speakers are invariably authorities on the topic and are excellent speakers. George V. Denny has used good judgment in developing the weekly programs and is himself a highly acceptable radio and face-to-face speaker.

The topic was a highly disturbing and controversial one in February 1950. Senator McMahon, for example, had addressed the Senate on the subject on February 2, and Kaltenborn in his radio commentaries had already discussed the problem several times.

In the Town Hall debate each speaker presented his case compactly and concretely. Kaltenborn's reply is largely a series of specific questions, which, however, go to the heart of the problem.

This Town Hall program is to be studied for the techniques of radio composition and for its demonstration of debating methods. The critic, judging the analysis, structure, language, audience adjustment, and refutation will attempt to answer the question, "Who won the debate?"

Senator McMahon is recognized as one of the outstanding Senate speakers. Mr. Kaltenborn continues with great success his long established career as radio news commentator. [7]

McMahon, both in Norwalk High School and at Fordham University, participated in forensic activities. He states: "My method of speech preparation is, I suppose, quite commonplace. Where a major address is concerned, I find it necessary to go through several rough drafts before

[5] Reprinted from the *Bulletin of America's Town Meeting of the Air*, vol. 15, no. 42, February 14, 1950. By permission of the speakers and by special arrangement with Town Hall, Inc., and through the courtesy of the American Broadcasting Company.

[6] For biographical notes, see Appendix.

[7] For further comment on H. V. Kaltenborn, consult the Cumulated Author Index in this volume.

the speech begins to please me. I am definitely a member of the blood, sweat, and tears school. Whatever pleasure I may derive from a satisfying phrase resides in looking at the finished product rather than going through the tortuous process of composition." [8]

ANNOUNCER: Of course, you've heard the press referred to as the fourth estate, but do you know how the name originated? So far as we know, the first reference to the press as the fourth estate was made by Thomas Carlyle about the reporters' gallery in the English Parliament. The three estates were the legislative, executive, and judicial departments of the government. "But," said Carlyle, "in the reporters' gallery yonder sits a fourth estate more important far than all."

Radio has been referred to, for much the same reason, as the "fifth estate," for its power and influence have already been used to elect and defeat candidates for public office, to stage revolutions, and to help hold the people of a police state in subjugation.

Wisely used, this fifth estate may inform and keep a nation free. Your Town Meeting is dedicated to this high purpose. You can help achieve this purpose by reminding your friends and neighbors to listen to Town Meeting each week.

Now to preside over our discussion, here's your moderator, the President of Town Hall, founder of America's Town Meeting, Mr. George V. Denny, Jr. Mr. Denny.

MODERATOR DENNY: Good evening, neighbors. On that fateful day in August 1945, when the atomic bomb destroyed the city of Hiroshima in Japan, we were at war. A feeling of elation spread over the country then. We felt sure that this would mean the end of World War II, and it did.

But when President Truman announced last week that we would attempt to build a hydrogen bomb one thousand times more destructive than the one used at Hiroshima, a feeling of fear and a sort of numbness gripped the hearts of men as they pondered the meaning of this step.

In desperate awareness of its meaning, Senator Brien McMahon, chairman of the Joint Committee on Atomic Energy, rushed to the floor of the Senate with a challenging plan to curb the armament race by devoting $50 billion [to peace], at the

---

[8] Letter to this editor, May 1, 1950.

rate of $10 billion a year, by reducing two thirds of our expenditures on armaments on condition that Russia do the same, and with the understanding that these funds would be administered by the United Nations for relief and rehabilitation around the world and including the people of the Soviet Union.

Obviously, Senator McMahon believes that this plan will promote peace. It's the first plan to receive nationwide recognition since the announcement that we would make a hydrogen bomb. So we invited the Senator from Connecticut to discuss it here tonight in company with Mr. H. V. Kaltenborn, dean of American radio commentators and a distinguished foreign correspondent, who has some questions to raise about the Senator's plan.

We hear first from Senator Brien McMahon, Democrat of Connecticut, member of the Senate Foreign Relations Committee, and chairman of the Joint Committee on Atomic Energy. Senator McMahon.

SENATOR MCMAHON: Thank you, Mr. Denny. Ladies and gentlemen, I'm very happy to be here before this fine audience tonight and particularly to be in the company of a most distinguished American, Mr. Hans Kaltenborn, to discuss this very grave question with him.

To understand what the hydrogen bomb means as a weapon, we should consult the scientists. They are the best qualified witnesses on this subject.

Dr. Urey, a Nobel prize winner, says that the hydrogen bomb will be one thousand or more times as powerful as the atomic bomb.

Dr. Hans Bethe, one of the foremost scientists of our time, declares that the H-bomb will exceed the A-bomb in destructive power as tremendously as the A-bomb exceeds old-fashioned TNT explosives.

Dr. Albert Einstein, the most famous scientist in the world, declares that the hydrogen bomb brings destruction of all life on earth "within the range of technical possibilities." Dr. Einstein adds, "There beckons more and more clearly general annihilation."

This, ladies and gentlemen, is what the scientists say about hydrogen warfare. Their words drive home and underscore in red what some of us have known and said all along.

A world which contains ever-growing stocks of atomic weapons, a world which tolerates a mad atomic-armaments race is not the kind of world in which human freedom can flourish or even hold its own. We Americans want peace with all our hearts. We seek a just peace whose terms and conditions will appeal to the consciences of all mankind, including the large fraction of mankind walled off behind Russia's iron curtain.

We have tried and tried and tried again to get a just agreement for international control of the atom. Why have all our earnest efforts to achieve atomic peace been stymied?

The Kremlin and the Communist iron curtain are responsible. The people of Russia, I am sure, want peace as sincerely and heartily as we do, but they have not been allowed to know the facts. The iron curtain has been used to keep them in ignorance of the danger from atomic energy.

The Russian people have not been allowed to know that our hand is extended in friendship. This is why I say that we must create a window in the iron curtain and through it deliver our message of peace and good will to the people whose minds have been poisoned against us.

At present, we transmit "Voice of America" radio broadcasts behind the iron curtain, but these should be called the "whisper of America." We spend less money on them than we do in the mere advertising of cosmetics.

I am confident that a bold and strenuous effort can pierce the curtain, can bring to the imprisoned Russian people the knowledge that we seek to be their friends and to join hands with them amidst the blessings of atomic control. But if we are to gain the ear of the Russian people, we must prepare a special, worthwhile, dramatic, and sincere message to send them.

In a speech before the Senate, I suggested the kind of message which might be sent. My suggestion is that we offer to take two thirds of the money we now spend upon armaments and use it through the United Nations to help all other nations, including Russia, provided that all other nations would agree to dependable atomic control and also agree to spend two thirds of their own armaments budgets for peace.

Such an American offer would give visible proof that we stand ready to do our share—and more than our share—in the great task of directing all our efforts, and particularly our efforts in the field of atomic energy, toward human welfare and ennoblement.

Such an offer might prove to be the prelude to a new spirit of cooperation among the nations. Such an American offer might set off a worldwide and irresistible moral crusade for peace.

The response of plain people throughout America to this speech has been truly amazing. I have received thousands of letters and telegrams expressing strong approval. They show that Americans everywhere are hungry for peace and eager to support any effort aimed toward peace, however bold and unconventional.

Ladies and gentlemen, we are engaged in a desperate race to fend off global disaster, with unimaginable benefits and blessings as our reward if we win that race. We cannot stand still and let disaster overtake us. We must act and act now through a daring new approach to atomic control.

MODERATOR DENNY: Thank you, Senator McMahon. Well, Mr. Kaltenborn, it's been your business since you started your newspaper work thirty-five years ago to analyze and appraise and sometimes criticize such plans as Senator McMahon has advanced. Will you give us the benefit of your counsel on this proposal? Mr. H. V. Kaltenborn, dean of American commentators.

MR. KALTENBORN: I join all true lovers of peace in thanking Senator McMahon for his challenging contribution to a momentous discussion. But let us not forget the important conditions that underlie his peace proposals.

In his Senate address, he told us that we cannot be less well armed than Russia. Hence, we must build the hydrogen bomb.

He admits that even the possession of this frightful weapon cannot give us positive security. But he labors under the delusion that we could live at peace with communism if the Kremlin would sign some kind of an agreement to reduce arms by two thirds.

His positive program has two parts: He would transform what he calls the present "whisper of America" into a resounding

"Voice of America," that would penetrate the iron curtain and sway the hearts and minds of the Russian people. Let us agree that this is worth trying. He would also offer $50 billion at the rate of $10 billion a year in return for a two thirds reduction in world armaments. Russia, of course, is to get her full share of the $50 billions if she will join.

The one solid feature of this arresting McMahon proposal is that it seeks to reduce *all* armaments. It admits that to limit only atomic warfare is futile. Germs, rockets, fire bombs, gasses, guided missiles can be just as deadly or destructive as atom bombs.

We killed more people in Tokyo in one two-hour fire raid than by dropping the atom bomb on Hiroshima. Let us not be so foolish as to believe that the mere elimination of atomic war would give us any positive security.

Will Russia sell us a guaranteed peace for X billion dollars? Would we believe her if she pretended to accept? Has the past taught us anything about the mentality of the Kremlin leaders?

Was the risk of war reduced when, at Teheran, we gave Russia Manchuria? At Yalta, when we gave her Poland? At Potsdam, when we gave her East Germany?

Did we promote peace in China when we sought to appease the Chinese Communists or was the risk of war reduced when we fought back and broke the Communist grip on Greece with American arms and American leadership?

Was the risk of war reduced or increased when we withdrew all military help from China, from her Nationalists, at a crucial moment because their government refused to share power with communism?

Was the risk of war increased or reduced when we broke the starvation blockade of Berlin by a proud demonstration of American air power?

If we buy off the Russians now, will they stay bought?

If we finally get an agreement by letting Russia whip us into more and more concessions, have we secured something that really binds the Kremlin?

Do Communists ever keep an oath, pledge, treaty, or agreement when they wish to break it?

As Senator McMahon told the Senate, an ineffective agreement is worse than no agreement at all. Look at Russia's record in the United Nations. Over a four-year period, she has vetoed every constructive proposal.

No, you can't buy peace from the Soviet Union. But we need not despair. We are strong and growing stronger. We have brought the major Atlantic powers into a pact of peace. That pact can be expanded to include other powers.

We are now providing the democratic powers with arms to halt aggression. We have rescued them from postwar depressions through the Marshall Plan. All the Communist powers, including Russia, were invited to share the benefits of the Marshall Plan. They can do so tomorrow if Russia has a change of heart.

I would have no objection to asking Russia once more if she wants to participate with us in European reconstruction, but we know from bitter experience that, in dealing with the Kremlin autocrats, we have only postponed peace by being too eager to buy peace. Yet, we have advanced the cause of peace whenever and wherever we showed ourselves prepared to fight for it.

Let us always be ready to lead the way whenever a new chance for peace is open, but let us always remain strong in arms, strong in allies among the world's free peoples, strong in generous dealing with those who need our help, and above all, strong in the justice of our cause—the defense of human freedom against those who challenge it.

MODERATOR DENNY: Thank you, Mr. Kaltenborn. Well, Senator McMahon, you can't answer all the editorial comments on your plan, but here is Mr. Kaltenborn who has laid himself open to your questions. Senator McMahon.

SENATOR McMAHON: Well, I would like first, Mr. Denny, to comment on the theme that seems to run through Mr. Kaltenborn's remarks that I suggested that we offer a bribe to the Russians. Now I contend, of course, that I didn't do any such thing. There were some editorial writers, a few of them, in fact I know, that wrote that headline who hadn't even read the speech.

Now what is the definition of a bribe? I looked in the dictionary for it the other day and it says "a bribe is a price or a gift given to corrupt the conduct of a person in a position of trust." I didn't know that I had suggested anything to corrupt the Kremlin. (*Laughter*)

MR DENNY: It might be a good thing if you did, Senator. (*Laughter*)

SENATOR MCMAHON: Well, if you would define corruption as the effort to get them to see some reason, it would be an unusual use of the word, but then I would agree with you. But, frankly, you see what I have suggested, I believe, is evidence to all of the world as to what we really intend—what is in our hearts. There is no bribe in that, no more than when we offered the Marshall Plan to the whole world. Was that denominated as a bribe?

In any international agreement when offers are made from one nation to another or one nation to the world—take the ill-fated Kellogg-Briand Pact—was that a bribe that we gave to one another when we pledged our words that aggression should be outlawed? Of course, it was broken, but that you would hardly denominate—the offer that was made—as a bribe.

Don't you see, too, Mr. Kaltenborn, that in addition to that, I suggested that the Russians put their two thirds ino a common pot to be put into the United Nations fund for the purpose of doing what? For the purpose of advancing mankind's welfare; for the purpose of—through this great agency which we could make to live—bringing hope, and bringing bread to men everywhere—bringing that instead of destruction. Do you want me to continue to comment, or shall I give Mr. Kaltenborn a chance?

MR DENNY: I think we'd better give Mr. Kaltenborn a chance, and then these people out here in the audience are ready to hop—hop on both of you.

SENATOR MCMAHON: Fine, fine.

MR. DENNY: Thank you, very much, Senator. Mr. Kaltenborn.

MR. KALTENBORN: Well, obviously, Senator, I am not afraid that you're going to corrupt the masters of the Kremlin. I am afraid that you are going to corrupt the American people into believing that when the Kremlin, perhaps, responds to some sort of an appeal that that means that we've gotten anywhere.

What I tried to point out was that, on the basis of our experience, we cannot rely on what the Kremlin says. We can only rely on what the Kremlin does, and we must judge that by what the Kremlin has done.

Now if you honestly believe that the Kremlin will agree to reduce its entire armament by two thirds and keep it reduced, well, you believe something that I don't believe and that I hope you couldn't persuade the American people to believe.

MR. DENNY: Thank you, Mr. Kaltenborn. The Senator has a rejoinder here for just a moment.

SENATOR MCMAHON: Mr. Kaltenborn, I think it would be very unfortunate if we should confuse the scheme for the reduction of armaments with mere written pieces of paper. I am not so naive—and I'm sure that the American people do not believe that I am—that I would take the Kremlin's word for anything. That is why I suggested that we should condition the proposal which I made upon the Kremlin agreeing to a control plant that would have as its basis an inspection system—an inspection system which would serve the value of letting us know when a fire was going to start. This way, we are going to spend all our time watching for a fire to break out and spending all of our efforts to do it, too.

No, I am for a self-policing agreement which is the only kind of an agreement that the Russians, of course, can be trusted with.

GOVERNMENT AND POLITICS

PARTY CONFLICT AND THE MODERN DILEMMA [1]

THOMAS E. DEWEY [2]

This lecture was the second in a series of four on "The American Political System," given by Governor Thomas E. Dewey of New York, in Alexander Hall, Princeton University, under the auspices of the Woodrow Wilson School of Public and International Affairs.

The first two lectures, given on February 8 and 9, were entitled "The Two-Party System" and "Party Conflict and the Modern Dilemma"; the next two, given on April 12th and 13th, were "Making Foreign Policy Under a Two-Party System" and "Domestic Policies Under a Two-Party System."

Some thousand Princeton students listened on each occasion. Each speech was followed by an extended rough-and-tumble period of question and answer, in which the New York Governor, without evasion, gave further clarification of his hour-long exposition of applied political theory.

The four lectures were of a high order in thought and composition. The Governor drew on his wide background of political experience for enforcement of his general theses. Political critics found in these lectures highly intelligent and statesmanlike exposition of our past political patterns and equally mature and plausible statements concerning the wisest course of action in both domestic and foreign policies.

The section of the lecture included in this volume should be examined in relation to the entire series. Aware that in the 1948 campaign Dewey was judged, perhaps necessarily so, on the record of the Republicans in the Eightieth Congress, Dewey at Princeton made plain that the voter should gauge that party by its record in those states—for example, New York, New Jersey, Minnesota—where Republicans had been in control and had produced much responsible legislation. He thus lined up with the progressive Republican wing that supported "welfare" legislation.

The New York Governor at Princeton was a "new Dewey." He thought and talked at a level distinctly above that of the seasoned politician of national leadership who has his eye on future national conven-

---

[1] The text was furnished by Paul E. Lockwood, secretary to Governor Thomas E. Dewey. Reprinted through the courtesy of Governor Dewey.

[2] For biographical note, see Appendix.

tions. Dewey's intellectual insight combined with organizational and compositional clarity and interest give these lectures lasting distinction— whether or not they meant "burning the political bridges" of their author.[3]

One of the standard weapons of party conflict both between conventions and during campaigns is the effort to pin labels on individuals or movements, attractive or sinister, depending upon the point of view. On the whole, the Democratic Party in recent years has been more successful, but less scrupulous, than the Republicans in their use of political semantics.

One of the most intriguing words in the political lexicon is the word "liberal." It is a touchstone eagerly sought by almost every political group. After a long and useful life, it still has warmth and confers a kind of pleasant aura upon those who garb themselves in its benign appeal. The trouble is that the word has been used to describe widely differing views and objectives and it has been greatly corrupted.

The traditional meaning of the word "liberal" described a movement to restrict the power of government over the lives of people. It came into active use in the new age ushered in by the eighteenth century when the Western world was striking off the shackles of royal absolutism. Society was to be governed by new concepts of individual freedom, equality under the law, limited government, and the rule of law instead of the rule of men.

Two hundred years later, the transmutation of the word, as the alchemist would say, has become one of the wonders of our time. Part of the change has come from a broadly based movement to use the powers of government for humanitarian ends.

It is evident that over the last hundred years there has been some loss of control by the individual over his own life. The swift advances of technology, the shift from rural to urban life, the rise of great corporate enterprise and of great unions of labor, the increasing sensitivity and interdependence of our economy— all these have stemmed from the industrial society we have built. While the industrial revolution has brought a far higher standard of living for the individual it has also brought him new kinds

[3] For other comment on Dewey as speaker and examples of Dewey's former speeches, see the Cumulated Author Index at the end of this volume.

of insecurity. This, in turn, has bred a collective sense of need for wider control of the forces which everyone now recognizes are far beyond the control of any individual.

After the Western world had achieved freedom from absolutism in government, the industrial revolution developed great economic powers in private hands. In the name of liberalism, the power of the state has quite properly been used to limit abuses by the strong and to protect the individual from hazards entirely beyond his control.

While our devotional words politically are still "freedom," "liberty," "independence," "self-reliance," and "individual initiative," many of us find that their meaning has become less clear since the machine came of age. People have looked for a new way to make the old and beloved words fit the new time.

This is the opportunity which Big Government and its advocates have seized. To resolve the dilemma inherent in their desire to claim the name "liberal," they have changed its meaning along with the meaning of the word "freedom." According to the new meaning employed by the neo-liberals of Big Government, freedom in its classic sense meant only freedom to starve. The new meaning says that freedom really means freedom to receive from government all the comforts and security of life. In exchange the individual is expected to do the bidding of government.

The higher purpose of the modern collectivists teaches that the legal liberty of the Western world is "formal liberty" without substance and that "actual liberty," as they call it, must be substituted for the traditional freedoms. The practitioners of Big Governmen say that the old kind of liberty was "license for the few and economic serfdom for the many."

Not only in America, but all over the world, we see men use the word "liberalism" to promote the very policies of government which liberals rose up to destroy. This sinister distortion of the word has led many well-meaning and genuine liberals into a state of confusion. The really disturbing thing about it is that it leads to the unwitting acceptance by an increasing number of people of the instruments of totalitarianism.

In addition to warping the basic concept of liberalism, the corrupters have gone further. I have already indicated that technical advances have prepared people to accept modified concepts of liberty. The supercharged word which Big Government uses to induce them to go further is "welfare." The Big Government people have taken it over as a latter-day Ark of the Covenant. Moreover, they have succeeded in tricking a lot of Republicans into appearing to attack all welfare and that, of course, seems to a good many Americans like something akin to firing on the flag.

It must have been some very clumsy Republican—I do not know the origin of the phrase or who perpetrated it—who tried to pin the label, "welfare state," on Mr. Truman's government. Others joined in the clamor and, of course, the apologists for Big Government joyously accepted the epithet as a new instrument of party warfare. They admit they are running a welfare state. They are proud of it!

Of course, they are running a welfare state. There has never been a responsible government which did not have the welfare of its people at heart. I am proud of the fact that we in the State of New York have made great social welfare advances, as have most of the states.

Anybody who thinks that an attack on the fundamental idea of security and welfare is appealing to people generally, is living in the Middle Ages. Everybody wants welfare and security in one form or another. It makes no difference whether he is a day laborer who wants his social security or a small business man who wants the value of his savings.

Here, in the words of a great Democrat, is the hard core of the Republican position today. It is the basic issue between the parties. It is not the issue between all Republicans and all Democrats. There are Republicans and Democrats who believe every social advance we have made toward personal security in the last twenty years should be abolished. There are Republicans and Democrats who believe we should rush headlong toward total government security and supervision from the cradle to the grave and some even include nationalization of industry as part of the program.

Disregarding the minority views within the parties, and judging preponderant sentiment by the standards I set up in last night's lecture, the essential difference between the parties lies in the way "to protect liberty when the government's purposes are beneficent." Or, to put it another way, the issue lies in the means of achieving objectives without injury to other objectives. . . .

I reach four basic conclusions: First, Big Government denies the great fundamental that the primary purpose of all government is to preserve liberty. By asserting that security is the chief aim of our society, it seeks to turn our people to the lotus and away from the basic truth that without working and producing we perish.

Second, Big Government requires a special kind of permanent control and continuity and therefore inevitably moves in the direction of the one-party system. It seeks to collect and pay out such a large share of the people's income that any interruption of its multifarious activities would produce hardship and crisis. To carry out this purpose will require the transfer of the power of the public purse from the Congress to the Executive.

Third, Big Government, like dictatorships, can continue only by growing larger and larger. It can never retrench without admitting failure. It feeds on the gradual obliteration of state and local governments as elements of sovereignty and tends to transform them into districts and prefectures. By absorbing more than half of all the taxing power of the nation, Big Government now deprives the states and local governments of the capacity to support the programs they should conduct. In place of their own taxing powers, it offers them in exchange the counterfeit currency of federal subsidy.

Fourth, Big Government gradually destroys the mainspring of our society. It offers no incentives to those who must create the goods and services which provide the security. In the words of the ancient writer, it sings a siren song: "Cast in thy lot among us; let us have one purse." It levels all down and throttles the source of our strength which lies in the restless ambitions of the ten million centers of initiative in our individual businesses and on our farms.

In its debut in this country Big Government has enjoyed considerable success. That is because it has been living on past accumulations of capital and techniques in a period of prosperity growing out of the postwar, worldwide demand for everything America can produce.

It is a fair weather system. One of two perils will catch up with it. The first peril is in the high taxes, oppressive regulations, delays and frustrations due to massive bureaucracies, inflation of prices and the ominous threat to adequate production. Each of these factors has an obviously destructive effect. Price inflation is especially virulent because it nullifies the value of the security programs which Big Government uses to justify its existence. It also falls hardest on those in the middle income range—the white collar groups—the people with moderate, fixed incomes, such as teachers, scholars, clergy and engineers. No free society has ever survived without a successful middle group.

The other peril that will catch up with Big Government is that, like all governments, it will make mistakes. Whenever government is so powerful that its mistakes can destroy the nation, then you may be sure the nation will be destroyed. To this truth the people of Germany, Italy and Japan bear eloquent and tragic witness.

Human freedom demands that we develop a better way than that of Big Government. First of all we must begin by agreeing among ourselves what the goal of our society should be. I propose that our goal should be the same today as it has been for 175 years: to foster individual liberty as the only means to a society of opportunity and abundance.

For government to act against the insecurities of life in our modern society is not at all inconsistent with a system based on individual competition and reward for everything above those minimum security levels. We can build a floor under the uncertainties of life in our industrial economy without putting a ceiling on the height of our building.

Our time is faced with the problems of unemployment, old age, medical care, housing, discrimination and agricultural price stabilization. Each of these problems can and will be met. But the road to Washington is not the only road.

We can believe in traffic control without agreeing that all traffic regulations should be promulgated from Washington.

We can practice our religion without agreeing that the Federal Government should appoint and pay the clergy.

We can approve of marriage without having all marriage licenses issued by the Department of the Interior.

We must have a tougher and wiser view of the modern dilemma than Big Government offers to us. I propose that we set up criteria by which to judge government action as we seek to reconcile the deep-rooted individualism of our country with the problems of the machine age.

Does the particular welfare measure of government build up the independence and responsibility of the individual citizen or does it make him dependent and subservient?

Does a particular intervention by government widen or narrow the bounds of personal liberty?

Does the proposal deprive any group or segment of our people of any legitimate individual freedom of action they now enjoy?

Does it do by governmental action what people can and should do for themselves by voluntary action?

Does it remove to a distant seat of government power or responsibility that belong in the locality?

Does it remove from productive work a substantial number of people in order to administer the program?

Does it have a sound fiscal basis?

Not all of these criteria may be relevant in each case. But they all stand as signposts of the right road.

Our only battleship in service recently showed what happens when the channel course is not kept. It happens more quickly to battleships but it happens just as surely to governments and their people.

In a later lecture I shall attempt to apply these criteria across the broad range of public issues today.

The central problem of twentieth century politics remains unsolved. No nation, no system of government has yet succeeded in reconciling the age-old conflict between liberty and authority.

It is our great responsibility, as a people, to press for the solution of that conflict within the framework of our free system.

THE DEMOCRATIC PARTY [4]

HARRY S. TRUMAN [5]

President Harry S. Truman gave this address at the Jefferson Day dinner at Washington, D.C., on the evening of February 16, 1950. The dinner, held in the National Guard Armory, the largest hall in the capitol, was attended by some 5,300 Democrats who had paid $100 a plate. After expenses, some $450,000 would go to the party treasury.[6]

The speech was broadcast and telecast over nationwide outlets.

Vice President Alben W. Barkley, Sam Rayburn, Charles Luckman, the dinner chairman, and others in addition to the President, spoke. Eleven Democratic governors, labor union leaders, members of the judiciary, members of the cabinet, and many other municipal, state, and Federal office holders attended.

The speech was the utterance of a strong party man rather than a statesman. Many of the stylistic turns that marked the Truman campaign speeches of 1948 were present. The substance was not too original or closely reasoned. Plenty of attention-getting-and-holding elements were used and expertly blended with the frame of logical continuity.

The usual types of personal proof were followed. The Republicans were identified with everything bad, and the Democrats, their ancestors and present friends and conduct, were splendid. The Republicans were users of scare words like welfare and state and socialism. They belonged to the Union League Club. They were of the 80th, the do-nothing Congress. In 1934, '36, '40, '44 and '50 they made absurd predictions that failed to scare or be borne out. The Democrats, on the contrary, were (1) inheritors of the Jefferson-Jackson tradition, (2) frank, (3) truthful, (4) constructive, (5) interested also in balancing the budget, (6) responsible for present prosperity, (7) non-socialistic, (8) determined to protect economic and other freedoms. There was no mention of the Taft-Hartley law, no eulogy of the 81st Congress. Rather the generalizations were skillfully calculated to appease many of the industrialists present.

The audience received the speech with applause and laughter, but hardly with the unrestrained enthusiasm evoked so often by Roosevelt and sometimes by Truman.

The Jefferson Day dinner speech should be compared in method and content with Truman's political speech at Kansas City on Thursday, September 29, 1949, honoring William M. Boyle, Jr., new chairman of the

[4] Text furnished by the White House.
[5] For biographical note, see Appendix.
[6] Carl Levin, in the New York *Herald Tribune*, February 17, 1950.

Democratic National Committee; and with the President's Labor Day speech at Pittsburgh on Monday, September 5, 1949. The Washington address echoes much of the sentiment of these earlier and more intimate utterances, but lacks some of the cleverness.

The President has become increasingly effective as a speaker since 1945. His constant formal speaking and press conferences, especially his "fighting" political speeches and rear platform talks, have given him fluency, confidence, and ample skill in audience adaptation.[7]

Fellow Democrats: This is a most remarkable dinner. This dinner and others like it throughout the land are evidence of the growing strength of the Democratic Party. They show that our party is determined, more than ever before, to carry its message to the voters of this country.

It is very significant that such great interest and enthusiasm are being shown in a Congressional election year. We know that Congressional elections are as important as presidential elections. We found out in 1946 how much harm can be done to our country when a Congressional election goes wrong. We are not going to let that happen again. We don't want another do-nothing 80th Congress.

These dinners carry forward a great tradition. The original Jefferson-Jackson dinner was held in this city in 1830, one hundred and twenty years ago. It was given in memory of Thomas Jefferson, and its guest of honor was President Jackson. At that first Jefferson-Jackson dinner, President Jackson gave his famous toast—"Our Federal Union, it must be preserved!"

Tonight, we meet again to think of our Federal Union, to be thankful that it has been preserved, and that it has grown in strength and in service to the people. As in Jackson's time, we meet to discuss some of the probems that our country faces.

We have some very serious problems today. We are living in a troubled period of the world's history. Our responsibilities, as a nation, have never been so great, and the decisions we face have never been more difficult. We confront serious questions of foreign policy. We have the problem of maintaing an adequate national defense. We have the task of maintaining prosperity

[7] For further comment on Truman as a speaker, see the introduction to and text of the "Madison Square Garden address," *Representative American Speeches: 1948-1949*, p110-21.

and protecting our economy from depression. We have the question of handling the nation's finances and the national debt.

These are grave issues. And the Democratic Party is meeting them squarely. We do not believe in trifling with the people about these issues. We do not offer to solve them with vague generalities or worn-out slogans. We know that the solution of these problems requires all the wisdom and energy we possess as a nation. We know that their solution requires heavy expenditures. The Democratic Party does not propose to deceive the people either about the problems we face or the cost of solving them.

The Democratic Party has confidence that the United States will meet these great responsibilities. It knows that the United States is a dynamic, growing nation. We believe that this country will make as much progress in the next fifty years as it has made in the last fifty years.

But we cannot meet the responsibilities of today or the challenge of the future by following the outmoded concepts of fifty years ago. The promise of the twentieth century cannot be fulfilled by those who would like to return to the days of McKinley.

We must go forward with our programs for peace through defense and foreign aid. We must proceed with our domestic programs for health, education, social security, and economic stability. Both our foreign programs and our domestic programs are necessary to answer the demands which this critical period of history makes upon us. We cannot have prosperity at home unless we play our full part in the defense and the revival of other free nations. We cannot have peace abroad unless we increase the strength, the freedom, and the well-being of our people at home.

There are some who would like to see us turn our backs upon the rest of the world and drop our efforts to strengthen our domestic economy. At the present time, they are spreading the mistaken idea that we can save money by going backward. They advocate slashing our expenditures for peace and for our domestic programs. These people are blind to the problems that confront us. They can see that a tax cut would help their own pocketbooks temporarily. They fail to see that in the long run false economy would endanger not only their pocketbooks but their lives and the continuation of civilization itself.

It is true that our present expenditures are large. But the Democratic administration is working toward a balance in the Federal budget. I wish we could balance the budget immediately by the simple expedient of cutting expenses. But that is out of the question. More than 70 per cent of our Federal budget goes to pay for past wars and to work for peace in the future. Anyone who says that these expenditures are extravagant does not understand the kind of world we live in. Our other expenditures are less than one third of the budget, and less in proportion to the national income than they were ten years ago.

I would like to cut expenditures further, and I intend to do so at every opportunity. But I do not propose to weaken the strength and security of this country. I do not propose to place the peace of the world in jeopardy to satisfy the advocates of false economy.

In this difficult world situation, some people are talking about general tax reductions. I regard this as political hypocrisy. We had one recent experience with an ill-timed, irresponsible tax cut. Much of our present financial difficulty is the result of the sweeping tax reduction which was enacted in 1948 over my veto—at a time when expenditures for defense and foreign policy were inevitably rising. We must not make the same mistake again.

In this election year, the Democratic Party will not play politics with the Federal budget. We will state the honest truth about the budget, just as we will about all other issues. We believe that the people are entitled to the plain facts about every issue, so that they can make up their own minds.

The Democratic Party can afford to be frank and truthful, because it is working for the general welfare of all our citizens. It does not serve any narrow group or clique. This makes it easy for the Democratic Party to put its program before the country openly and completely. We have nothing to hide from the people. Our strength lies in explaining our program and our policies to the people. And the more thoroughly we explain to them what the Democratic Party is trying to do, the more certain we can be of their continued support.

There are many differences between the Democratic and the Republican Parties. But I think the greatest difference is that the Democratic Party is the party of affirmative action—it is for measures to achieve prosperity and progress. The Republican Party is the party of negative inaction—it is always against things.

The principal thing that Republicans are against, of course, is the Democratic Party. But they can't win on that plank alone. They must try to find reasons for being against the Democratic Party. They must persuade people to vote against the Democratic Party. And that is getting harder and harder to do.

One reason it is hard to do is that the Republican Party has no affirmative program of its own. It refuses to face the problems of our economy. It refuses to take thought and make plans for the future. Instead of presenting a positive program of their own, the Republicans sit around waiting for us to make a proposal. Then they react with an outburst of scare words. They are like a cuttlefish that squirts out clouds of black ink whenever its slumber is disturbed.

Right now, the main problem of the Republican leaders seems to be to find some new scare words. They have not had much luck along that line, lately. They tried using the phrase "welfare state" as a scare word for a while, but they discovered that the people are in favor of a government that promotes their welfare. So they dropped that scare word. Then they tried "statism." But my good friend Governor Lehman took care of that one in the New York election—so they had to drop it, too.

Now, the Republican leaders have had to go back to an old standby. Frankly, I don't think it's as good as some of the others, but it appears to be the best they can think of. Their current scare word is "socialism."

It's perfectly safe to be against "socialism." The difficult thing is to make the country believe that the Democratic Party stands for socialism. How in the world can the Republicans persuade people that all you Democrats at all these dinners are Socialists?

It can't be done. But the Republicans will try it just the same. That's what they've been trying to do ever since 1933. For the last seventeen years they have called every new Democratic measure "socialism" or "communism," and they have made constant predictions of doom and disaster. The plans and proposals that we have advanced for improving the condition of the people of this country have been greeted with these same old scare tactics during all these years.

And I'm going to prove that to you. Let us take it step by step.

In 1933, this country faced some of the greatest problems in its history—the problems of providing food and work for millions of jobless persons and their families, of saving millions of farms and homes from foreclosure, of restoring a banking system that had collapsed, of placing the entire economy on the way to recovery.

The Democratic Party rolled up its sleeves and went to work. It took steps to provide relief and jobs, to save farms and homes, to restore banks and businesses. Bit by bit the economy responded to those vigorous measures. Income began to grow, confidence returned, business activity mounted. This was the response of the economy to our farm and labor and business programs—our programs for resource development and public works and the building of homes.

As this miracle of recovery unfolded, what was the attitude of the Republican Party?

In 1934, the Republican National Committee issued a policy statement. And in that statement they said: "American institutions and American civilization are in greater danger today than at any time since the foundation of the republic."

That sort of talk may have frightened the members of the Union League Club. But it didn't frighten the people who had been saved by the New Deal from bread lines and bankruptcy.

In 1936, the Republicans thought the danger was worse. In that year, the Republican platform cried out: "America is in peril. The welfare of American men and women and the future of our youth are at stake. . . The New Deal Administration"— this is from the 1936 Republican platform—"has bred fear and hesitation in commerce and industry, thus discouraging new enterprises, preventing employment, and prolonging the depression."

People weren't scared by that one either. They knew it just didn't make sense, because the national income had risen more than 50 per cent in the previous four years, and it was still rising.

In 1940, the Republicans tried to scare us again. This time their platform said: "The Administration has imposed upon us a regime of regimentation which has deprived the individual of his freedom and has made of America a shackled giant. . . . The New Deal administration has failed America."

That's what the Republicans said, but the America that the New Deal had saved—the economy that the New Deal had freed and made productive again—became the arsenal of democracy that overwhelmed the forces of totalitarian aggression.

But that still didn't teach the Republicans anything. In 1944, when we stood at the peak of our wartime production—the economic bulwark of the free world—the Republican Party platform proclaimed: "The fact remains that under the New Deal, American economic life is being destroyed." That's what they said in 1944—"American economic life is being destroyed."

Apparently, they never learn anything. Today, when we have a national output of over $250 billion a year and a higher standard of living than ever before, the Republican Party still cannot see anything good about the situation. In their policy statement issued ten days ago, the Republican National Committee declared: "The major domestic issue today is liberty against socialism. . . Basic American principles"—they said—"are threatened by the Administration's program. . . ."

It's the same old story—the same old words and music—the same empty and futile attempt to scare the American people—in complete contradiction of the plain facts that are visible to every citizen in his daily life.

For the past seventeen years, the same outcry has greeted every proposal advanced by the Democratic Party—whether it was for better housing, social security, rural electrification, farm price supports, minimum wages, or any other program for the general welfare.

In 1944, Representative Joseph W. Martin, Jr., summarized the Republican attitude toward all these progressive steps in one brief paragraph when he said: "For eleven years we have been steadily drifting into a regimented nation, with absolute control vested in a power-mad group of bureaucrats and social planners. Unless there is a change in government this year"—that was in 1944—"we can be reconciled to some kind of totalitarian, Socialist government."

That is what the Republicans said about our programs in 1944. That is the way they talked about them in 1948. That is what they are saying about them now.

Today, we are proposing further development of our resources, further strengthening of our economy, new measures for the welfare of the people. And what do we hear? The same old story. It is all repeated in that latest statement of the Republican National Committee: "This program"—they said, and they were talking about the program of the Democratic Party—"This program is dictated by a small but powerful group of persons who believe in socialism, who have no concept of the true foundation of American progress, and whose proposals are wholly out of accord with the true interests and real wishes of the workers, farmers and businessmen."

Well, let's look at the record. What is our program? Where did it come from? Our program is the platform adopted by the Democratic Party in its Convention of 1948. And it has been voted on by the people of this country, including the workers, farmers, and businessmen.

If our program was dictated, as the Republicans say, it was dictated at the polls in November 1948. It was dictated by a "small but powerful group" of twenty-four million voters. And I think they knew more than the Republican National Committee about the real wishes of the workers, farmers, and businessmen.

Of course, this program is not socialism. It is based upon a firm faith in the strength of free enterprise. It is designed to strengthen the markets of free enterprise and to expand the investments of free enterprise. It will make our citizens economically secure, well educated, and confident of the future. Only in a nation of such citizens can free enterprise grow and expand and reach its full possibilities.

The program of the Democratic Party is aimed to promote the prosperity and welfare of the American people. It is aimed to increase the freedom of the American people.

Freedom is not an abstraction. Freedom is a reality in our daily lives. The programs of our party have freed workers from economic subjection to their employers. They have freed farmers from the fear of bankruptcy. They have released farm wives from the bondage of ceaseless drudgery. They have freed older people from the fear of a dependent old age.

Our programs look forward to the day when our people will be freed from the fear of inadequate medical care and crushing medical expenses. They are aimed at freeing our young people from ignorance and poor education. And on these foundations for greater freedom for all our people, we are going forward to break down the barriers to economic opportunity and political liberty that have been created by prejudice and discrimination.

This is the record and the promise of the Democratic Party in expanding the freedom of the American people. And when the Republican Party proclaims that we are engaged in restricting freedom—that we are the enemies of freedom—I ask, "Whose freedom?" Let the American people look into their own lives and ask themselves whether they enjoy greater freedom or less than they did eighteen years ago.

About the only freedom we have limited is the freedom of Republicans to run the country. Maybe that is what they are complaining about.

For the Republicans to drag out the same old moth-eaten scraecrow of "socialism" again in 1950—after having used it, or something very like it, in opposition to every progressive step the nation has taken since 1933—is an insult to the intelligence of the American people. Out of the great progress of this country, out of our great advances in achieving a better life for all, out of our rise to world leadership, the Republican leaders have learned nothing. Confronted by the great record of this country, and the tremendous promise of its future, all they do is to croak— "Socialism!"

The Democratic Party is going right ahead to meet the needs and carry out the aspirations of the American people.

Our objective is to advance in freedom—to create a system of society that is ever more responsive to the needs of the people —to establish democratic principles so firmly in the hearts of the people that they can never be uprooted.

In the present anxieties and troubles of the world, the real strength of our country lies not in arms and weapons, important as they may be, but in the freedom of our citizens and their faith in a democratic society. Among the nations of the world, we stand as an example of what free men can do when they are in control of their own affairs and dedicated to the concept of a better life for all.

To work for the prosperity, the welfare, and the freedom of the American people is to work for the vindication of democratic institutions everywhere. And it is only through the growth of democratic institutions that a just and lasting peace can finally be achieved.

In this troubled world, it is more than ever important that the Democratic Party remain steadfast in its devotion to these ideals. It is more than ever important this year that the Democratic Party present its program to the people so plainly that it cannot be misunderstood. If we do that, I am confident that the people will again voice their approval of the principles which lead to increased prosperity, welfare, and freedom—not only for this country, but for free nations everywhere.

THE WELFARE STATE [8]

JAMES ROOSEVELT [9]

James Roosevelt gave this address before the Commonwealth Club at San Francisco, on December 2, 1949.

On November 15, 1949, the speaker had announced his candidacy for nomination on the Democratic ticket for the California governorship.

In that formal announcement the candidate had stressed (1) the development of California resources accompanied by the declaration that "we will not permit them to be wastefully dissipated for the profit of the few," (2) full employment, (3) the spread of tolerance, (4) extension and strengthening of social security laws, (5) the development of the Central Valley project, (6) the further protection of the interests of farmers and fruit growers, (7) the promotion of public education, and (8) extension of health services. These matters were, of course, familiar politico-social aims, and were generally subscribed to by California citizens. The question had to do with the extent to which the liberal approach of Franklin D. Roosevelt would shape the implementation of aid to labor, agriculture, and so on.

In the San Francisco speech, the younger Roosevelt delineated his New Deal, Fair Deal position, and elaborated on the political philosophy implicit in the earlier declarations.

Note the care and detail with which *individualism* and *welfare state* are defined and illustrated. Are his interpretations satisfactory? What was the extent of unemployment in California that led Roosevelt to note at length that problem?

Note the completeness with which Roosevelt meets the objections to the welfare state. What refutatory methods does he use for each of the six points to be refuted? Would his techniques be apparently adequate for an audience of economic conservatives? Are the arguments to be refuted arranged in the best order? Does he give undue space and attention to any one of them? What, of these arguments to be refuted, are most important? What, if any, major objections to the welfare state does the speaker ignore?

Early in February 1950, Governor Earl Warren announced his candidacy for a third term. Twice he had been elected by large majorities, running as he had been on both major party tickets.

Young Roosevelt, arriving in California in 1938, became a Los Angeles insurance broker. Later he entered politics, deplored the Old Guard

[8] Text and permission to reprint were furnished through the courtesy of James Roosevelt.

[9] For biographical note, see Appendix.

leadership of the Democratic party, and became a Democratic National Committeeman. The "invisible" leader of that Old Guard was allegedly E. W. Pauley, Jr., wealthy oil operator and close friend of Harry Truman. Other powerful Democratic leaders of California vigorously opposed the liberal leadership of James Roosevelt.

Warren's success in California politics was attributed to his popular personal qualities, the freedom of his administration from machine party politics, and his financial skill in balancing the state's billion dollar budget at a lower tax level than previously, in spite of a sudden population expansion from seven to ten million.

Roosevelt, after January 1950, made hundreds of speeches throughout the state. As speaker and campaigner he had had much experience earlier in supporting and often speaking for his father's candidacy in the campaigns of 1932, 1936, and 1940. The son closely resembles the father in gestures, smile, voice quality, and vocal inflections. Observers were still wondering to what extent James could produce the political wisdom and persuasive oral style of Franklin D. Roosevelt.

It is a pleasure and an honor once again to appear before the Commonwealth Club. For nearly half a century this organization has demonstrated the value of open-minded inquiry, of unbiased discussion, and of a hard-headed determination to get the facts. These things must be preserved if we are to retain the key to progress.

I am particularly grateful for the opportunity to discuss the subject which is before us today. Reactionaries are telling ghost stories again. They are trying to frighten the American electorate with a new bogey. They have even given it a name—the "Welfare state."

Today I propose to put that ghost to rest. I propose to show why the American people, who have never been notably subject to fears in the night, will not be frightened by this synthetic apparition. In short I shall defend the welfare state—the proposition that our government should work for the general welfare—and I shall do so without apology.

Yet I cannot refrain from expressing wonder and indignation that it should be necessary for *any* American to stand before his fellow citizens and defend an idea which has been written from the beginning into our Constitution, which has been reaffirmed throughout our history, and which has served more than anything else to distinguish our American society from societies based on caste and special privilege. From its very birth this nation has been committed to the proposition that welfare must be general, and that it is the business of the state to promote it.

Those who have chosen thus to draw the lines of battle, who cheapen the word "welfare" and say it with a sneer, have made, I think, a tactical blunder. They have led with their right. They have betrayed their weakness. They have shown their hand. They have demonstrated their ignorance of what American history means. They have misunderstood human nature. And the weakness of their principles is equaled only by the shortcomings of their logic.

For it is obvious, is it not, that this is no battle over the meaning of a mere word. The issue can't be settled by consulting a dictionary. It goes far deeper than that. It is a moral issue. It involves the whole question of the aims of society, of the function of government, and of the relation of the citizen to his government.

It has been said many times that our democratic government rests on a basis of individualism. This certainly is true. But what does individualism in this context mean? Surely it stands for something other than an inalienable right to drive through a red light or to refuse with a show of melodrama to pay a withholding tax to the treasurer of the United States. The moral history of Western civilization suggests a more profound and fruitful answer. It is an answer which has its basis in religion— in the moral insights of the prophets and in the social teaching of Jesus. It was deeply rooted in the minds of the men who brought this nation into being and who wrote the most glorious pages of our history.

For individualism means the principle that each human being is uniquely valuable; that he is a child of God; that he is endowed therefore with dignity and sacredness. His highest good consists in developing the best powers that lie within him. He is an end in himself. And, because he is an end in himself, he should always be so treated, and never be regarded as a mere commodity. This view of man is the moral foundation on which our democracy rests.

I emphasize this point because it is essential to the question before us today. This principle of individualism, this belief that every human being is an end, is not universally accepted. Throughout history and throughout the world today men have been used as means or commodities merely, and their unique value as ends is lost sight of.

Individualism, conceived in this way, is no empty platitude. There follow from it consequences of the greatest significance. If *men* are ends in themselves, if the *individual* has the highest value, then the *state* cannot be supreme. The state is a *means* and not an end. This is the reason we Americans and all freedom-loving men everywhere detest totalitarianism. To elevate the state to supremacy, to endow it with a sanctity of its own, to permit *its* demands to override the welfare of the individuals who make it up—this violates the deepest moral convictions that we have. This is why both fascism and communism are evil.

Now if these things are true, and I profoundly believe that they are, I think we can derive a more definite idea as to what the function of the state really is. Its business is to foster and maintain that kind of economic and social environment in which the *individual* has a real opportunity to develop his full stature as a *man*. This gives us a principle, a criterion by which to judge the rightness of proposed courses of action: Every collective action, every piece of legislation, should contribute toward the perfecting of a society in which the *individual* can be really free to develop his higest capabilities.

Obviously this is not a matter of material well-being merely. It has to do with the development of the total individual, whose motives and goods are not exclusively economic. I certainly do not maintain that government can or should concern itself directly with every aspect of human life. Spiritual, intellectual, and artistic values lie completely outside the proper sphere of direct legislation. In this country we don't establish truth in science, or critical standards in music, for example, by passing laws. But it cannot be doubted that this economic and social environment of which I have spoken *affects* every aspect of human life. It imposes conditions and limitations; it is an inescapable, bed-rock fact, it can either stifle human aspirations or it can help make their achievement possible.

The "general welfare," then, means the establishment and preservation of those conditions which give real, substantial freedom to individuals. If the people, through the democratic process, choose, as they have always done in this country, to use their instrument, the state, for this purpose, I maintain that they are using it properly. This is why I hold that to contrast the welfare state with what is called the "opportunity state," and to say that the two are opposed, is completely false. Welfare, on American principles, *means* opportunity; it means *real* opportunity; and it means opportunity for *all*.

It is for these reasons that the American people have approved measures for unemployment insurance, old-age security, minimum wages, insurance of bank deposits, low-cost housing, and emergency loans to home owners—and incidentally, gentlemen, emergency loans for business. It is for these reasons that they will approve further expansion of social security, extension of employment opportunities, the planned development of natural resources, the passage of civil rights legislation, the restoration of more workable rules of collective bargaining, and provision for medical care within the reach of the middle and lower income groups. . . .

Such measures as unemployment insurance, social security, commissions for fair employment practices, and adequate labor legislation are intended to adjust the admittedly imperfect machinery of our economy. They are not handouts. They are designed to help provide the conditions under which men and women can work in honor and in decent security. The American people as a whole understand this, even if people like Senator Taft don't. And they will reject the libellous charge that they merely want something for nothing. When the reactionaries say—as they do—that we are trying to eat our cake and have it too, let us remind them that the American people own the bakery.

Another common argument against recent legislative measures for the general welfare is that such legislation robs us of our freedom and is leading us ultimately into dictatorship. The electorate is being bribed, it is said; the people are selling their birthright of freedom for a mess of pottage. This is the charge.

Now of course this is another libel against the American people, but apart from that, it doesn't even make good sense.

One writer for an Eastern financial publication recently put it into a neat formula which gave the whole thing a mathematical flavor. "As welfare expands," he wrote, "freedom dwindles." Let's examine this for a minute. Welfare and freedom on this view are inversely related. As one increases, the other diminishes. Thus it must follow that as welfare diminishes, freedom increases. The conclusion is inescapable, is it not?—the country is most free when the people are most destitute, most poorly housed and fed, most disease ridden, and most illiterate. Can you wonder, gentlemen, that I sometimes question even the intelligence of the opposition?

Further, this sort of argument completely ignores the true causes of dictatorship. Dictatorship thrives on mass poverty and insecurity. A society whose members make ample provision for their own security through the democratic process is in no danger of becoming a dictatorship. Those who find the threat of "statism" in every effort of the people through their government to promote their general welfare are themselves inviting some form of dictatorship. By reducing democratic government to impotence, by denying it the power to cope with the problems which face it, they would subject it to the very strains and tensions which would-be dictators shrewdly exploit. A people which has known democracy will not willingly surrender it until it has lost faith in the power of democracy to act.

Still another argument of the anti-welfare faction is that the government has no business tinkering with our economic machinery. But hasn't the American government, in order to promote the general welfare, always concerned itself with how our economic machinery runs? Such powers were given it in the Constitution and have been repeatedly confirmed by decisions of the Supreme Court. The very first Congress of the United States adopted a protective tariff for the purpose of aiding manufactures and promoting the development of industry. This came about on the recommendation of Alexander Hamilton. Later the railroads were given subsidies in the form of public lands—lands which finally equalled in total size the area of the whole state of Texas. The government has provided funds for roads, canals, and harbors. More recently it has subsidized shipping and the airlines. The Reconstruction Finance Corporation has lent millions to American industries. The list of similar measures could go on for pages.

It is when the government concerns itself with measures which more directly benefit the people that the reactionaries really protest. They don't literally believe the principle they invoke. They conveniently forget such measures as the Homestead Act, which was passed during the administration of President Lincoln. What they really appear to believe in is a kind of trickle-down theory of general welfare. This is illustrated in their opposition to the public housing measure which finally passed the 81st Congress only after a long and bitter fight. The difficulty with the trickle-down theory is that not enough trickles down.

Let me turn to a final objection. It emphasizes our already great tax burden and our alleged inability to afford a comprehensive program of direct measures for the general welfare. First of all we must balance the cost of such a program against the cost of failure to provide it. For example we must weigh the cost of decent housing for everyone against the heavy cost of not having it. The costs of delinquency and expenditures for mental institutions, for example, are directly related to this social failure.

But also we must consider the cost of a welfare program in light of our total national income and our total national production before we predict that the welfare state will spend us into bankruptcy. Not only is our national income rising—and our national productivity,—but so is the per capita productivity of our workers. For example, the output in manufacturing per man-hour more than doubled in the twenty-year period between 1919 and 1939. There can be no doubt that we have the resources and the productive skill to create an economy in which every citizen has security and an opportunity to work. To maintain otherwise is to take a pessimistic view of our economic system which the facts do not warrant.

The Director of the United States Bureau of the Budget reminded this organization in a recent address that approximately

80 per cent of the money we pay in taxes goes to meet the cost of past wars, and to pay for insurance against future wars. The current needs of national defense and international affairs consume more than 50 cents out of each dollar we spend. I am convinced that if our democracy in America can demonstrate to the world that it can and will enable the just needs of all Americans to be met, the millions of people in Western Europe, India and China will turn to democracy. That is the only way to reduce the threat of Soviet Russia and eliminate the necessity of spending for war.

I should like to conclude, gentlemen, with some general observations. The Republican Party has chosen to make the welfare state the issue of the coming elections. In doing so I fear it has chosen to fight again the campaigns of the 1930's instead of the 1950's. The real issue before us is not whether in fact we shall have the welfare state. The American people have already decided that. They want more than freedom in the abstract. They have already decided that a society as fabulously wealthy and productive as our own can and must make adequate provision for *all* of its members. Such provision must come, not as a grudging concession, but as a forthright recognition of the rights of free people.

As a Democrat I might rejoice over what is assuredly a major strategic error on the part of the opposition. But as a citizen I must regret that we are diverted from the issues that ought really to concern us. We ought to be in agreement on the goals and devote our effort to the measures necessary to achieve them. One thing, for example, that certainly is required is a productive and continuously expanding economy. In the end, welfare for all the people depends upon production and continued full employment. This is the practical issue which should most concern the American people. This is the issue to which the parties should be addressing themselves.

The achievement of a genuine welfare society, whose government chosen by the people acts in the interest of *all* of them, may be delayed and hindered. But it cannot be averted. The American people have decided this. The certainty of this achievement is not a calamity, as the reactionaries would have us believe. Rather it is an assurance of the fulfillment of the American ideal. The achievement will not come without heroic effort. But it will be a righteous struggle—a struggle, in the words of Abraham Lincoln, "for maintaining in the world that form and substance of government whose leading object is to elevate the condition of men—to lift artificial weights from all shoulders; to clear the paths of laudable pursuits for all; to afford to all an unfettered start." This is our best hope for justice, security, and peace.

CHARGE TO JURY [10]

HAROLD R. MEDINA [11]

Federal Judge Harold R. Medina gave this charge to the jury, on October 13, 1949, at the conclusion of the nine-month Communist trial, in the Federal Court House, Foley Square, New York City. The charge occupied two hours.

Eleven members of the Communist Party's American Politburo were charged with criminal conspiracy to organize the party, under orders from Moscow, to "teach and advocate the overthrow of the government and destruction of American democracy, by force and violence."

The judge's instructions called for a verdict of (1) guilty for all eleven, or (2) acquittal for all, or (3) guilty for some, or (4) disagreement.

The judge agreed with the prosecution that the right of free speech is not absolute. The issue was whether the defendants were advocating governmental change by peaceful means or by violence and revolution. The jury was thus urged to weigh carefully the testimony that would answer this issue. Said the judge, the case required "calm, cool, deliberate consideration of the evidence." The jurors must not be governed by "conjecture, passion, prejudice, public opinion, or public feeling."

The judge read his charge swiftly, clearly, calmly, and dispassionately. "In his black robe he leaned back in his chair and rocked back and forth gently under the American flag and the great seal of the United States in the high ceiling of the court room." [12]

The jury followed him closely.

On the next day, the jury declared the eleven guilty. Would such decision mean the end of the Communist Party in this country? General opinion so concluded—provided the Federal Court of Appeals and the Supreme Court sustained the verdict. The Constitutional question was whether the Smith Act of New York State, as applied to Communists, violated the first Amendment to the Constitution with its safeguarding of freedom of speech. The question at stake (to echo the language of Justice Oliver Wendell Holmes) was in this case, "whether the words used are used in such circumstances and are of such nature as to create a clear and present danger."

On October 21, Judge Medina sentenced ten of the eleven to a term of five years in prison and a fine for each of $10,000. Robert G. Thomp-

---

[10] Text and permission for this reprint furnished through the courtesy of Judge Medina.

[11] For biographical note, see Appendix.

[12] New York *Times*, October 14, 1949.

son received only three years because of his army record—he had won the Distinguished Service Cross in World War II.

The Judge denied bail; the verdict was appealed.

Judge Medina has practiced at the bar for almost forty years, where his time has been devoted almost entirely to the argument of appeals and the trial of cases. He also has had experience on the faculty of the Columbia Law School for some twenty-five years.

LADIES AND GENTLEMEN OF THE JURY: You now approach the performance of one of the most sacred duties of citizenship, the meting out of justice. Just after you were sworn in as jurors I took occasion to make a few remarks which I shall now repeat in somewhat different form, as the thoughts I then expressed are peculiarly applicable to the period of your deliberations in order to reach a just and true verdict. I then told you to be patient and said that there are few qualities in life so important. I said that if you once get yourself in the frame of mind where you know that you have a task ahead and it has to be done carefully and it has to be done just right and you know that it will be wrong to let little things disturb you, then there comes a certain calm and peace of mind which are of the essence in the administration of justice. When you get yourself in that frame of mind, you find not only that the task ahead becomes much easier, but in addition that the quality of your work in the administration of justice is of the quality that it should be. Justice does not flourish amidst emotional excitement and stress.

The rich and the poor, and persons of every race, creed and condition stand alike before the bar of justice; and you must consider and weigh the evidence carefully, calmly and dispassionately, without the slightest trace of sympathy or prejudice for or against any party to the proceeding. The very importance of the case makes it all the more urgent that you heed these words of caution. In this connection you will bear in mind at all times that these eleven men are charged here as eleven individuals. The guilt or innocence of each of which must be passed on by you separately, pursuant to and in accordance with the instructions which I am about to give you. . . .

And so I come to the construction and interpretation of the statute. You will have noticed that, to infringe this law, a defendant must not only have conspired to organize as the Communist Party of the United States of America a society, group and assembly of persons who teach and advocate the overthrow or destruction of the Government by force and violence, and to advocate and teach the duty and necessity of overthrowing or destroying the Government by force and violence. The statute makes such conduct unlawful only when persons have so conspired "wilfully" or "knowingly"; and the indictment so charges these defendants.

Thus the question of intent also enters into the offense charged. If you find that the defendants, or any of them, participated in the conspiracy charged in the indictment, one of the questions for you to consider and determine is whether they acted wilfully. This is a question of their intent. You must be satisfied from the evidence beyond a reasonable doubt that the defendants had an intent to cause the overthrow or destruction of the Government of the United States by force and violence, and that it was with this intent and for the purpose of furthering that objective that they conspired both (1) to organize the Communist Party of the United States as a group or society who teach and advocate the overthrow or destruction of the Government of the United States by force and violence and (2) to teach and advocate the duty and necessity of overthrowing or destroying the Government of the United States by force and violence. And you must further find that it was the intent of the defendants to achieve this goal of the overthrow or destruction of the Government of the United States by force and violence as speedily as circumstances would permit it to be achieved.

In further construction and interpretation of the statute I charge you that it is not the abstract doctrine of overthrowing or destroying organized government by unlawful means which is denounced by this law, but the teaching and advocacy of action for the accomplishment of that purpose, by language reasonably and ordinarily calculated to incite persons to such action. Accordingly, you cannot find the defendants or any of them guilty of the crime charged unless you are satisfied beyond a reasonable doubt that they conspired to organize a society, group and assembly of persons who teach and advocate the overthrow or destruction of the Government of the United States by force and violence and to advocate and teach the duty and necessity of overthrowing or destroying the Government of the United States by force and violence, with the intent that such teaching and advocacy be of a rule or principle of action and by language reasonably and ordinarily calculated to incite persons to such action, all with the intent to cause the overthrow or destruction of the Government of the United States by force and violence as speedily as circumstances would permit.

No such intent could be inferred from the open and above-board teaching of a course on the principles and implications of communism in an American college or university, where everything is open to the scrutiny of parents and trustees and anyone who may be interested to see what is going on. That is why it is so important for you to weigh with scrupulous care the testimony concerning secret schools, false names, devious ways, general falsification and so on, all alleged to be in the setting of a huge and well-disciplined organization, spreading to practically every State of the Union and all the principal cities, and industries.

It is obviously impossible to ascertain or prove directly what were the operations of the minds of the defendants. You cannot look into a person's mind and see what his intentions are or were. But a careful and intelligent consideration of the facts and circumstances shown by the evidence in any given case enables us to infer with a reasonable degree of accuracy what another's intentions were in doing or not doing certain things. With a knowledge of definite acts we may draw definite logical conclusions. We are in our affairs continually called upon to decide from actions of others what their intentions or purposes are. And experience has taught us that frequently actions speak more clearly than spoken or written words. You must therefore rely in part on circumstantial evidence in determining the guilt or innocence of any of these defendants.

Circumstantial evidence may be received and is entitled to such consideration as you may find it deserves depending upon the inferences you think it necessary and reasonable to draw from such evidence. No greater degree of certainty is required when the evidence is circumstantial than when it is direct, for in either case the jury must be convinced beyond a reasonable doubt of the guilt of the defendants. Circumstantial evidence consists of facts proved from which the jury may infer by process of reasoning other facts sought to be established as true.

Different inferences, however, may be drawn from the facts and circumstances in the case, whether proved by direct or circumstantial evidence. The prosecution asks you to draw one set of inferences while the defendants ask you to draw another. It is for you to decide and for you alone, which inferences you will draw. If all the circumstances taken together are consistent with any reasonable hypothesis which includes the innocence of the defendants, or any of them, the prosecution has not proved their guilt beyond a reasonable doubt, and you must acquit them. On the other hand, if you find that all of the circumstances established by the evidence in this case, taken together, satisfy you beyond a reasonable doubt of the guilt of the defendants, in accordance with these instructions, it is your duty to find the defendants guilty.

Thus, if you find that the evidence has established to your satisfaction beyond a reasonable doubt that any defendant has violated the statute as thus construed by me, you will find such defendant guilty. Otherwise you will acquit him by a verdict of not guilty. Under these instructions you may find all the defendants guilty or all of them not guilty or you may find one or more of them guilty and the others not guilty.

If you are satisfied that the evidence establishes beyond a reasonable doubt that the defendants, or any of them, are guilty of a violation of the statute, as I have interpreted it to you, I find as a matter of law that there is sufficient danger of a substantive evil that the Congress has a right to prevent to justify the application of the statute under the First Amendment of the Constitution.

This is matter of law about which you have no concern. It is a finding on a matter of law which I deem essential to support my ruling that the case should be submitted to you to pass upon the guilt or innocence of the defendants. It is the duty of counsel for both sides to present by way of objections, motions, and similar procedural devices, matters of law affecting the case for my consideration and determination. All such matters of law and their presentation by counsel, including motions of every name, nature and description, challenges, questions relating to the admissibility of evidence and things of that sort must be entirely disregarded by you. These are matters of procedure with which you have no concern. Neither the presentation of such matters by counsel for either side, nor any argument made in support or in opposition to any of them, has any bearing upon your deliberations. Put all such matters out of your minds. They should not influence you in any way in arriving at your verdict.

I charge you that in arriving at your verdict you must not consider anything which the court has said with respect to the conduct of either the prosecution or counsel for the defense in the course of this trial as being any indication or suggestion or direction of the court to you as to what your verdict should be, nor shall you be influenced thereby in arriving at your verdict. . . .

Now, ladies and gentlemen of the jury, one last word. If you find that the evidence respecting the defendants or any of them is reasonably consistent with innocence, such defendant or defendants should be acquitted. If you find that the law has not been violated, you should not hesitate for any reason to render a verdict of not guilty. But, on the other hand, if you find, in accordance with these instructions, that the law has been violated as charged you should not hesitate because of sympathy or any other reason to render a verdict of guilty.

The exhibits will be gathered together by counsel and will be available for the jury if the jury wish to have them.

SOCIO-ECONOMIC RELATIONS

THE CHALLENGE OF HUMAN RELATIONS [1]

RALPH J. BUNCHE [2]

Dr. Ralph J. Bunche, acting assistant Secretary General, Department of Trusteeship and Information from Non-Self-Governing Territories, United Nations, gave this address at an Abraham Lincoln celebration, sponsored by the City Club of Rochester (New York), at the Eastman Theater, on the evening of February 11, 1950. On the same program was Mrs. Franklin D. Roosevelt. Earlier that day these two speakers had addressed a student conference on human rights at the University of Rochester, part of a program to celebrate that University's 100th Anniversary.

Dr. Bunche at Rochester carried the prestige of his United Nations success as Acting Mediator for Palestine in the war between Israel and its neighbors. On the island of Rhodes, in 1949, he succeeded in setting up an armistice between Israel, on one hand, and Egypt, Iraq, Saudi Arabia, Lebanon, and Transjordan on the other. For his splendid results in ending hostilities and effecting an armistice until permanent peace terms could be signed, Dr. Bunche was awarded the Spingarn Medal in 1949, given annually since 1915 "for the highest achievement of an American Negro."

Dr. Bunche was educated at Michigan, Harvard, Northwestern, the London School of Economics, and the University of California. He has been head of the Department of Political Science at Harvard University since 1929.

His addresses show mature thinking and wide research. His language is original and forceful.

His diagnosis of the problems of race relations and his fresh affirmation of his own faith in American democracy were timely. After a scheduled concert by the Negro baritone Paul Robeson, at Peekskill, New York, in August 1949, had ended in a riot, many Americans looked to Dr. Bunche for leadership in stemming the tide of racial prejudice.

We are gathered here tonight to pay tribute to a man of rare greatness—one of the most stalwart figures of our nation's history. But it is not within our feeble power to do honor to

---

[1] Text furnished by the United Nations Department of Public Information. Permission to reprint given through the courtesy of Dr. Bunche.
[2] For biographical note, see Appendix.

Abraham Lincoln except as we may dedicate ourselves to the fulfilment of the imperative objectives which he sought.

Lincoln, the man, was mortal, and being mortal was fallible. History records his moments of indecision, his groping, his bows to political expediency. But in the crucial hours of decision, he found a boundless strength which flowed from his unwavering faith in the "plain people," from the equalitarianism of the West in which he was born and reared, from his undecorated belief in the equality and dignity of man.

I am impelled to deviate for a moment and to say that on this platform tonight there is another great American personality, whose greatness history will also record, and from whose untiring efforts posterity will reap an abundantly rich harvest. A great lady, who walks unerringly in the hallowed tracks of Jefferson and Lincoln, and whose greatness, like theirs, is grounded in the dedication of her life to the high principles of true democracy. Mrs. Roosevelt, herself identified with a group —women—which is still not fully emancipated from traditional and unjust inequalities, is, in her own right, a twentieth century emancipator.

I have been chosen to speak tonight to the topic—The Challenge of Human Relations—for two reasons.

In the first place, it seems to me to be a rather appropriate subject for this occasion. Lincoln, himself, was called upon to save this nation from as great a crisis and conflict in human relations as has ever confronted any nation. And though he met the challenge and saved the nation, even Lincoln could not avert a cruel, tragic, devastating internecine war. Indeed, eighty-five years later, that war is still not fully liquidated, and at times it may seem not entirely clear who won it.

In the second place, the greatest danger to mankind today, in my view, is to be found in the sordid human relations which everywhere prevail.

Were Lincoln alive today, he could scarcely avoid taking a dark view of the relations among peoples the world over, not by any means excluding his own country. It would be understandable if even a quick view of the situation should induce in him one of those occasional moods of melancholia which some historians have attributed to him.

For what is the situation? The relations among peoples are broadly characterized by dangerous animosities, hatreds, mutual recriminations, suspicions, bigotries and intolerances. Man has made spectacular progress in science, in transportation and communication, in the arts, in all things material. Yet, it is a matter of colossal and tragic irony that man, in all his genius, having learned to harness nature, to control the relations among the elements and to direct them as he sees fit—even to the point where he now has the means readily at hand for his own complete self-destruction—has never yet learned how to *live* with himself; has not mastered the art of human relations. In the realm of human understanding the peoples of the world remain shockingly illiterate. This has always been and today remains man's greatest challenge: how to teach the peoples of the world the elemental lesson of the essential kinship of mankind and man's identity of interest.

We live in a most dangerous age—an age of supersonic airspeeds, of biological warfare, of atomic and hydrogen bombs, and who knows what next. In no exaggerated sense, we all today exist on borrowed time. If we of this generation deserve no better fate, surely our children do. They, certainly, can never understand why we could not do at least as well as the animal kingdoms.

We need peace desperately. But the world has always needed peace. Today, however, the question is not peace or war, as it has been in the past. The question now is sheer survival—survival of civilization, survival of mankind. And time is short, frighteningly short.

How is the question to be answered! We may improvise, we may build diplomatic dams, we may pile pact upon pact. The United Nations, as it is doing, may scurry about valiantly with its fire-fighting machinery and put out a war-fire in Indonesia today, in Palestine tomorrow, and in Korea or Kashmir or Greece the next day. But new war-fires will continue to flare up, and one day one of them, fanned by a furious windstorm of human conflict, may very well get out of hand. And then the final havoc will be upon us. Indeed, it is a sign of the deplorable state of human affairs in our time that unless we blind ourselves to the realities we must always think and speak of the future in terms of sound and fury, of fire and brimstone. Yet I do not believe that either the present or the future is by any means irretrievably lost, that all is hopeless.

No strength is ever to be gained from sheer imaginings and escapisms. Let us be not like the figures in Plato's parable of mankind in the dark cave. We must see and face reality and truth rather than shadows and images, distortions and illusions on the wall of the cave. The truth is that there can be but one really secure foundation for peace in the world. And that foundation must be in the attitudes which reflect the state of the hearts and minds of man. Without great changes in human attitudes, without massive strides toward human understanding and brotherhood, the most perfect international machinery for peace will ultimately be unavailing. No mechanical device, no international charters or pacts, no diplomacy however ingenious, can serve to save mankind from itself if man in his relations with man remains mean and brutish.

It is ourselves that we must fear more than the atomic or hydrogen bomb. It is in man's perversities, in his brooding suspicions, in his arrogances and intolerances, in his false self-righteousness and in his apathy that the real danger is to be found. In the final analysis, there is but one road to peace and that is the road of human understanding and fellow-feeling, of inflexible determination to achieve peaceful relations among men. That, clearly, is a long, hard road, and today it is too little travelled.

I repeat that the fundamental weakness and danger of the world today is the universality of bad human relations. If these relations were everywhere, or let us even say *almost* everywhere, internationally and domestically, good, there would be little to fear. For then the free peoples of the world would have unassailable strength, and more than that, unwavering confidence in their ability to protect themselves collectively and fully against any maverick who might go on the loose. On the other side of the coin, bad human relations are, indeed, an encouragement and stimulus to the adventures of mavericks. It is on the disunity of peoples that Hitlers prey.

By "human relations" I mean simply the ability—or inability —of mankind to live with itself in peace and order, in harmony and understanding, in honor and mutual respect.

I am optimistic enough about my fellow beings to believe that it is human *attitudes,* not human nature, that must be feared —and changed. On the international scene, it is these attitudes which have brought the world to the menacing state of affairs of today—the "cold war," the maneuverings for power and dominance, the dangerous rivalries, the propaganda battles— cannibalistic struggles in which ethical principles, and moral law are often callously jettisoned. If peoples could not be induced to suspect, to fear, and finally to hate one another, there could be no wars, for governments, from whatever motivations, can only lead peoples into wars—the peoples must fight them. And in these wars, countless numbers of human beings—by nature essentially good, whatever their immediate attitudes—must be sacrificed solely because the peoples of one society or another embark, or permit themselves to be embarked, upon fatal adventures of conquest or domination. On the domestic scene, it is human attitudes, not human nature, which nurture the racial and religious hatreds and bigotries which today permeate many soceities, and even in democracies thrive in the fertile soil of complacency.

The picture is foreboding and the future looms ominously. But perhaps there lies the hope. Can man, a thinking animal, capable of both emotion and cool calculation with regard to his self-interest, be brought to his senses in time? Can he see the black doom which awaits him at the end of the path he now follows? I have enough faith in the potentiality of mankind for good to believe that he can save himself.

Certainly, there is nothing in human nature which renders it impossible for men to live peacefully and harmoniously with one another. Hatred, intolerance, bigotry, chauvinism are never innate—they are the bad lessons taught in society. Despite the fact that in recorded history, mankind has been as much at war as at peace, it cannot be concluded that war is inevitable—a natural state of mankind. Nor do I believe that because hatreds, bigotries, intolerances and prejudices loom large in the pages of history, these are the natural conditions of man's societal existence on earth.

I am under no illusions about mankind and I do not for a moment underestimate his capacity for evil doing. All of us, no doubt, are painfully aware of some individuals who live up to the hilt—and then some—to the Hobbesian characterization of man as "nasty, poor, mean and brutish." Yet, I am persuaded that such persons are the exception rather than the rule, and in any case, they are the unfortunate end-products of society. I believe, with Julian Huxley, that there is a sharp distinction between human nature and the *expression* of human nature. War and bigotry are not reflections of human nature but rather collective expressions of it in the particular circumstances in which man finds himself at a given time. Ironically enough, modern man has given some of the best demonstrations of how peoples can work together in a close bond of understanding during the adversities of war itself. Human nature may be relatively constant, but its expression is subject to change. That man has the *ability* to change the circumstances which influence the expression of his nature and lead him down disastrous paths is undoubted. The great decision involves his *will* to do so.

It may be that man's will can be activated only by an impending sense of catastrophe; that only on the brink of disaster may he turn to human solidarity as his last chance for salvation. If so, he finds himself today precariously on that brink.

I think it no exaggeration to say that unfortunately, throughout the ages, organized religion and education have failed miserably in their efforts to save man from himself. Perhaps they have failed because so often they have merely reflected the mean and norrow attitudes of the very peoples they were striving to save.

Human understanding, human brotherhood and solidarity, will be achieved, if at all, only when the peoples of many lands find a common bond through a compelling sense of urgency in achieving common goals. The purposes and principles of the United Nations—with peace as the universal common denominator—afford that bond and the common goals. The implements of modern warfare afford the urgency, if people once understand the frightful implications and elect to survive.

Lincoln, instinctively a true democrat, believed deeply in the essential justice of the plain people, whose better impulses and good will he trusted ultimately to prevail. Given half a chance, I believe that the peoples of the world today, in their collectivity, will justify Lincoln's faith.

It is not necessary to seek to transform people into saints in order that impending disaster may be averted.

Throughout the world today, thinking and psychology have not kept pace with the times. That people inevitably think in terms of their self-interest is something very little can be done about. But is it not equally tenable that a great deal can be done about influencing people to think and act in terms of their *true* self-interest? In this dangerous age, notions of exalted and exaggerated nationalism, of chauvinism, of group superiority and master race, of group exclusiveness, of national self-righteousness, of special privilege, are in the interest of neither the world nor of any particular group in it. They are false views of self-interest and carry us all toward the disaster of war. And in the war of tomorrow there can be no victor; at best there will be only survivors. The old concepts and values are no longer valid or realistic. The future may well belong to those who first realign their international sights.

I sincerely believe that the generality of peoples throughout the world really long for peace and freedom. There can be no doubt that this is true of the American people. If this is true, it is the one great hope for the future. The problem is how to crystallize this longing, how to fashion it into an overpowering instrument for good. The United Nations recognizes acutely the desperate need, but has not yet found the ways and means of mobilizing the peace-loving attitudes of the peoples of the world over the stubborn walls of national egoisms.

I sincerely believe that the generality of peoples throughout the world really long for peace and freedom. There can be no doubt that this is true of the American people. If this is true, it is the one great hope for the future. The problem is how to crystallize this longing, how to fashion it into an overpowering instrument for good. The United Nations recognizes acutely the desperate need, but has not yet found the ways and means of mobilizing the peace-loving attitudes of the peoples of the world over the stubborn walls of national egoisms.

Every nation, every government, every individual, has a most solemn obligation to mankind and the future of mankind in the fateful effort to rescue the world from the morass in which it is now entrapped and to underwrite a future of peace and freedom for all. This is a time of gravest crisis. Constructive, concerted actions—not negativism and recrimination—are called for. There are many motes in many eyes. There is no nation which can stand before the ultimate bar of human history and say: We have done our utmost to induce peoples to live in peace with one another as brothers.

It must be very clear that what the world needs most desperately today is a crusade for peace and understanding of unparalleled dimension; a universal mobilization of the strong but diffused forces of peace and justice. The collective voice of the peoples of the world could be so irresistible as to dwarf into insignificance both A and H bombs and to disperse and discourage the warlike and war minded.

In the existing state of affairs, societies admittedly owe it to themselves to be prepared and protected against any eventuality. With that, given the international circumstances, reason and reality might perceive no quarrel. But it would also appear that reason and reality would dictate that since armament is never an end in itself and must expand itself, if at all, only in war, the only way peace-loving societies might cover their mounting losses from the tremendous expenditures on armaments would be to exert an effort of at least equal magnitude for peace—to the end that the armaments would never have to be used. This, it seems to me, would be at once good economics, good humanitarianism, and good self-interest.

And now, if I may take advantage of my nationality and speak for a moment simply as an American citizen, I may ask where do we, as Americans, stand with regard to the challenge of human relations?

The United States is in the forefront of international affairs today. The eyes of the world are focussed upon us as never before in our history. A great part of the world looks to us for a convincing demonstration of the validity and the virility of the democratic way of life as America exalts it. It would be catastrophic if we should fail to give that demonstration. We cannot afford to fail.

But it is only too apparent that our democratic house is not yet in shipshape order. There are yawning crevices in our human relations; the gap between our democratic profession on the one hand, and our daily practices of racial and religious intolerance on the other, while less wide than formerly, is still very wide.

Race relations is our number one social problem, perhaps our number one problem. It is no mere sectional problem; it is a national—indeed an international—problem. For any problem today which challenges the ability of democracy to function convincingly, which undermines the very foundations of democracy and the faith of people in it, is of concern to the entire peace and freedom loving world. Surely, it must be abundantly clear that it is only through the triumph of democracy and the determined support of peoples for it as an imperative way of life that secure foundations for world peace can be laid.

That race relations are gradually improving, both in the South and elsewhere in the nation, cannot be doubted. But neither can it be doubted that these relations remain in a dangerous state, that they are a heavy liability to the nation, and constitute a grave weakness in our national democratic armor.

Certainly the costs of anti-racial and anti-religious practices are enormously high. Attitudes of bigotry, when widely prevalent in a society, involve staggering costs in terms of prestige and confidence throughout the rest of the world, not to mention the contamination and degradation resulting from the presence of such psychological diseases in the body of the society.

Throughout the nation, in varying degree, the Negro minority —almost a tenth of the population—suffers severe political, economic and social disabilities solely because of race. In Washington, the nation's capital, Lincoln, the Great Emancipator, sits majestically in his great armchair behind the marble pillars, and

overlooks a city which does not yet admit his moral dictum that
the Negro is a man; a city in which no Negro can live and work
with dignity; a city which, administered by Congress itself,
subjects one fourth of its citizens to segregation, discrimination
and daily humiliation. Washington is this nation's greatest shame
precisely because it is governed by Congress and is the capital of
a great democracy. Washington, of all American cities, should
symbolize and vitalize that democracy.

Lincoln saw that slavery had to be abolished not only because
as an institution it was contrary to human morality, but also
because it was inimical to the interests of the "plain people" of
America. By the same token, present-day practices of racial segregation and discrimination should be outlawed as inimical to the
interests of all who believe in and derive benefit from democracy,
whatever their race or religion.

The most valuable resources of any country are its people.
But in our country today, and in the South particularly, our
human resources, white and black alike, are being recklessly
squandered. They are being squandered in interracial conflict, in
prejudices and animosities among two groups of citizens—
Americans all—which prevent that unity of purpose and that
cooperative effort which alone could insure the full realization of
the nation's potential in its human resources; and this at a time
when it vitally requires its maximum strength.

The vitality of this great country derives from the unity of
purpose and the devotion to its democratic ideals of the diversified
peoples—by race, religion and national origin—who make up its
population. Disunity and group conflict constantly sap that
vitality.

As a nation we have also found strength in the fact that we
have always been able and willing to face our shortcomings
frankly and attack them realistically. It is in this spirit and in this
knowledge that I, as an American, take occasion to point to our
shortcomings. I do not imply, in any sense, that the rest of the
world is free of such imperfections, or in given instances, even
greater ones.

To enjoy our maximum strength, we need more *applied* democracy. We need to live up to the principles which we believe

in and for which we are hailed by the world. We too need a mobilization—a mobilization throughout the country of men and women of good will, of men and women who are determined to see American democracy fulfill its richest promise, and who will ceaselessly exert their efforts towards that end.

This nation, by its traditional philosophy, by its religious precepts, by its Constitution, stands for freedom, for the brotherhood of man, and for full respect for the rights and dignity of the individual. By giving unqualified expression to these ideals in our daily life we can and will achieve a democratic society here so strong in the hearts and minds of its citizens, so sacred to the individual, that it will be forever invulnerable to any kind of attack.

Because I believe in the reason and essential goodness of human beings; because I have deep respect for and faith in my fellow man, I look to the future of race relations in our country with reasonable optimism. I know that there are very many men and women of good will in the North, South, East and West, that their ranks increase daily, that their influence is being widely felt, and that this influence is gradually clearing away the race-relations fog which has enshrouded us. But I must add that where rights and birthrights are concerned, gradual progress can never be rapid enough for those deprived, since rights and birthrights can never be enjoyed posthumously.

If I may be pardoned for a personal reference, I am proud to be an American and I am proud of my origin. I believe in the American way of life, and believing in it, deplore its imperfections. I wish to see my country strong in every way—strong in the nature and practice of its democratic way of life; strong in its world leadership; strong in both its material and spiritual values; strong in the hearts and minds of all of its people, whatever their race, color or religion, and in their unshakable devotion to it. I wish to see an America in which both the fruits and the obligations of democracy are shared by *all* of its citizens on a basis of full equality and without qualification of race or creed.

The United Nations ideal is a world in which peoples would "practice tolerance and live together in peace with one another as good neighbors." If this ideal is far from realization it is only because of the state of mind of mankind. Man's reason and calculated self-interest can be powerful forces for changes in that state of mind. No ideal could be more rewarding. Every individual today has it in his power—in his daily living, in his attitudes and practices—to contribute greatly to the realization of that ideal. We must be strong in our adherence to ideals. We must never lose faith in man's potential power for good.

FOR THE FEDERAL FAIR EMPLOYMENT PRACTICES ACT [3]

ADAM CLAYTON POWELL, JR. [4]

Congressman Adam C. Powell, Jr., gave this short debate before the House of Representatives, on February 22, 1950. This speech should be reviewed in conjunction with that of Congressman Sims which follows.[5]

The proposed Federal Fair Employment Practices bill was a highly controversial one. More than a hundred Southern Democrats met in caucus on February 21 to map out their opposition strategy. The Administration bill, sponsored by Congressman Lesinski of Michigan, Chairman of the Educational Labor Committee, was scheduled for floor consideration under a House rule that provides for "Calendar Wednesdays," days on which chairmen of many bills, blocked by other House procedures, might call up their measures. Alphabetically the Committee on Education and Labor was entitled to its turn on this Wednesday. A House rule also stipulated that a measure at issue must be brought to a final vote before that legislative day ends. Each side was to be given an equal amount of time—with speeches usually limited to five minutes. A filibuster, as often developed in Senate debate, was thus hardly possible.

The bill would make it illegal for any employer of fifty or more persons to discriminate in hiring because of a job applicant's race, color, religion, ancestry, or national origin.

The setting for the debate was dramatic. Crowds packed the galleries and, in long lines on the floor below, more people waited admission.

Involved parliamentary tactics occupied five hours after the House convened at twelve o'clock. There was reading of Washington's Farewell Address, followed by eight roll calls on one pretext or another, including motions to adjourn. Reading the bill in full, for example, was resorted to "as a road block."

It was one of the most turbulent House sessions in years. Language and delivery were bitter. There were constant shouts. "Southerners interrupted with rebel yells."

Congressman Lesinski opened the debate with a brief statement and then yielded to Congressman Powell, who controlled the debate, and who, after his argument in support of the motion, recognized in turn many affirmative speakers. His argument was a compact debater's brief.

[3] *Congressional Record* (81st Congress, 2nd session). 96:2211-14. February 22, 1950 (daily edition).

[4] For biographical note, see Appendix.

[5] See below, p159.

It exemplifies the condensed argument given in the House when time limitations are imposed.

Powell, a graduate of Colgate with an advanced degree from Columbia, has been since 1937 a minister of the Abyssinian Baptist Church of Harlem, New York City, and since 1945 a member of Congress. As speaker he is fluent, physically and emotionally highly active. In his Congressional speeches, he usually adheres closely to argument without much rhetorical embellishment.

Toward the end of the debate many amendments were offered and at 3:14 A.M., on February 23, fifteen hours after the debate started, by a vote of 221 to 178, the House accepted amendments that defeated the Lesinski measure. Later that day, 240 to 177, the House passed and sent to the Senate a "voluntary" fair employment practice program. For enforcement reliance would be placed on conciliation, education, and public opinion. The outcome was regarded as a major defeat for the Administration. The measure, scheduled to be introduced in the Senate, was expected to result in a filibuster. Even the "voluntary" bill had little chance of passage in the Eighty-second Congress.

Mr. Chairman, I would like to express my thanks to the members of the FEPC [Fair Employment Practice Committee] subcommittee for the cooperation they gave me in the hearings on this bill. I would like to publicly thank our colleague from Ohio [MR. BREHM], whose cold has been plaguing him and developed into laryngitis. His actions on the subcommittee were greater than any words he could utter today. Also I want to thank members of the full committee on Education and Labor, and I refer to Members on both sides, those who agreed and disagreed, for the cooperation and understanding that we had in committee. I trust that further debate on this bill will be in an atmosphere of dignity, even though we may oppose it bitterly or we may be in favor of it wholeheartedly.

I have allotted myself only five minutes because there are scores of members who want to talk and I do not want to cover myself with any personal glory.

I would like to say one or two things concerning the bill so that we can remove from our minds anything that we may not know concerning the details. . . .

I. Does job discrimination exist? There can be no serious question that employment discrimination is widespread. In its final report, the wartime FEPC predicted that even such gains as it had made were dissipating and predicted further, accelerated dissipation. . . .

II. Should it be eliminated? Without going into the vast wealth of detail available in answer to this question, it should suffice here to indicate briefly some of the areas adversely affected by employment discrimination.

(a) The democratic principles on which the nation was founded are flaunted by discrimination. Any violation of these principles has an adverse effect. Futhermore, the general moral code to which we pay allegiance, demands that all men be considered as individuals and rated according to their individual worth. As the bill states, "it is essential that this gap between principle and practice be closed."

(b) Our foreign relations are hampered by the publicity our enemies give to our discriminatory practices. Secretary of State Acheson describes discrimination as "a handicap in our relations with other countries." Senator Dulles when a United States delegate to the UN said that FEPC is necessary to "erase what today is the worst blot on our national escutcheon." The United States is bound by its international agreements to eliminate discrimination—for example, the Inter-American Conference in Mexico City, 1945; the Charter of the UN; and the Universal Declaration of Human Rights proclaimed by the General Assembly.

(c) The economic waste of discrimination cannot be totally computed. One economist estimated before the House subcommittee that we send at least $15 billion annually down the drain because of discrimination. Contributing to this total is the cost of training those whom we will not allow to use their training; the cost to industry of using artificially limited pools in selecting what should be the most skilled manpower; the creation, in minority populations, of a disproportionate degree of unemployment, resulting in an island of depression which affects its surroundings—"a man who can't earn can't buy"; the breakdown in morale among those who know that no matter what their skills, they cannot compete on an equal basis with those whom they are taught to believe are their equals; the personality difficulties resulting from lack of home life when mothers are forced to work to supplement inadequate income brought in by fathers. The only remaining question, then, is—

III. Can S.-1728 [the FEPC bill] properly do the required job? Since the testimony at the various hearings in support of FEPC, combined with the analysis of the S. 1728 above, seems to make out a prima facie case for an affirmative answer to this question, it would appear sensible to put the burden on the objections raised.

The chief ones are as follows:

(a) "The bill is unconstitutional; it violates States' rights."

But, first, the Federal Government has the right to impose any reasonable regulations regarding its own employment relations, including regulations against discrimination—United Public Workers against Mitchell.

Second, it can do likewise re employment relations of those who contract with it—Perkins against Lukens Steel Co.

Third, it may regulate the employment relations of private businesses engaged in commerce—NLRB against Jones & Laughlin Steel Corp.

Fourth, it can therefore impose regulations against discrimination in such businesses, (i) logically, from first, second, and third above, and (ii) on the basis of cases like New Negro Alliance against Sanitary Grocery Co.

(b) "Even if constitutional, this matter should be left to the states; it is a Southern problem."

But, first, the problem is not a Southern problem—nor a Negro, or Jewish, or Catholic, or Mexican problem. Discrimination exists in the North, South, East, West, and middle of America; it is an American problem.

Second, cutting across State lines as it does, discrimination is of national legislative concern.

Third, in general, the greater number of discriminators in a given area, the more difficult to enact local antidiscrimination laws; so the areas which do practice the most discrimination will be just those with no statutory inhibition.

Fourth, many large businesses have their affairs spread out into many states; where one sells may not be where it hires. Federal legislation is the only feasible way to meet this problem.

As an impartial study made by the Library of Congress states, education alone is not sufficient to do the job.

These various studies, together with the testimony presented during the hearings on H. R. 4453, demonstrate all too strikingly that in virtually every section of this country qualified workers are being denied an opportunity of making a living—and a life—solely because of their race, color, religion, or national origin.

Gentlemen, let us conduct this debate in dignity. Let us now proceed to the business of restoring integrity to this body. Both parties and presidential nominees pledged this in their platforms and we will now show the world that at least the House of Representatives is a place that keeps its word.

AGAINST THE FEDERAL FAIR EMPLOYMENT PRACTICES ACT [6]

HUGO S. SIMS, JR. [7]

Representative Hugo Sims, Jr., of South Carolina, gave this speech in the House of Representatives, at Washington, D.C., on February 22, 1950.

Through the late hours of that day and far into the night determined debaters argued for the passage of the Fair Employment Practices Act. Equally vigorous opponents of the measure replied. Each side was given its proper allotment of the limited time allowed for the debate. And each speaker was usually restricted to not more than five minutes.[8]

Prominent supporters were T. H. Nurke of Ohio, Helen Douglas of California, Chet Holifield of California, Jacob Javits of New York, John Lesinski of Michigan, Vito Marcantonio of New York, Mary Norton of New Jersey, Adam C. Powell of New York, John M. Vorys of Ohio, John Walsh of Indiana, and Sidney Yates of Illinois. Important negative debaters were Thomas Abernathy of Mississippi, Paul Brown of Georgia, Donald Jackson of California, Wingate Lucas of Texas, Samuel McConnell of Pennsylvania, John Rankin of Mississippi, Hugo Sims of South Carolina, William Whittington of Mississippi, and Arthur Winstead of Mississippi.

Congressman Sims, whose short speech was among the more impressive for his side, had been a high school debater at Orangeburg, South Carolina, and at Wofford College, Spartansburg, South Carolina.

Sims had also studied law (LL.B., University of South Carolina, 1947); had considerable experience as a columnist; had practiced law and had served one term in the State legislature of South Carolina; and during his war experience had made many speeches as company commander. In his candidacy for nomination and election to Congress, he had campaigned widely and ably. Thus, although young in years and in Congress, he had established his reputation as an effective speaker.

Of his methods of speech preparation he writes: "I have no set plan for preparing a speech. Sometimes I write out a whole speech word for word, then throw the speech away, make an outline of it, throw the out-

[6] *Congressional Record* (81st Congress, 2nd session). 96:2225-6. February 22, 1950 (daily edition). Text furnished through the courtesy of Congressman Sims.

[7] For biographical note, see Appendix.

[8] For details of the speaking situation, see the Introduction to Congressman Powell's speech, p154.

line away and then make the speech. On other occasions I make speeches without any preparation at all. Except for radio speeches, I do not use notes of any kind." [9]

Mr. Chairman, I am opposed to this legislation; I am opposed to any legislation of this type, because I do not believe that civil rights is an end in itself. I do not believe there is anything sacred about civil rights legislation; I think that whether civil rights legislation is right or wrong depends entirely on whether it accomplishes its ultimate end of attaining and preserving human rights. As I understand it, the enactment of civil rights is merely putting human rights into law; consequently, if by passing the law you do not attain and preserve human rights then I feel that civil rights legislation is wrong. . . .

If the proponents of FEPC really want to give the Negroes in America equal opportunity, if the proponents of FEPC accept the minority problem as a national problem (and I agree with you, it is a national problem), then the proponents of this legislation should step boldly forward with a program for providing basic needs to this minority group—basic needs so that they can properly develop their personalities.

The argument is used by proponents of FEPC that we cannot sell democracy and the idea of equal opportunity to the world if we do not practice it at home—that we must close the gap between principles and practices. I agree with them completely that solving the race problem and providing equal opportunity is a national problem. Let us face it realistically.

Let us not make the same mistake that we made in America back in the nineteenth century when slavery was abolished. The problem then was exactly the same problem as it is today; that is, two races living together harmoniously with human rights for all. What was the situation then? We had many people from outside of the South shouting, "Pass a law that makes all people equal and then we will have political freedom and human rights." And on the other hand, within the South you had an equally loud group that were so busy shouting "States rights" that they did not have time to try and solve the race problems that did exist in the South. Neither group recognized the problem of the South for what it was, an economic problem.

[9] Letter to this editor, April 5, 1950.

Perhaps the War Between the States could have been avoided, if, instead of abolishing slavery, the slaves had been bought by the government, and freed, and had been given education, and training, and land, and an opportunity to be economically independent individually. But Congress then did not recognize the problem as an economic one. They thought that by passing laws they would secure political freedom and human rights for the Negro. Let us not make that same mistake again.

Fair employment practice legislation will not give to the Negro an opportunity to become economically independent. Let us give the Negro the opportunity to develop his personality and his capabilities. After all, the Christian religion uses as a standard the development of the personality, to determine right from wrong. The Christian religion is not nearly as concerned with the rewards that one receives on this earth, even if that reward be fair employment, as it is with the opportunity to develop one's personality.

Education is certainly one way toward solving this problem. But education is not enough. Education should be coupled with legislation and that legislation should be designed toward providing those basic needs for all people. Actually, legislation designed toward lifting up those people on the bottom rungs of the economic ladder will, in the long run, eliminate most of the causes for prejudice and will provide opportunities for millions and millions of Negroes who are not given an opportunity to develop their abilities.

However, if the proponents of FEPC legislation feel that we cannot wait on legislation designed to lift up all people who are on the bottom rungs of the economic ladder because of our position as the leading advocate of democracy in the world, I suggest that we pass legislation designed specifically to provide these opportunities to the Negro minorities.

I suggest, first, that we make a huge federal appropriation to the states on the basis of their Negro population for the purpose of providing adequate educational, health, housing, and recreational facilities for the Negro. I suggest, secondly, that we establish a minority employment agency for the purpose of finding jobs for Negroes all over the United States. In other words, it would encourage voluntary migration of Negroes from the South to those parts of the United States where better employment opportunities exist. And, thirdly, that a national education program should be conducted with the objective of eliminating discrimination by education and publicity.

My suggestion of legislation to eliminate the causes of prejudice would help the common man within the Negro race. It is not designed like FEPC to help only a small percentage of the Negroes, perhaps 3 to 5 per cent who could be classified as the elite members of that race.

My objection to FEPC is, first, that the Commission will, in my opinion, use its authority in an effort to end segregation in the South. Secondly, FEPC legislation, or the consideration of FEPC legislation, stirs bitterness and hatred among the races in the South. It does not work toward harmonious race relations and the rank and file of the people will not accept it—consequently, it will be unenforceable.

If this FEPC law were passed it is reasonable to assume that the President of the United States in appointing members for the Commission would appoint people genuinely interested in the success of the legislation. I think that it is also reasonable to assume that all of the members of the commission would feel that segregation is discrimination in itself and that, consequently, they would have no sympathy at all with the people in Southern states who are opposed to ending segregation. I think it is entirely reasonable to assume that these people would agree with the report of President Truman's civil rights committee that the nation should force the South to end segregation and they would use what authority they have toward furthering this aim. I think that the activity of the wartime FEPC justifies these expectations.

President Truman's Committee on Civil Rights recommended that the nation force the South to end segregation by withholding federal funds. And, since the South would not end segregation, it would be bled economically—just as it has been bled by discriminatory freight rates, high protective tariffs, and so forth. This would destroy human rights by lowering per capita income, lowering ability to meet basic needs in a section of the country with an already low per capita income.

A vote for FEPC is not a liberal vote—it is a vote against human rights. I refuse to vote to throw a sop to minority agitators not genuinely interested in the Negroes in South Carolina. I shall continue to oppose vigorously this and similar legislation.

INDUSTRY, LABOR, AGRICULTURE

DETOUR AHEAD [1]

BENJAMIN F. FAIRLESS [2]

Benjamin F. Fairless, President of the United States Steel Corporation, gave this address before the Baltimore Association of Commerce, Baltimore, Maryland, April 21, 1950. The address is a clever, well-reasoned argument, buttressed by specific instances, of capital's defense against the charges of "big business," "monopoly," and "concentration." Because of the investigations of big business and monopoly early in 1950, under Senator Joseph C. O'Mahoney, chairman of the Senate Committee on Interior and Insular Affairs, and those under Emmanuel Cellar, of the House Judiciary Committee, United States Steel was under special scrutiny. Its raising of the price of steel after the end of the strike of 1950 produced much new criticism of that company as monopolistic.

President Fairless' speech is highly personal, informal, humorous, at times sarcastic, and certainly interesting and lacking in stuffiness.[3]

Gentlemen, I am about to deliver a critical speech, and at the outset I want to make it clear that I am neither attacking nor defending either political party as such. Neither am I attacking nor defending any individual or individuals of either political party. I am, however, attacking anyone who, in my opinion, is attempting to destroy the free competitive American industrial system which has made our country the greatest on earth. I offer this statement for clarification purposes only and it is not in any way to be construed as an apology for what I am about to say.

This visit to the Free State of Maryland is a pleasure which I have been promising myself for a long time. In fact, I had planned to be with you months ago, but unfortunately I hit a

---

[1] Text supplied by J. Carlisle MacDonald, assistant to the Chairman of the United States Steel Corporation, with permission for this reprinting.

[2] For biographical note, see Appendix.

[3] For details concerning the CIO Steel Strike of 1949 and President Fairless' leadership in negotiations, see Introduction to Philip Murray's "CIO Labor Policies," p179.

detour and wound up in a notorious suburb of yours, over near Bladensburg—a place called Washington, I believe.

I guess that's what always happens to people these days when they start heading for a free state. Some traffic cop shunts them off on a rough and bumpy road they did not want to travel, and they end up at an unhappy destination they never wanted to reach at all.

It is about detours that I want to talk to you today—and about Washington. I had expected, of course, to talk about the steel business, and some day I hope to get back to Pittsburgh long enough to find out what's happened to it. But during the past few months, I have been specializing in our National Capital, and our National Capital has certainly been specializing in me. Up to now, as you know, I've spent most of my time in O'Mahoney's doghouse; but next week I move to Emmanuel's cellar.

So it is a pleasant relief indeed to escape for a few hours and to enjoy your hospitality here in Baltimore.

I have already spent a most interesting morning. Mr. Charles E. McManus took me over to the Crown Cork and Seal Company to see the fine new cold reducing mill they have installed there. To me there is something really beautiful about machines like that. They have majesty, dignity and grace of motion; and I never cease to be fascinated by the miracles they perform.

The magician who first produced a live rabbit from a silk hat had a great deal of ingenuity and skill, and people of every age still marvel at the trick; but to me it is not nearly as mystifying or as breath taking as the process by which modern American industry produces even such seemingly simple things as bottle caps.

My visit to this plant today, however, was not merely a pleasure; it was definitely a matter of business as well—not that I am thinking of going into the bottle-closing business; and not that Crown is a customer of ours, either. They are not. They buy their steel from one of our rivals. I hate to say that, because I know what a shock it will be to some of our Washington critics who insist that there is no competition in the steel industry. Apparently they never heard of Bethlehem—or a couple of hundred other competitors of ours who are doing very nicely, thank you. You know, sometimes I wish these critics could join our sales force for a few weeks and try to sell a little steel. I think they would find out for themselves what competition really is.

When I say that my visit was a matter of business, I mean that I think it is part of my job—and the biggest part of my job, perhaps—to know how American industry produces and engineers the millions of intricate things that it turns out—to study the ingenious processes that it has devised and to see how it meets and solves the hundreds of operating problems that it has to face.

I do not believe that any man who has not seen these things for himself can hope to understand our American industrial machine. I do not see how he can hope to discuss our American enterprise system intelligently, factually, or even honestly.

If you happen to detect a note of feeling in my voice as I say that, it is because of my recent experiences in Washington. From the time it was organized fifty years ago, U. S. Steel has been subjected to almost constant investigation by various agencies of the government and for the past ten years and more, I myself have been on the business end of most of these investigations. Gentlemen, I have been through so many Congressional inquisitions that no self-respecting skeleton would hide in my closet on a bet.

So far this year, Senator O'Mahoney has already had me on the griddle once, and Congressman Celler starts dissecting me next week. After that, O'Mahoney wants me back again, it seems; and Representative Macy is proposing that I become the permanent victim of a continuing investigation. I shall never know why.

What with the T N E C [Temporary National Economic Committee] report, the voluminous records which we file regularly with various government agencies, the frequent Congressional inquiries we have faced, the proceedings before the Federal Trade Commission, and the evidence we have presented in numerous court actions, I don't suppose there is a single statistic about United States Steel which could possibly be of any real interest or significance to anyone, that is not already a matter of public record. And yet to this day, most of our inquisitors remain blissfully ignorant of the most important fact of all—how steel is made.

Among all the members of all the public bodies we have faced in the past dozen years, I don't suppose that more than two or three, at the outside, have even been inside a steel plant, or have ever seen for themselves what a gigantic opration steel making is. Yet until he *has* seen these things for himself, I do not believe that anyone has any right to tell anybody how big a steel company should be; for any views he may hold on the subject can hardly be regarded as the reasoned opinion of a qualified and competent authority.

During the hearings next week, I intend to invite Mr. Celler and the members of his committee to visit our steel plants. I hope most earnestly that they will accept that invitation; for, by doing so, I believe they could add richly to public knowledge and public understanding of this whole controversial issue of "bigness."

I am aware, however, that such action by them would constitute a radical departure from established Congressional practice as I have seen it. So far as I can discover from personal experience, Congressional investigations of businessmen follow a standardized pattern that has not been in vogue in America since the old days of the western frontier, when the established procedure was to shoot first and ask questions afterwards.

Nowadays, the Chairman sends you a letter "inviting" you to appear before his committee on a certain date. Then he starts issuing a barrage of statements to the newspapers telling the world what a dangerous and nefarious character you are. When you no longer have a friend left in the world, the hearing begins, and the chairman starts out by reading a statement in which he finds you guilty and pronounces sentence upon you. Then he announces that the committee will proceed to a full and "impartial" investigation of the facts, which seems to be a great waste of everybody's time, because when the evidence has been fully presented, the chairman ignores it completely, writes a report setting forth all of his preconceived notions, and quotes at length from his opening statement to prove he was right all the time.

Throughout the proceedings, of course, there is a great deal of talk about the "public interest," but I cannot help wondering what "public interest" a committee is serving when it conceals, distorts, and openly misstates the facts—the basic, all-important facts—which the American people must have if they are to plan their economic future intelligently and wisely.

Now, gentlemen, I am not an alarmist. I don't run around crying "wolf." I never see bogeys under the bed—and seldom see them on a golf course, these days. But I am gravely and sincerely disturbed by what I have seen in Washington.

In my opinion, our American economic system is in deadlier peril today than it has ever been in my lifetime. I say that knowing that it has always defended itself successfully against its enemies abroad; but I honestly do not know how it can be protected against its self-styled "friends" in Washington who would literally hack it to death on the pretext of saving its immortal soul. I am convinced that if these misguided planners and politically ambitious officeholders have their way, three of our most precious liberties—freedom of opportunity, freedom of initiative, and freedom of enterprise, will vanish from this earth.

I have always had great faith in the plain, cracker-barrel, common sense of the American people, and so long as they are permitted to know the facts, I have no fear that they will ever allow their economic system to be engulfed by foreign "isms" and ideologies.

I do not fear communism because every passing day proves its utter failure. The American people know that if communism were really working successfully there would be no need for police state oppression, phony trials and slave labor camps behind the iron curtain.

I do not fear fascism because it has killed the three great nations which adopted it. The American people want no part of any economic system that feeds only upon war and conquest.

I do not fear outright socialism because, in Europe today, socialism itself is living on the dole, and America is the only country on earth that is able to foot the bill for it. No American taxpayer is likely to fall for that kind of an economic system, at least until he has found some other nation that is rich enough and generous enough to indulge him in his folly.

But when somebody in Washington starts telling me how much he loves the free enterprise system and how he proposes to save it from itself, I shake in my very shoes. I wonder why it is that these self-appointed saviours of our national welfare always seem to miss the point—the one magnificent lesson that should be apparent to anyone who looks about him at the world today.

The point is, gentlemen, that our American system of free competitive enterprise is the only one left in the world that is NOT controlled by power-hungry politicians; and whether you call it the Square Deal, the Fair Deal, the New Deal or just plain federal regulation, the fact remains that once the dead hand of politics gets its convulsive grip on American business and industry, free competition will be strangled, and our economic system will be no different—and no more successful— than those noble experiments which are crumbling into dust in Europe.

Of one thing, I am convinced. The American people will never knowingly travel that foreign road to economic disaster. They have built the most magnificent industrial machine this world has ever seen and they are certainly not going to wreck it *that* way as long as the road itself is clearly marked by signposts which honestly reveal its destination.

But in Washington today there are theorists and bureaucrats and economists and Congressmen who are switching the signs. They are trying to take down all the honest guideposts and put up others reading: "Detour—to Utopia."

To my way of thinking, gentlemen, that is nothing less than economic murder; and it is hard for me to believe that all of these signpost-jugglers are so innocent and so credulous that they can sincerely suppose they are pointing the way to salvation.

We are all riding in the same machine, and we are all going to end up in the same place whether we like it or not. So I think it might be wise indeed to examine the signposts closely. Now it seems to me that the most dangerous deception which has been practiced upon us is the fallacy that our whole economy can be divided into two parts labelled "big" and "little" business. This deception has been used so long and has become so familiar to us that we have begun to accept it, unthinkingly, and without question. Because some statistician has arbitrarily drawn an entirely imaginary line between companies employing more or less than five hundred persons, we argue about big business and little business as though they were two hostile armies warring against each other. And so we fall into the trap that Washington has set for us, by creating class distinction in the industrial world.

How silly that concept is, if we stop to analyze it. There are four million individual business units in this country and they are all part and parcel of one great industrial machine. They are very much like the parts of that cold reducing mill I was watching this morning. Some of them were big and some of them were little. There were tiny electrical contacts and huge steel rolls that weighed several tons each. Some parts ran at high speed, while others ran slower; but all of them were intricately fitted together, and each had a particular job to do. So this mechanical giant went grinding along, rolling the hard, tough steel into strips, as smoothly and as easily as grandmother used to roll piecrust.

But of what use would that machine be to anybody if our Washington theorists once went to work on it? Our economists would cut it up into half a dozen pieces because it is so big. Our statisticians would sort out all the parts into neat piles according to size. Some members of Congress would pass a law decreeing that all the parts must be the same size, or that all must run at exactly the same speed. And in the end, there would be no machine at all. All the parts—the big parts and the little parts—would be junk.

So before the jugglers start taking our American industrial machine apart, there is one simple question I want to address to them. I just want to know *who* is going to put Humpty-Dumpty together again.

Of course, no one *ought* to understand all of this better than our government because never, probably, has the complete interdependence of so-called "big" and "little" business been as clearly demonstrated as it was during the recent war when this great industrial machine of ours shattered all records, and when every part and gear and piston in it was running at breakneck speed.

That was the first time our jugglers had ever had any real opportunity to put their theories to the test and to try to drive the wedge of class distinction into the machinery. They did their best.

They persuaded Congress to set up a special agency whose job it was to funnel war contracts into the hands of "small business." On many items, the Army and Navy agreed to pay small businessmen as much as 15 per cent more than they paid "big business" for the same work. And some government planners so far forgot themselves as to look with favor upon the idea of a *merger*. Heresy of heresies! They proposed to consolidate the efforts of all the small machine shops in an entire region in the hope of creating an industrial establishment big enough to handle large prime contracts.

So what happened?

You gentlemen know the answer as well as I do. When the shooting was over, we found that in spite of all the futile efforts of all the theorists in Washington, 75 per cent of the prime contracts had gone—of necessity—to the hundred largest manufacturing companies in the land.

The theorists were terribly unhappy about it, of course, and great were their lamentations. They could only see it one way, and without bothering even to consult the facts, they jumped despondently to the conclusion that the big had gotten richer and the small had gotten poorer.

They were wrong.

Over in the Department of Commerce and in the Federal Reserve Board, research experts went quietly to work with their calculating machines and came up with some amazing facts.

It was true, they found, that "big business" had been handed the lion's share of the war contracts; but it was *small business* that ended up by scoring the greatest increase in sales, in profits, and in assets. Small business had gained in size and it had gained in wealth at a vastly greater rate than the so-called industrial giants.

The explanation, of course, was all very simple. Big business had merely succeeded in doing what the government had failed to do. It had loaded up small business with contracts— just as it always does, in peace or in war.

It did the biggest jobs on its big machines in its own big plants; but it subcontracted the other jobs that could be done on smaller machines in smaller plants. It took a big company to deliver a finished B-29, but it took hundreds of companies of every conceivable size to make it—to make all the parts and materials that went into it. Which of these companies did the most important part of the job? . . . The big ones? . . . The little ones? Gentlemen, you might as well ask which soldier won the war.

So let us beware of the dangerous and deceptive signpost that would send big and little business down two separate and divergent roads. It is just as dishonest as the second of these fatal frauds that the jugglers would perpetrate upon us—the one they call "monopoly."

Now "monopoly" is a common, and highly unsavory word that all of us understand. Properly employed, it is a useful noun meaning the exact opposite of competition; but our jugglers do not use it as a noun—they use it as an epithet which they hurl freely and with great abandon at any large and successful enterprise on which they may hope to move in.

With impeccable logic, they declare that it is the inalienable right of any man to try to establish himself in any business he wants—even the steel business.

And that is undeniably true.

But then, with fallacious cunning, they insist that he can't go into the steel business because "the monopoly" won't let him.

And that is utterly, completely, absolutely and ridiculously false.

What is this "monopoly power" that big business is supposed to possess? What power does United States Steel have, for example, to prevent some intrepid small businessman from setting up shop in the steel business? How could we go about it? What could we do?

Those are questions which our Washington critics, I notice, conveniently ignore; and until somebody answers them for me, I frankly confess that I haven't the slightest idea how I can keep any would-be competitor out of the field. I know of no way to keep him from getting the raw materials he will need or from buying the furnaces, mills and plants he must have. And if he can beat us out on quality, price, or service, I know of no power whatever that can keep him from taking our customers away from us.

No, gentlemen, it isn't "monopoly power" that keeps any small businessman from making steel today. It is simply a little matter of money.

A blast furnace alone will cost him about $12 million, and when he gets his coke ovens, open hearths, his mills, his power and fuel lines and all his auxiliary equipment, he might start turning out hot-rolled bars for an investment of $50 million or so. If he wants to make light plates and cold-reduced sheets, his plant will cost him something over $200 million at today's prices.

And if any businessman has that kind of money, there is nothing "small" about him—not in my book, at least, for he would be one of the world's richest men, and his business would be one of the very largest manufacturing companies in the United States.

Even a large new corporation, with plenty of capital behind it, might hesitate prudently before venturing into the business of making steel—not because "monopoly" exists in the industry, but for exactly the opposite reason—because of the competition which prevails in it today.

In the face of this competition, any newcomer would be at a great disadvantage, because his plant and equipment will cost him from two to three times as much as his competitors had to pay for the same facilities ten years ago—before a quarter-trillion dollar national debt, and a governmental weakness for deficit spending, transformed the almighty dollar into the not-so-almighty sixty-cent piece.

But just because a small businessman may not be able to go into the business of *making* steel, that does not mean that he cannot go into the steel business. Not at all. He can set himself up in the business of *fabricating* steel whenever and wherever he wishes, and for a relatively small capital investment, he can turn out any one or more among thousands of useful, salable, profitable products.

Sometimes I think our Washington theorists ought to turn back to their own governmental records and find out what has really been happening in the steel industry during the past generation. Thirty-three years ago, it is true, there were nearly twice as many establishments *making* steel as there are now, but their product was so crude by comparison with today's steels, that the opportunities for *fabricating* it were limited. Today fewer companies make the steel, but 12,000 more establishments are able to fabricate it. For every steel-making company that has disappeared, sixty new metal-fabricating plants have been successfully established. And for every wage earner who had a job in the industry thirty-three years ago, three are employed today.

Now, is that bad? Is that "monopoly"?

Well, let's look at another trick word the jugglers have been palming off on us—"giantism." It's a beauty. It's effective. Nobody loves a giant, and why should they? From the earliest days of our childhood we have thought of giants as monstrous, wicked, bloodthirsty creatures. So, naturally, a giant corporation must be evil. It's all very simple; but what are the facts? How many big companies are there?

According to the government's latest count there are nearly 7,500 of them in America today. A century ago there were none. But wait a minute! For every single company that has grown big in this country during the past hundred years, 440 healthy new enterprises have been born. And, gentlemen, that didn't just *happen*. The truth is that had it not been for the fact that there *are* giants, most of these small establishments could never have existed at all, and could not, today, survive.

No, there is nothing sinful about size, and there should be nothing unlawful about it either.

The *size* of any company depends, in the first instance, upon the product which it intends to manufacture—upon the amount of money it is going to take to buy the plants, machines and tools that will be necessary to produce that product efficiently and competitively. From that point on, the *growth* of the company depends on its customers. If they like the product and want to buy more of it, the company will have to expand in order to meet their demands. If they don't like the product there is no way on earth that the company can force them to buy, no matter how big and how powerful it may be.

That is why today's giant must be useful, helpful, and necessary or he simply goes out of business because he failed to serve his customers to their satisfaction, and therefore failed to serve the public interest.

So when our Washington theorists attempt to place an arbitrary limit on size, they are saying, in effect, that certain products shall not be manufactured at all—except, perhaps, by the government. And when they try to put a limit on growth, they are denying to the American people the right to buy as much as they want of a particular company's product.

For my part, I don't believe that the American people will ever stand for that kind of a restricted, second-class economy.

Finally, there is one more treacherous signpost which we see everywhere these days and which menaces all of us far more seriously than many of us may suppose. The jugglers call it "concentration." It is based on the fallacy that there is something evil and dangerous about the fact that four, or eight, or sixteen, or fifty companies, do 40 or 60 or 80 per cent of the business in their particular industry.

Well, of course they do—and they always will as long as free and honest competition exists in our American economy. In industry or in the field of sports, concentration is the *result* of competition. If the top teams in any baseball league don't win the highest percentage of the games, how are they going to stay on top? And when the top companies in any industry win the highest percentage of the customers, they naturally are going to have the highest percentage of the business.

Any time you see any league or any industry where everybody has come out even, you can be reasonably sure that somehow and somewhere the boys got together in the back room, plugged up the keyhole, and indulged in a little high-handed conspiracy, otherwise known as the "fix." How else could it happen?

That's why there always is and always must be a certain amount of this so-called "concentration" in every American industry; but our inquisitors in Washington insist that "concentration" is especially marked in the steel industry. And gentlemen, I want to take that one apart right here and now, because I think the facts will amaze you.

In the first place, let me say that the steel industry has no special characteristics that could conceivably justify its classification as a public utility, or that could possibly warrant this feverish desire on the part of our Washington bureaucrats to subject it to federal regulation.

Now of *course* steel is vitally necessary to our people and our national economy. So are oil and coal and automobiles, and rubber and lumber and glass, and refrigerators and cookstoves and radios. But certainly steel is no more necessary than clothing, and it is even less necessary than food. If the Washington jugglers are going to regulate every product that is necessary to our national economy, *then, gentlemen, they are going to regulate every single business in America.* Including yours!

And if they are going to break up every industry which is as highly "concentrated" as the steel industry, *nearly half of the units in our American industrial machine will be torn apart.*

Yes. That is the exact, indisputable fact.

The United States Census Bureau has recently completed its latest count of more than four hundred American industries, and has reported on the degree of so-called "concentration" in each. And remember, I am speaking of entire *industries*—not individual companies.

Now how many of these industries do you think are more highly "concentrated" than the steel industry? Three? . . . Ten? . . . Fifty?

Well, guess again. The Census Bureau's own report on "steel works and rolling mills" shows that this industry is not anywhere near the top at all. It is in the great middle, along with the great body of all American industries. In fact, it stands 174th on the list. *So there are 173 entire industries which are more highly concentrated than steel.*

Now what are some of these industries where the "concentration of power" in the hands of the "big four" is so great as to menace our national welfare and to arrest the pursuit of happiness?

You'd never guess.

There is the pretzel industry for one. Honestly, that's right. I mean it.

And there are the candle-makers too.

Then there are straw hats, and streetcars, breakfast foods and chewing tobacco, wallpaper and cigar boxes, lead pencils and pianos. Then we have women's neckwear and boys' underwear. And, oh yes—window shades and garters.

Now if every one of these—plus 159 other industries—is more highly "concentrated" than steel, and if "concentration" is really as wicked as our theorists tell us it is, I can't for the life of me, understand why all these high-priced Congressional committees are wasting their time on me.

Seriously, gentlemen, make no mistake about it. U. S. Steel has been singled out as the target for this present attack on "bigness"—but only temporarily, and if our Washington jugglers now succeed in placing U. S. Steel on trial before the court of public opinion, then they also will have managed to put every successful, growing business in America on trial beside it.

So I wonder if it isn't time to have an entirely new Congressional investigation—one that will hale before it all the other government agencies and Congressional investigating committees which seem to be trying so desperately to destroy the finest and the only successful economic system that exists in the world to-day.

I wonder if it isn't time someone took these gentlemen aside and found out just what public interest *they* are serving—and why?

In short, I wonder if it isn't time to get back on our high-speed highway to progress and growth and production, before we get mired and lost forever on a detour to Utopia!

CIO LABOR POLICIES [4]

PHILIP MURRAY [5]

President Philip Murray, of the Congress of Industrial Organizations, gave this address at the opening of the eleventh annual convention of that organization, in the Public Hall, Cleveland, Ohio, on Monday, October 31, 1949.

Two major issues confronted the convention: (1) Should the strike against United States Steel, then in progress, be prosecuted by labor until its demands should be accepted in full? (2) Should left wing "Communist dominated" unions be expelled from the CIO?

President Murray's address reviewed the strike situation. On June 15 the steel industry flatly rejected the proposal for negotiating with the union the questions of wages, non-contributory pension plans, and the development of related social insurance programs. On July 7th negotiations broke off. President Truman intervened on July 13 and appointed a fact-finding body to report and recommend. On September 10 the Board gave its findings and recommendations. On the 13th the steelworkers accepted, but the next day the steel industry rejected the proposals. The strike started on October 1.

Benjamin F. Fairless of United States Steel was spokesman for the steel industry, comprising some sixty major concerns. The United Steelworkers had a membership of almost a million.

The issues were: (1) Should the steel industry accept a plan costing six cents per hour per worker for pensions and four cents per hour per worker for other social security? (2) Should the management pay all the costs of such pension and social security program?

On the day of Murray's speech, Bethlehem Steel agreed to a "noncontributing" pension plan providing for at least $100 per month for workers retiring at the age of sixty-five after twenty-five years of service. The pension would include old-age benefits payable under the Federal Social Security System. A contributing social insurance plan was also agreed to that would provide for life insurance and other benefits, the company and worker each to pay 2½ cents per hour for such program. On November 13, the United States Steel agreed to similar terms, and the strike was thus ended as a Philip Murray victory.

An aftermath was that "Big Steel" boosted prices of steel on the average of $4 a ton. Labor vigorously denounced the price increases and

[4] *Daily Proceedings of the Eleventh Constitutional Convention of the Congress of Industrial Organizations*, Monday, October 31, 1949, Cleveland, Ohio. Permission for this reprinting given through the courtesy of President Murray.

[5] For biographical note, see Appendix.

pointed to U. S. Steel profits for nine months of 1949 as $133,233,409 larger than for any previous comparable period. As Murray in his speech put it: "This giant industry . . . will be able to report . . . profits of approximately one billion dollars, the highest in the entire history of that great industry."

The second great issue raised by President Murray concerned left-wing unions. On November 8, 1935, eight unions of the AFL joined together to promote industrial unionism and established the CIO. Its membership rose from 900,000 to some 6,000,000.

During President Murray's speech most of the 620 delegates vigorously applauded his denunciations of the "Commies" and his recommendations for their expulsion. The left-wing delegates "sat on their hands." Whereas the CIO pressed for the "Fair Deal," the Marshall Plan, the North Atlantic Pact, and similar measures, the left wing (after 1945) allegedly followed the "Moscow-Stalin" line of obstructing these moves.

The Convention voted (1) to bar from membership on the CIO Executive Board all Communists, (2) to expel the United Electrical and the Farm Equipment Workers and to set up a new International Union of Electrical Workers (IUE), and (3) grant to the Executive Board power to expel other left-wing unions.

As speaker, Mr. Murray has accomplished much in round table negotiations. He has believed that most problems can be settled in such conferences, where his considerable storehouse of facts concerning industry and economics can be brought into play. On the platform he speaks quietly, earnestly, with occasional humor. He has excellent voice control. He is little given to overwhelming oratory. He is at his best in open forums and in extempore give-and-take.[6]

I desire to take advantage of this opportunity to express to the Mayor of the City of Cleveland, Archbishop Hoban and others, the sincere appreciation of the delegates participating in this convention, to the City of Cleveland and all of its citizens for their very splendid manifestations of hospitality to the officers and delegates attending this, the Eleventh Constitutional Convention of the CIO.

I should like also to take advantage of this occasion to express to our organizations affiliated with the Congress of Industrial Organizations, the appreciation of the President of this Union for the manner in which most of them have cooperated with me in the promotion of our organization's affairs during the past year. Your Union, the CIO, has taken a leading part

_____
[6] For further comment on Murray as a speaker, see *Representative American Speeches: 1946-47*, p 177-89.

in the conduct of fights, if I may refer to them in such language, in the halls of Congress for the enactment of progressive legislation designed to promote and to protect the wellbeing of not only the members of our own Union but also of our entire citizenry. This mighty organization has won for itself the respect and admiration of all right-thinking people throughout our great land for the courageous, intelligent and constructive manner in which it has fought for the protection of our people and the welfare of our country.

Beginning with the Ninth Constitutional Convention of the Congress of Industrial Organizations in the City of Boston, your organization gave its unanimous approval to the adoption of the European Recovery Program. We loaned our influences in securing through Congress the enactment of this most important piece of legislation. Your organization, through its Executive Board, has given approval to the adoption of the North Atlantic Pact as a necessary adjunct to the furtherance of the work of the European Recovery Program.

In conformity with the expressed desire of the Tenth Constitutional Convention of the CIO your International Executive Board, meeting in the City of Washington last May, adopted a resolution authorizing the accredited officers of this organization to disaffiliate membership in the World Federation of Trade Unions.

We expect to have this convention give approval to the action of your Executive Board upon these all-important matters. Together with our great departed leader, Sidney Hillman, I assumed a substantial measure of responsibility for the formation of the original World Federation of Trade Unions. In so doing I, together with other members of the CIO Executive Board, expressed the hope at that time that the World Federation of Trade Unions would promote the wellbeing of the peoples of the universe, would promote peace, and would promote the healthy development of true democratic trade union movements throughout the world.

Contrary to our expectations the World Federation of Trade Unions was used by certain elements within its structure, to propagandize the world for the purpose of spreading diabolical, subversive communism. Because of our experience as representatives of the CIO within the World Federation of Trade Unions, as well as those of other unions in democratic countries, it became necessary to sever our relationship with the World Federation of Trade Unions this year. In pursuit of our desire to secure the formation of a truly democratic world trade union movement we have joined with the British Trades Union Congress, the American Federation of Labor, and other democratic trade unions in an effort to form a new world labor movement. We hope by the end of the present month, as a result of conferences which are scheduled to begin in London on or about November 26th, to frame a constitution and to create all of the necessary mechanisms incident to the formation of a new democratic world trade union movement.

Since your convention last met in the City of Portland the workers of the United States of America have experienced what I have commonly referred to as a man-made recession in employment. I have consistently contended, since the beginning of the present recession during the spring of the present year, that the unemployment situation in the United States grew out of a desire on the part of leading industrialists to force upon our country widespread unemployment. There was no necessity for the prevalence of unemployment in the United States of America. The extreme and extraordinary demand for American products, not only here in the United States but all over the world, made it quite obvious to all of those of us who had an understanding of our situation here at home that our country should continue to enjoy prosperity—and, if I may add, prosperity of an unprecedented nature. It has been the goal, therefore, of the Congress of Industrial Organizations to correct the evils growing out of this man-made recession by deliberately charging that the responsibility for the creation of unemployment in our country lay directly at the door of the leading manufacturers and industrialists and bankers in this country.

Marvelous changes have taken place in our economic system in the course of the past four or five years—the introduction of new technological devices designed to increase productivity, per capita productivity, lower costs of manufacture and production are evident in almost every line of endeavor. It is particularly notable in a few of the major industries. Witness the giant steel industry, during the year 1948, establishing a record of unprecedented profits, which, in the course of the year 1949, will undoubtedly be surpassed. These tremendous profits are attributable to two factors: one, the great technological improvements that have taken place in the steel industry; and two, the extortion practiced by the employers in the steel industry in charging American consumers extremely and extraordinarily high prices for goods.

It is anticipated that for the present year, although we have had a strike in the basic steel industry for a period of approximately one month, that this giant industry, if it gets back to work quickly, will be able to report to its stockholders and the American people profits of approximately one billion dollars, the highest in the entire history of that great industry. . . .

The presidential fact-finding board, in its recommendations, recommended to the industry and to the Union that the first charge against revenues of the industry should be the investment of moneys for the wear and tear on the human machine, the human being. The Board said so, the President said so, the Union said so, and I believe the American people say so.

I addressed a great meeting in the City of Homestead just about two weeks ago. Homestead is a great steel center, and there were some 25,000 or 30,000 steelworkers there. At that meeting I endeavored to express in graphic form the real, true meaning of this issue. There was an old man there 67 years of age. Forty-four out of those 67 years had been spent in the service of the United States Steel Corporation. He stood beside me, broken down, no money, in a state of complete poverty. He could not pay his rent, he could not buy his medicine, could not provide himself with clothing or purchase his food—44 years of loyal service to that Corporation. I asked him to tell that great crowd of steelworkers what kind of a pension the Steel Corporation was paying him, after 44 years of service, and he said, "The Steel Corporation, Mr. Murray, is paying me 29 cents a month." Twenty-nine cents a month! His frame broken, in a state of complete destitution—and 29 cents expended on that man, that human being who bears the dignity of a man and the dignity of God! Twenty-nine cents, and right across the hill, in a great modern plant, where the machinery is carefully nursed and protected, the same industry had expended in the year 1948 $146,000,000 to maintain the health and the efficiency of its machine —the inanimate machine, a piece of metal.

That is an issue of major consequence. The industry at the moment is resisting the recommendations of the presidential fact-finding board that has said to the industry: "It is your bounden, God-given responsibility to arise now to your social consciousness, to a position where you might meet the needs of a human being"—like the man I have just referred to.

The Steelworkers are fighting to support the recommendations of the Board, and let me say this to you, this is the first time in the history of our government that any governmental agency or board has recommended to industry the institution of non-contributory pension plans. This is the first time, and we are fighting for it, and we are going to fight for it until we get it.

Wall Street is fighting our Union—we know that. The steel industry is fighting our Union. The President of the American Federation of Labor, in the course of the American Federation of Labor Convention over in the city of St. Paul a few weeks ago, took occasion to castigate me personally because we accepted the recommendations of the presidential fact-finding board. Old Bill! Need I say anything more there? He joined the procession of Wall Streeters and barons of the steel industry.

When the presidential board's recommendations were made to the Steel Union, Wall Street not only attacked us, the steel industry not only attacked us and forced us into a strike, but the Communist Party attacked us as well. I observed when the original attack was made upon us by the Communist Party and by Wall Street that perhaps that is where they both belonged, they ought to get together and sleep in the same bed. They both have the same objectives in mind—totalitarian dictatorship in some form or other; American business on the one hand, communism on the other and decent American labor caught between them fighting, fighting, fighting every day of their lives to improve the lot of people whom they are privileged to represent.

That is the type of strike we have been engaged in. Why, just after the steelworkers had accepted the Presidential Fact-Finding Committee's report, to show you the far-reaching repercussions of the union's decisions in matters of this description, there were transmitted over the shortwave radio system from the City of Moscow three radio addresses. Each of them charged me with being a Wall Streeter, claiming that I was not a fighter, I did not defend my people, criticized the policies of our union —all the way out of Moscow, a distant and remote land. And the same radio addresses transmitted overseas were proclaiming to the universe the militancy of some of our left-wing unions, naming them.

We have had a combination of interests to contend with in the conduct of this strike. But with this combination of interests at work, as they have been until very recently, to undermine the Steelworkers in their strike, like they did the Mine Workers in 1928, these interests, big interests, big money interests, and the Communist Party joined hands in 1928 to destroy the United Mine Workers of America, and they attempted just recently to carry out the same program in 1948. What do they care about trade unionism? Their interests are the interests of the Soviet Government. If that means the disruption of the democratic trade union movement in the United States, the Communist Party will say to you tomorrow, "To hell with trade unionism, I am going to support the Soviets." No devotion to their union.

At meetings of my own Executive Board and the CIO Executive Board, in recent months I have taken occasion to say that I didn't know whether I could talk freely to the members of my own Board or not, I didn't know whether I was talking to a Fink, a Commie, or an FBI man. Now I can't tell you, if I had to take an oath before God Almighty on this platform this morning, whether the fellow I meet who proclaims to be a Communist or serves the Communist Party's interests is an agent of the FBI or the agent of a corporation.

They have said that if we in the CIO are going to cleanse this movement—which, by the way, we are going to do in this convention—it has been surreptitiously scattered around, at least the reports indicate that they might go underground. I don't know where that hole in the ground is they are talking about going to, but I am going to make quite sure that hole in the ground is not under the CIO.

This is a fundamental question that touches the lives of not only the members of the labor movement in the United States of America, but its effects are felt in the home of almost every citizen. No subtlety that might be engaged in by representatives of these organizations to the effect that they are not serving the interests of the Communist Party in this convention will be sufficient to meet the requirements of this delegation.

I became the President of this organization in November 1940. I was ushered into this office against my will. Throughout the early part of 1941 I was treated with a great deal of reserve by certain of the leaders of some of the organizations affiliated with CIO. There was a question mark as to whether or not the new President of the CIO was reliable. The 7th day of December 1941, Japan attacked our country, resulting in a Congressional declaration of war against Japan, which eventually brought our country into this great big international holocaust, World War II, and from December 1941 on to August of 1945, when Japan capitulated or surrendered, almost everything within the family of CIO unions was serene. Some of the extremists who purported to represent the Communist-type of thinking during those days went to the greatest extremes, even to the point of almost abjectly surrendering their trade union principles. For a period of four years I had a great amount of cooperation while there was a war on. The nation needed its production, it had to win a war, it was fighting a war against Hitler and all that Hitler stood for.

And then along came the capitulation of Japan and the ending of the war, and before the end of 1945 the line had changed —the line had changed, there was no longer any unanimity in the Board on matters of policy.

In 1946 we endeavored to correct some of the misgivings in the organization by writing up some new rules for the regulation of our councils, eliminating so far as humanly possible the evil propaganda of the Communist Party in our state and city councils.

In 1947 we reviewed the Communist situation within the CIO, and there was a Convention declaration to the effect that we were definitely and unalterably opposed by communism or any other kind of totalitarianism, including fascism. And the convention adopted that. But that was not sufficient to meet the requirements of our situation.

During the Portland convention in 1948, we again reexamined our situation, and at that time the convention carefully reviewed the situation and gave greater emphasis in its pronunciamentos to the effect that this organization of ours could no longer tolerate the infiltration and propaganda of the Communist Party into the trade union movement of America.

In May of the present year the CIO Executive Board met in the city of Washington. In pursuance to instructions given it by the last National Convention of the CIO, it adopted another resolution, and that resolution proclaimed to our membership the fact that no one who adhered to the communistic philosophy and propagated communism to the detriment of our trade union movement in this country could hope to serve in office or be a member of our International Executive Board. The May declaration of the CIO Executive Board was fought bitterly by certain elements within the Board. This servile process of serving the interests of the Communist Party continued following the May declaration of the CIO Executive Board.

We come around now to another convention, the 11th Constitutional Convention of the Congress of Industrial Organizations. As the President of your organization I have exhausted every measure of tolerance and patience in an effort to compose the difference between those groups who serve our organization as members of the CIO Executive Board. I find it impossible for the President of your organization to resolve the issues. I am, so far as I am concerned, just as far apart from the philosophy of those who advocate support of the communistic cause as the two poles might be, just as far apart. There is no way, no decent way by which we can hope to resolve these issues in the International Executive Board. It cannot be done. The issues have their roots, and those roots are deep, and they are fundamental, and there will therefore be recommended to this convention certain definite, constructive, constitutional changes designed to put an end to these practices within the Congress of Industrial Organizations.

It is my hope that this convention will respond to the recommendations of your committees when they are placed before you on this all-important subject.

I have covered a number of the more important aspects of problems which in due course will be presented to the convention and acted upon by you.

I do express the hope—I always do—that we will have a good convention, a constructive convention, a convention designed to serve the best interests of the millions we represent.

We have thrust upon our shoulders great and very grave responsibilities, obligations that not only run to the membership of our own unions, but grave obligations and responsibilities which run to our people and to our country. This convention has a prime interest in protecting the welfare and the well-being of our people and our nation. We seek the preservation of the CIO as a forward-looking, militant, constructive, democratic trade union movement. We will lend our services in that direction to not only the members of our own organization here at home, but to the new world labor movement which will undoubtedly be created before the end of the present year.

I wish at this juncture, therefore, to express to you my appreciation for the patience which you have exercised while I have taken the liberty to express my point of view to you on some of the more important issues to come before this convention. I thank you.

UNITED AUTOMOBILE WORKERS: AIMS AND PROGRAM [7]

WALTER P. REUTHER [8]

President Walter Reuther of the United Automobile Workers, Congress of Industrial Organizations, gave this address at the opening of the Twelfth Constitutional Convention, at Milwaukee, Wisconsin, on July 10, 1949.

The speech aimed to stir the delegates to unwavering support of the coming showdown concerning wages and pensions with the Ford, Chrysler, and other automobile companies.

The address enunciated vigorously the labor philosophy of Reuther. To him and his million-member union, government legislative programs and policies favored big business; industry's profits, although necessary for the continued prosperity of labor, were unduly swollen. A disproportionate share of these earnings and profits was going to stockholders and management, or reserved for future dividends. To labor, demanding a larger percentage of these profits, it was clear that wage increases and pension provisions could be effected without increasing prices. General prosperity, to Reuther and his UAW, depended on full employment at relatively high wages and in a market with sufficiently low prices to ensure general purchasing power and thus wide distribution of goods and services. Reuther had been a Socialist, an organizer of automobile workers, and a powerful spokesman in negotiations with management since 1935.[9]

President Reuther, in this speech, closely articulates with the needs, attitudes, and stereotypes of his audience. He uses freely personal references, specific examples of his points, detailed evidence, occasional colorful and idiomatic language (e.g., "twilight period," "hifalutin' "), sarcasm and invective ("They are sitting there in Wall Street on their fat money bags. . . . The people in Wall Street who are doing these things that drive us down the road to depression are Joe Stalin's real fifth-column agents in America").

Reuther is a vigorous debater, intelligent in his analysis of a problem, in marshalling of facts and in quick reply. Many conservatives who fear labor domination look to Walter Reuther and to his brother Victor as stabilizing agents.

[7] Text supplied by the public relations department of the United Automobile Workers, CIO, Frank Winn, director, and by permission of President Walter Reuther.

[8] For biographical note, see Appendix.

[9] For introductory comment on Reuther and for examples of his speeches, see *Representative American Speeches: 1945-1946*, p165-79; *1947-1948*, p103-17.

In November 1949, UAW negotiations with the Ford Company resulted in an agreement generally regarded as a victory for labor. That company was to contribute 8¾ cents an hour per worker to provide a pension at the age of 65 of $100 per month, including Social Security benefits. The company was to continue a contribution of 1¼ cents per hour for social welfare. Thus the plan and settlement gave the UAW a strong lever in its effort to exact similar terms from other automobile companies during 1950.

Mr. Chairman, distinguished guests, delegates to the twelfth Constitutional Convention, fellow workers and friends:

I want first to thank Mayor Ziedler, in behalf of this convention for his words of welcome. Milwaukee truly is a progressive community, but Mayor Zeidler is a modest citizen, he did not advise you of the most important function that he has performed with respect to this convention.

When he learned that 2,400 thirsty Automobile, Aircraft and Agricultural Implement Workers were going to convene in the hot days of July he called an emergency conference over at the City Hall, and who do you think he invited? Mr. Pabst, Mr. Blatz, and Mr. Schlitz, and he said, "You don't know these guys in the UAW; they have capacities that are unlimited." And Mr. Schlitz, Mr. Blatz and Mr. Pabst put on a third shift in every plant in Milwaukee, and we thank the good Mayor for that special service, because we will need it before the convention is over. I speak as a guy who knows.

Twelve years ago we met in this same auditorium. We were a young organization. We had just come out of the sit-down strikes. Since that day twelve years ago the UAW-CIO has been in the vanguard of the struggle of American labor to move forward in the building of that kind of world in which the people, whose sweat and skill and labor create the wealth, can realize their full equity of the fruits of their labor.

In those twelve years we can be proud of the fact that we wrote some glorious and militant chapters in labor's struggle.

We meet today in a difficult period, a period of great decision, a period when, throughout the world, there is fear and anxiety in the hearts and minds of men, because they are uncertain and afraid of what tomorrow will bring.

This is a kind of twilight period in the world. We have neither war nor peace. We have neither prosperity nor depression. But we can't stay balanced in that middle position; we are either going forward to peace and freedom and abundance, or we are going to slide back to depression and war and disaster. And what this convention does during this week—how effectively we mobolize our power to implement the current contract negotiations, how effectively the steelworkers fight on their front, and the coal diggers on their front, and how effectively labor fights in every aspect of the economic struggle—will be decisive in determining whether we go forward or backward.

As the banner says, we can drift to depression and war and disaster. But we have to plan and work and fight for peace and security and freedom and abundance.

They tell the story that when the Marines were storming the beachheads in the South Pacific one group of Marines, after they had made themselves secure on the beachhead, put up a sign that read: "Golden Gate in '48; Breadline in '49."

The atomic bomb changed the calendar date of the first item, but the atomic bomb will not solve the problem of growing breadlines in 1949. That will be solved only if you and I and millions of other Americans who believe that we fought a war in order to have an opportunity for free men to work out their economic and political destinies, will mobilize the productive power for building the peace as we did for war and destruction. If we fail we lose all. We will shatter the common hopes and aspirations of people everywhere.

This convention has got to speak out in clear and unmistakable language. We have got to ask the same question which those Marines asked, the same question that five million unemployed Americans are asking, the same question that hungry people all over the world are asking. That is this question: if they could give us a gun to fight in war, if they could give us a job producing for destruction, producing to kill life in achieving the negative ends of war, why can't they give us employment and a job making the good things in life for people in peacetime?

You can dress up the problems of the world, you can put them into hifalutin' sounding language in the United Nations, or you can write them in noble resolutions, but fundamentally the struggle in the whole world is for men to find the answer to the age-old problem, how do you solve the basic economic problems and get economic security for the great mass of people without at the same time robbing them of their basic political freedoms? That is the problem we have to find an answer to, and people all over the world are looking to America for the answer, because we have everything it takes to find the answer. The American economy, our human and material resources, our technical know-how, our tremendous productive capacity—these are freedom's greatest asset. But they will not find the answer unless we help them intelligently in finding that answer. And unless we can find the answer in America it cannot be found any place in the world. We say to the world, we are going to find that answer, and that is part of the job of this convention.

We know that the answer will not be found in the magic formulas of totalitarianism, Fascist or Communist. They offer a promise of economic security at the price of freedom and spiritual enslavement. Nor will the answer of America—and we have got to make this clear—nor will the answer be found in the kind of reckless socially irresponsible Wall Street economics of "boom and bust," which offer you freedom at the price of security.

We take the position in America that we want both bread and freedom, and it is possible to have both bread and freedom living in democracy's house side by side. You don't have to trade one for the other; we can have both. . . .

We have lost $23 billion in the first half of 1949. If we had full employment we could be making about $273 billion in production in goods, but we are only getting $250 billion, so we are losing $23 billion worth. That is enough to pay for all these things we are asking for. But the boys down in Washington who are beating the economic drums just don't understand these elementary things, or they don't want to.

The world is going to judge America, and we in America must judge ourselves, not by our technical progress, not by our ability to split the atom or make a jet ship go seven hundred miles an hour. We have got to judge ourselves as the world would judge us, by our ability to translate technical progress into human progress, human security, human dignity and human happiness.

It is of little consolation if you happen to be among the five million unemployed in America, to sit down in your kitchen with a bare table and tell your kids, Mary and Johnny and Susie, "Don't feel too badly about the fact daddy is unemployed and we can't get you all the things you want and need to eat. Remember America is a great country, we know how to split the atom, and down in Oak Ridge at the Atomic Energy plant, they are building a bigger and bigger stockpile of atomic bombs every day." I say that will not feed the hungry stomachs of the kids in America. Human needs have to be taken care of. That is what we are fighting for when we talk about these things in this convention. I say the hour is getting late, and if we let things slip we can lose everything, and labor has the opportunity to take the lead in America and demonstrate that leadership, that vision and courage and that imagination necessary to formulate democratic solutions to our complicated economic and political problems and translate those solutions into programs of action.

That is the challenge before us. We have all the tools in America to conquer human insecurity. We have the material resources and everything. It is a question of whether the people are going to use them or whether we are going to be blocked by the powers that be in Wall Street. You hear a lot of talk about planning in America, and the Wall Street boys would have you believe they don't plan. Well, they plan, but it's the wrong kind of planning. The conflict in America is between two kinds of planning. It is privately planned economic scarcity by companies for profits or publicly planned economic abundance for people. That is really the struggle. I say the challenge can be met. We have to build a broad coalition of labor and farmers in America and weld a joint political and economic program. With a program that makes sense, these forces, welded together in America, can be the architects of tomorrow. It is a big job, but we in the UAW-CIO come into this convention better equipped than ever before to discharge our broad responsibilities. During the past several months we have had more than a million dues-paying members. Since the last convention we have organized

366 new shops, with more than 200,000 new members, the biggest peacetime increase in our membership in the history of our union. Financially we are stronger, but we are not strong enough, and this convention must address itself to that problem.

Internally we are in the healthiest condition we have ever been. By and large we have broken up the destructive power of factional political blocs. We have tried to weld together the forces in this union around a militant, democratic program, around the slogan that we raised at last convention, "Teamwork in the Leadership and Solidarity in the Ranks." We still have a little more progress to make on that, but we have gone a long way in welding together the forces of this union—not on a personal or political basis, but on the basis of a sound, democratic, militant trade union program.

We have got to go out and complete the organization of the unorganized in every segment of our jurisdiction. We have got to work to build, first a practical working unity among American labor unions, and some day to have organic unity, one powerful union in America representing all the workers, and when we do that we will be in a position to do something that has to be done. We have got to take steps to see to it that we get a national labor daily newspaper with regional supplements in every community in America. We have got to have these things.

Since the last convention we have taken a step forward in our radio program. Some months ago we dedicated WDET, the first UAW-CIO radio station in Detroit. Two weeks ago we dedicated the second UAW-CIO radio station, WCUO in Cleveland. We ought to urge at this convention that every labor union that can get the money, every farm group, every co-op group that can get the money, do so and build a radio station, so that we can tie together a national labor-farm-co-op hookup covering the whole country. We have got to get the tools to fight this battle with, because we are up against powerful opposition. We have to work with the farm groups, we have to support their basic program to get security in our economy, and we have got to build the co-ops.

There are many other problems that I will not discuss now, but which we will discuss in detail at the various committees on them. I only want to say that this convention can be an important milestone in the forward march of our great union. Let us work together, plan together and act together in this convention in the spirit and in the tradition of our great union. And I say, working together, planning together, acting together for the great, broad sections of America with the people of goodwill in America, with the help of God we can go forward and build that better world where men can be free and secure, where they can live in dignity and brotherhood and peace with the rest of the world.

I thank you.

A LONG RANGE FARM PROGRAM [10]

ALLAN BLAIR KLINE [11]

Mr. Allan Kline, President of the American Farm Bureau Federation, and Charles F. Brannan, Secretary of the United States Department of Agriculture, debated before the National Farm Institute, Des Moines, Iowa, in the KRNT Theater, on February 18, 1950. The four thousand members of the audience often cheered or booed.

The Institute was sponsored by the Agricultural Department of the Des Moines Chamber of Commerce in cooperation with the Iowa Farm Press and farm organizations. J. S. Russell, farm editor of the Des Moines *Register and Tribune*, presided over the debate. The purpose of the Institute was "to promote free discussion and objective study of farm questions as related to national and world economy."

Mr. Kline gave the opening address, and Mr. Brannan followed. The debate took almost two hours. Professor T. W. Schultz, of the University of Chicago, afterward conducted a turbulent panel.

The issue of the debate was: "Shall the Brannan plan be adopted?" Secretary Brannan proposed his plan early in 1949 as a method of dealing with farm surpluses. The government would support farm income at "relatively high levels" by crop purchases, loans, and direct payments to farmers. Farm prices would be allowed to reach their own levels in the open market, to the advantage of the consumer. The government would pay the farm producer the difference between this open market price and the "support" level. The government would determine the acreage to be permitted to each farmer for a given crop.

The Farm Bureau, representing some 1,400,000 farmers, at their 31st annual convention in Chicago on December 12, 1949, denounced the plan as "regimentation" and "nationalization of agriculture."

The Des Moines debate developed into a personal and bitter clash. Kline as speaker is forceful and even eloquent. He had public speaking courses at Morningside College, Iowa, but most of his experience, as he states, "has been with actual public speaking. My objective has been rather uniformly to create understanding of problems, and also to create both desire and intention to act on issues which listeners might confront." [12]

Mr. Brannan was vocally less relaxed, tended to elevate unduly his pitch and tighten his voice. He gesticulated frequently and often at ran-

---

[10] *Proceedings of the Twelfth National Farm Institute, 1950.* Text supplied by the Des Moines, Iowa, Chamber of Commerce, and permission to reprint given through the courtesy of Allan Kline.

[11] For biographical note, see Appendix.

[12] Letter to this editor, March 11, 1950.

dom. He resorted to personalities and sarcasm more than did his opponent.

Professor Schultz criticized both speakers for by-passing important issues. According to him, both arguers completely ignored the discussion of basic commodities—tobacco, cotton, peanuts and wheat. Both proposed to retain acreage allotments, marketing quotas, and marketing controls. "Neither is prepared to abandon them in good times. Why not?" "Neither debated the problem of poverty in agriculture." "More than a million farm families have been by-passed by the economic programs." [13]

The Brannan plan, supported by President Truman, continued to be a major domestic issue in the political speaking of 1950.

It is under rather peculiar auspices that I am here today. I have been on the National Farm Institute program for many years, and have assisted in a good many ways. But I have been reading in the papers and hearing on the radio that this session is a sort of contest—a peculiar sort of contest. That makes it a little difficult for me, and I want to take a few minutes to explain why.

For one thing, you have also on the program a fellow who is a recognized political exponent. He is a member of the President's cabinet. He is frankly, honestly, aggressively partisan and political in his approach to this question. That makes it difficult to have a contest, because I am president of the American Farm Bureau Federation. I was elected by Farm Bureau members— 1,409,000 of them. They set the policies and they are half Republicans and half Democrats. All of them are agreed that we should decide agricultural policy on a nonpartisan basis, that we should make every possible effort to consider issues on their merits and decide them on the basis of what is right and what is wrong. That makes it difficult for me.

I will give you an illustration—one peculiarly pertinent to this state in which many of you live. During the past year there has been much national publicity to the effect that during the last presidential campaign I campaigned for Mr. Dewey in Iowa, and that in spite of my efforts I was unable to switch the farmers of Iowa to Mr. Dewey. Some of you may have said, "It must have been over in some other part of the state." But the people who live there thought it was in your part of the state. Because I

[13] Des Moines *Register and Tribune*, February 19, 1950.

wasn't in your state, I didn't make a speech. I didn't write a speech, I didn't make a telephone call, I didn't send anybody out, and nobody came to see me. It is that sort of thing that I want to get out of your minds.

I am going to roll up for you some ideas. All I want you to do is to twist them, turn them, look at them from both sides, and see whether they stand up. Let's think together on this proposition of agricultural policy as it fits into the present scene and see whether we can make up our minds about the direction in which we would like to go.

As a representative of farmers and as a farmer myself, I think I know what farmers want. What they want is prosperity and all the things that go with it, all the advantages created by the sort of situation in agriculture that we think we must have and to which we think we are entitled. . . .

The approach of the farmers who are members of the American Farm Bureau Federation is based on the philosophy that the American system of regulated free enterprise really works, that it has been as peculiarly successful as it is peculiarly American, and that we ought to make whatever we do consistent with that kind of economy.

At the same time, of course, we ought not lose sight of the necessity of preventing monopoly in business and out of business, nor of the necessity for maintaing a high production per man in agriculture. The only chance you will have of getting a high standard of living—build a new house, buy new furniture, landscape the front yard, or plant a tree and sit in the shade and tell the world to go rest—the only chance you will have depends on the service you render to society. Whenever you lose sight of that fact, or allow something to come in and restrict your capacity to render service, look out! You are the people with the most to lose, and if you lose, America loses, too, because it has been that pattern of progress which has made possible what we have done in the past.

There was a time when you went 'way out to the well to get water. We made a great improvement when we put a pump in the back yard. How did we get the job done? We did it by improving the capacity of farmers to earn—the most fundamental requirement of all. Any price support program must be fitted into that kind of a proposition. That is the reason, for instance, why we are in favor of flexible price supports.

Some of you who were at this meeting last year remember that I said there was faulty economics in the notion of some farmers that loans on corn were all pure gain. It might not have been too bad an idea if we had fed more corn—if we had fed a few more cattle and if they had not reached $41.50—because then the corn would have been used up. Any time you take a half billion bushels of corn off the market, you have added to demand. But any time you put that corn back on the market, you subtract from demand. There is an equal and contrary effect. You have to keep that in mind if you want to think straight—and we need desperately to think straight because we are dealing with the question of whether agriculture is going to continue to be more prosperous or whether we are going to give up.

Now there is another philosophy—the philosophy that you can't afford to take a chance, that you can't afford to depend on yourself, that you have to depend on a guaranteed fair price, or alleged fair price, set by the government. As much as I regret it, I suppose I have to identify that philosophy as the Brannan plan.

In considering that plan, I have two choices: First, I can assume it means exactly what it says; second, I can assume it does not. If I take the second choice, then I am assuming it is pure hokum. I don't assume that. I take it for granted that it means what it says, that it is the idea presented by Secretary Brannan to the agricultural committee of the house, that it is the plan being presented by employees of the Department of Agriculture to farmers here and there over the country. I take it for granted that it is a proposal to support prices until they reach the income support standard.

I want to refer to my business. I raise pigs. I have raised pigs all my life since I was old enough to raise anything. Long before I was able to raise hell I raised pigs. That is my business. Now here is a proposition which says that we will be guaranteed $19 for pigs and $1.46 for corn. That is a 13-to-1 corn-hog ratio, and I don't need to tell you what that means. Everybody decides to raise more pork, and a lot of people who didn't raise any pork before now decide to keep two sows. Here is a profitable level, a supposedly guaranteed profit. So you get a lot of pork.

Presumably that is a good idea. But let's look at what would happen. Over the past two months you fellows have been selling hogs for about $15. If they had been supported at $19, it would have cost the taxpayer $4 a hundred plus the costs of administration. And, mind you, if we went ahead and produced still more and they went on down in price—and demand for most food products is such that if you increase supplies by 20 per cent you get more than a 20 per cent reduction in price—the tax would still be up there, plus the cost of administration.

I have said that we must live with big government and we do, because there are a lot of things that you and I want government to do for us. But we have the problem of keeping it responsive to the people. When you have the expansion in production I have described, you have not only the problem of cost but also the difficulties caused by a very large, centrally administered government. When you have an expansion in uneconomic production and then start controlling—and you must control because you couldn't get the appropriations required if you don't—you soon get into the ridiculous. . . .

Finally, there is this question: Is it appropriate and proper for farmers and others to build on the record of the past—to use the means which have been successful in America? Or must we go over to a system of letting the government figure out on a statistical basis who is to produce what for whom and how much each is to produce? You may think we aren't heading that way. The best example I know is the tobacco program. I recommend a little compulsory reading of the debate on the Chapman amendment to the Agricultural Act of 1949—an amendment sponsored, not by people against the tobacco program, but by congressmen from Kentucky and Tennessee. The proposal was that minimum tobacco allotments were reduced from 9/10ths of an acre to 5/10ths of an acre, with everybody entitled to the minimum. And, as Senator McKellar pointed out, 72 per cent of all tobacco allotments are at the minimum of 9/10ths of an acre. Is that the direction in which you want to go? Where would America be if we did that? With everybody trying to get an allotment of 5/10ths of an acre of tobacco because there is a guaranteed profitable price, you would, of course, squeeze economic production. And you don't get plenty that way.

Is our peculiarly successful regulated free enterprise worth fooling with any more? Maybe we ought to discard the blooming thing and start over. Maybe we ought to copy another pattern. After all, we are in a period of great confusion following a great world war, and we are cutting the pattern for the future today. Maybe we ought to cut out a new one. Maybe we ought to base it on some new plan. Maybe we ought to say that we shouldn't let these things be decided by too many people. Maybe we ought to have more controls so we can guarantee more to everybody.

Or we can increase opportunity, then restrain ourselves and keep the rest of the money to do with as we please. That is my philosophy and the philosophy of the American Farm Bureau. Has it worked? I recommend that you read, in the January issue of the *Atlantic Monthly* the article by Sumner Slichter, a great business and management-labor analyst, recognized not only in this country but throughout the world.

Suppose someone had told you in 1900 that this country was going to have to fight two great wars in the next fifty years. Suppose he had described those wars and had said: "We are going to take out all the men, materials and production necessary to fight those wars to a successful conclusion, and at the same time we are going to cut working hours from 58 to 40 a week, increase consumption of goods per capita by 250 per cent, increase the percentage of kids in college three times as fast as the population grows, and have three out of four of all children of high school age in school." You would have said: "You're crazy. That can't be done. It is ridiculous." But it is in the record: That is what we did do in America.

I think I know why we did it. I think it was because there was something fundamentally right about America—something which said to every individual citizen: "This is the land of opportunity. We are going to try to help you and you are going to help yourself. If you render an unusual service to society— whether you raise pigs, cattle, corn or cotton, or whether you are a worker in a factory, a schoolteacher, coal miner, ditch digger or whatever you are—we are going to try to create opportunity, we are going to try to make it possible for you to use your imagination, and you will get paid on the basis of the service you render to society." Look at the record. Did it work? The whole world is coming to America's door to see how we got it done. The only people who would sell America short are Americans. (Applause.)

We have done another thing. I confidently believe that Americans are better than before. If they are, it is because this kind of system encouraged a man to use what he had, to be a little better each generation than in the generation before, to somehow fan the little spark of divinity in every man, and we had millions of people doing it. What it did was to create a great light. It is the light of the whole world here in the middle of the twentieth century. It shows up over the horizon of tomorrow, and it is the only possible light that shows to free men any place in the world the capacity or possible capacity to dispel the dismal gloom of a philosophy that is completely opposite—a philosophy which says, "Man is nothing; the state is everything," a philosophy which has a ruthless recklessness about it which submerges the individuality of every citizen and denies the existence of God.

This thing we have is a different thing. This is the proposition that it is the citizen that counts—that the important question is: Are we better today than we were yesterday? This is the time to stick out your chest, take a full breath, and say that you have the same kind of courage as did the men who left you the most magnificent heritage in the history of the world.

A FARM PLAN FOR THE FUTURE [14]

CHARLES F. BRANNAN [15]

Charles F. Brannan, Secretary of Agriculture, gave this speech at Des Moines, on February 18, 1950, as a continuation of the debate on the Brannan plan for agriculture. For detailed comment see the introduction to Kline's speech, p 196.

These kinds of programs going on over this country and participated in by farmers—by the people who are directly and immediately affected—are as fundamental expressions of our democracy as can be found anywhere. I believe that out of American agriculture have come many of the roots of American democracy. We got cooperatives and we got the cooperative spirit; we got the method of working together to develop and improve the things we were doing; and I believe that the residual depository of that influence in America is still among the farmers. It is there more so—as demonstrated by our farm cooperatives, as demonstrated by our committee system—than you will find in any place else in the country.

In his opening, Mr. Kline made the personal reference to the fact that I am a politician. Ladies and gentlemen, I plead guilty. (Laughter and applause.) I thought that in a democracy people expressed their point of view about what was going on and about what had gone on. So last year when Mr. Kline, as he eloquently told us, maintained hands off of everything mildly suggesting politics, I confess that I was out telling the American people in my inadequate way that I thought there was a threat to farmers' cooperatives in legislation which had been proposed to the Congress, and that the threat was coming from people who called themselves politicians because they were members of the House

[14] *Proceedings of the Twelfth National Farm Institute, 1950.* Text supplied through the courtesy of the Agricultural Department of the Des Moines Chamber of Commerce. Permission to reprint given through the courtesy of Charles F. Brannan. Because of the extreme length of the debate, it has been possible to include here only a part of the argument.

[15] For biographical note, see Appendix.

and Senate and who perhaps were under the influence of people outside.

I went about this country telling American farmers that there had been a group in Congress which had taken away the right of your government to assist you in providing adequate storage for the ever-increasing crops we have been able to produce. I went about this country telling the people of America that I thought the gentleman then in the White House was a great human being and that he was entitled to your consideration for the position of President—and that is a political position if there ever was politics in this country.

Ladies and gentlemen, I am guilty of being a politician. And I say to you that again this year I shall go to the American people and I shall tell them that cooperatives are being threatened again. I shall tell them that there is another attempt to deprive us of the right to have adequate storage facilities. I shall tell them all the rest of the things that I think should be known by citizens with the right to vote—and this is one of the few countries on the face of the earth with that right. I shall exhort them to cast their ballots—I don't care how—but to cast them intelligently. And I say above all that I shall not sit back in a holier-than-thou attitude and say that I do not participate in politics. (Applause and whistles.)

We have before us for consideration today some serious problems of farm policy—problems which demand an early solution, not only in the farmer's interest but for the welfare of the entire nation. There are undoubtedly a number of approaches that would help us try to get at this problem, but I would like to suggest today—because we are objectively trying to reach some understanding as to where we ought to be going from here—that we take this approach:

At my request a bushel of corn has been placed on the platform. If you will assume that this bushel of corn is the first extra bushel beyond our assumed domestic need, beyond export requirements, and beyond even the safe reserves required to protect the nation against crop failure or other emergency, then it is a symbol of our major national farm problem.

It is the extra bushel. It is the bushel for which a satisfactory market must be found if the men who produced it are to get a fair price and if it is to do anybody any good. Its counterpart is to be found in many other kinds of crops whether measured in bushels or bales or tons or in any other fashion. Yet it is no different from any other bushel of corn. Time and effort and money are required to produce it, and it contains the same essential feed values as does all the rest of our corn.

Farmers may accidentally produce it in good faith as part of their effort to earn a living for their families and to help feed our nation adequately and properly. They can produce many like it through more efficient use of their resources, through new and better farm practices, through better care of the soil, through new varieties developed by long and painstaking research, and through mechanization to cut down man-hours of labor.

What are we going to do with that extra bushel of corn? In my opinion, there are just two alternatives: We must either consume it by transforming it into meat, milk, eggs or poultry and by getting that extra food eaten; or we will have to lock up that extra bushel of corn and go back to the American farmer and say, "Next year, don't produce quite so much."

Of course, there are some industrial uses for a small portion of that extra bushel of corn. But the alcohol manufacturer who is one of those industrial users could not pay the American farmer more than fifty cents for that bushel and still produce alcohol and stay in business. He has to compete with sorghum from Cuba and with potatoes from a lot of places. (Applause and laughter.)

So that is all the choices we have, unless I don't understand this economy. That is all the choices we have and that about sums up our farm problem today. There it is—that extra bushel of corn. The future course of our farm policies will determine what shall happen to it, whether we use its potential nutritional values for better diets or whether we stop producing it—if it is possible to stop. Making use of it will benefit both farmers and consumers. Abandoning its production will be a sacrifice for both of us. . . .

Nor do I believe that the farmers or the rest of the American people are willing to concede that more efficient use of resources is a waste because it produces that extra bushel, or that we should give up the know-how for producing that abundance. We want to learn, and must learn, to live with our abundance. That is why I have advocated a farm program aimed at making use of that abundance rather than shackling it.

I want to discuss some of those recommendations with you today. I want to point out to you that we have not suggested that you abandon a single one of the things that have been put into legislation since 1935, when we first began to get good, sound farm legislation in this country. But just as any other program must be dynamic or adapted to the new things we know, learn and have done, so must we make in our farm program the necessary improvements required by changing conditions.

There still appears to be some misconception—and I have been listening to another evidence of it—and lack of understanding of our recommendations and even of my motives for having made them. Some of this is the natural result of insufficient information, but I say to you in complete candor and without any feeling of malice at all that some of the misinformation and misconception has been intentionally manufactured by the leadership of a great farm organization. (Applause, boos and whistles.)

But whatever the cause, let's do a little objective study about it. Let's get down to some of the basic concepts. (Applause.) I am for parity. I am for the original concept of parity and a standard of equality for agriculture—a fair share of the national income for the farmers who contribute so greatly to creating that income. I am thinking in terms of people rather than just in terms of commodities. I want parity of opportunity for the farmers to earn a fair return from investment of capital, of labor and of skill, and of their management ability—not just parity for the bushel of corn. I want parity of living opportunity for the farm family and for all of the farm families.

I am against any form of regimentation. (Applause.) I am against any form of controls that can reasonably be avoided and which may not have the affirmative support of a large majority of the producers affected. I am for the widest possible freedom of choice by the farmer himself in the management of his enterprise. I am for the farm programs that will make the maximum use of our farm production so we can avoid the strict controls that will be inevitable if we fail to provide profitable and useful outlets for the extra bushel of corn. I am for efficiency of production and for constantly increasing it. But I do not agree with those who hold that the only path to efficient production is industrialized mass farming.

I want to see no collectives taking over the farms of America, whether of the Soviet design or of the corporate pattern. (Applause.) I believe that the family-type farm can be efficient, and I believe we should concentrate our efforts for increased efficiency upon the family-size farm and the family-size farm unit, because of the important human value it contributes to our society, if for no other reason. I am for encouraging, strengthening and preserving it as the backbone of American agriculture, not for turning our backs upon it and destroying it in the false name of increased efficiency.

I am for government economy—for economy by eliminating the uneconomic practices . . . (Laughter.)

Now let me speak to the hecklers a moment: Do you remember the summation of Mr. Kline a few moments ago when, if I understood it, he even accused anybody who didn't follow the program he sponsors of being un-Godlike? Is that what he said? (Applause, cries of "yes" and "no".) Who was he talking about? He had been talking about me all afternoon, so you can't say it was a gross assumption. But let's get down to the hecklers: Come right on any time; this is a grand America where everybody has a right to say what they want to say. I don't know whether the radio will hold out, but if you will be patient with me—those of you who did not come to heckle—I am going to try to say what I intended to say. (Applause.)

I want to remind you again that I am your servant. I am your employee; you pay my salary. I do in the Department of Agriculture what I conscientiously think is my best. It may not be good enough. But I do say to you that when I come out here to talk to you about these problems and to express what is in my heart and mind—and I sat quietly while my opponent made considerable light of the serious recommendations we have made—it occurs to me that in line with something we used to call "American" you might hear the guy out. (Applause.)

Now for the benefit of the hecklers I say again: I am for government economy. I am for economy eliminating the uneconomical practices of present price support methods that waste good food and penalize the consumers by making them pay the costs twice—first in their tax bill and second in their food bill. I am for doing everything in our power now to avoid the tremendous cost to government of another disastrous depression, and to avoid its cost in human misery to the people of our nation. . . .

But just what is our situation today? Are we making progress toward our objective? Are we slipping backward or are we on the right track? Unfortunately, both farm prices and incomes are headed in the wrong direction. Farm prices have dropped an average of almost one fourth in less than two years. They are still going down, but farmers still have to pay within 5 per cent as much for what they buy as they paid two years ago. In 1947, farm operators had a net income of nearly $18 billion. Last year it was down to around $14 billion. The forecast for 1950 is for a net income of under $12 billion. That is a net decline of almost one third in net farm income at a time when national income is at its all-time peak.

Is this the way to parity? Is this a desirable trend? The gap between farm and non-farm income is widening instead of closing. Even at the peak of agricultural income total per capita income of persons on farms—and I am talking about both commercial and non-commercial farmers—was only 60 per cent as high as for persons not on farms. In 1949 this income gap widened and in 1950 it is expected to widen still more.

The people on farms constitute one fifth of the total population, yet the year before last they got from their farms less than 10 per cent of the national income and last year they got only 7.8 per cent of the total national income. We are headed away from, instead of toward, our real concept of parity—which in my opinion is equality of opportunity for agriculture.

Should we not be disturbed about this? Should we not seek its cause and should we not offer some kind of remedies and suggestions which might reverse that trend? Must those in public office whose duty it is to be particularly sensitive to these trends be attacked as "stupid," "dishonest," or as "nuts" because they speak out about such trends and seek to offer some kind of remedy?

Behind and around all the pros and cons, the underlying conflict is in the very philosophy of our farm policy itself. You are confronted with two entirely different ways of thinking about what objectives we should seek for the American farmer.

One group, of which the present administration is a part, believes it is in the best interests of the entire nation to use price supports as a means for providing agriculture the opportunity to earn a fair income. It does not propose to guarantee that income to anybody. But it does propose to assure diligent farmers the opportunity of achieving a level of income that would bring them closer to the goal of equality with other groups.

On the other hand, there are those who preach that the only role of price support is to protect the farmer against bankruptcy. In other words, they see no reason for stopping price and income declines until the farmer's back is against the wall.

The Farm Bureau's present national leadership, if I understand it correctly, may fall in that category. It advocates "stop-loss" price supports—whatever they are. Sometimes it uses that terminology and sometimes it uses more exact language. Sometimes they say they are only against "unreasonable" price declines. What do you mean by "unreasonable" price declines? Farm prices already have dropped 23 per cent. How much farther must they fall before we begin to call the decline "unreasonable"? Must the farmer almost go broke before he can expect the steadying hand of his own government to be extended? And where is the fine line between being almost broke and just plain broke? For my part, I can't fix that line.

If I understand it correctly, and if that quotation I gave you was correct, then the Farm Bureau's leadership at this moment has turned its back on the historic position of its own great organization, when it so often declared—and I quote again from its own former statements of policy: "The fight of organized agriculture has been and is now for equal opportunity and parity position with the other great groups." Why aren't those words still true today? Will somebody tell me? (Applause.)

Now, because the gentleman who now heads the American Farm Bureau is here today, I would like to take the opportunity, for just this once, of addressing him directly, in the hope of reaching a better understanding of his attitude and perhaps of the attitude of some of us in the Department of Agriculture. I would like to ask the president of the American Farm Bureau Federation in all seriousness: Does it aid agriculture in any way to say of the administration's proposals, "People who propose such a program to farmers are very dumb or downright dishonest?" How will that kind of attack help us to solve the hog-price-support problem?

I would like to ask the gentleman: Do you actually expect to halt the decline in farm prices by calling the administration's recommendations a "statement of politico-economic philosophy, not a farm program"? Or by calling those recommendations "a supreme delusion"? Or, as you have also done, by saying that the proposals are "nuts"? (Applause.)

And I would like to ask in all sincerity: Do you think it fair to farmers in your membership to be openly favoring still lower price supports for farmers in the hope of forcing some of them out of business so that farming can be more profitable for the big-scale farmers with large cash reserves who are able to survive? (Applause.)

I would like to ask if you really feel that the Farm Bureau is fulfilling a constructive role in behalf of agriculture by having its spokesmen spend their time tearing down the recommendations of others with such abusive remarks as, "It shines and stinks and stinks and shines like rotten mackerel in the moonlight?"

Ladies and gentlemen, again I say to you that I am a public official; I realize that all public officials are entitled to or must expect abusive language addressed to them, and I assure you that I am neither offended nor bothered by the laughter and applause. As a matter of fact, if it gives some release to the feeling of frustration at not having an adequate program, I am for their doing it and I want them to. (Applause and laughter.) . . .

Let's keep that bushel of corn in mind. What do you want to do with it? Shall we find a way to get it used—fully used and into the stomachs of the American people? Do you know that the Irish eat more meat per capita than the people of the United States? We are not eating all the meat we can eat. So we can convert that corn into meat and get it into the marketplace and get it consumed, and then we won't have to come back to the American farmer and say, "Quit producing corn."

There are just two ways you can go: Find a good use for the things we can produce—get them into the marketplace at attractive prices and keep the government out of the channels of trade; or go back to this thing called regimentation and ask American farmers to cut down production. I don't want to go to the American farmer and ask him to cut off the production of anything until I have satisfied myself beyond any reasonable doubt that we have exhausted every effort to get that corn converted into the things people want to eat and into the marketplace at prices which are attractive. And I think we have a long, long way to go.

We ate eight eggs less per person this year than last and five to six less pounds of meat. We have eaten a lot less of everything these past few years because we have priced ourselves out of the marketplace. And we have a lot of things down in the cave and potatoes down in the ground.

Thank you for hearing me out. This has been a grand audience. I was told when I came to Iowa, the home state of Mr. Kline, that the going would be tough. But I don't think it is tough anywhere. People are people and human beings, and the problems in Iowa are no different than the problems anywhere else. I think there is so much of good human Americanism in every one of us that I will be happy to talk or accept an invitation to talk to any audience anytime anywhere.

EDUCATION

THE PLIGHT OF THE CONSERVATIVE IN PUBLIC DISCUSSION [1]

JAMES H. MCBURNEY [2]

James H. McBurney, Dean of the School of Speech, Northwestern University, and President of the Speech Association of America during 1949, gave this address at the first general session of the thirty-fourth annual conference of that organization, in the Grand Ball Room, Stevens Hotel, Chicago, Illinois, on December 28, 1949. This conference was held in conjunction with the annual meeting of the American Speech and Hearing Association (Silver Anniversary) and the American Educational Theatre Association (fourteenth annual meeting).

The theme of this first session was "Areas of the study of speech—what do they have in common?" Horace G. Rahskopf, University of Washington, First Vice President (and President-elect) of the Speech Association of America, presided. On the program also were the Honorable Ralph E. Church, Representative of the 13th Illinois District in the United States Congress; President Delyte W. Morris of Southern Illinois University, President of the American Speech and Hearing Association; and Hubert Heffner of Stanford University, President of the American Educational Theatre Association. More than a hundred registered for the convention, and some one thousand, including teachers, research specialists, graduate and undergraduate students of speech, and other educational groups, were in the audience.

The convention, a three day conference, included sectional meetings on oral interpretation, semantics, business communication, secondary and college teaching, preaching, experimental phonetics, forensics, public address, voice and diction, television and radio, debate and discussion philosophy and techniques, library and the speech teacher, speech and human relations, clinical procedures, discussion, rhetoric, listening, history of speech education, British oratory, stuttering, acting, play production, and new trends in theatre education.

The address reflects the speech philosophy of its author; is closely adjusted to the immediate listeners; conveys much of the speaker's personality; is well organized.

[1] Permission for this reprint through the courtesy of Dean James H. McBurney. Text supplied by the author. See also *Quarterly Journal of Speech.* 36:164-8. April 1950.
[2] For biographical note, see Appendix.

Only indirectly is it addressed to the business conservatives themselves, few of whom obviously were in the audience. The language is oral, unhackneyed, personal, animated.

Mr. McBurney has been dean of the School of Speech, Northwestern University, since 1942. Previously he had taught speech at Northwestern, the University of South Dakota, University of Michigan, Columbia University, and at several secondary schools. At the University of Michigan McBurney was awarded the doctorate in speech. The chairman of his doctoral committee was professor J. M. O'Neill, one of the two or three national leaders in speech education.

The speaker, a former school and college debater, is an excellent platform speaker and discussion leader. He has demonstrated the principles of effective discussion in his widely used *The Principles and Methods of Discussion* (with Kenneth Hance), and in his more recent *Discussion in Human Affairs* (also with Hance).

The plight of the conservative in American public life is a fact which hardly needs documentation. An analysis of this plight was presented in a recent issue of the Chicago *Daily News* in which opinions from grass-root voters to political and educational leaders were reported. Says the *News*: "Whether it was called a 'welfare state,' 'creeping socialism,' 'fascism,' 'a regimented state,' or something else, it boiled down to a belief that individual freedom and initiative are being threatened by the government." When queried by the *News*, Franklyn B. Snyder, President Emeritus of Northwestern University, added this: "Complacency today is the greatest foe of the conservative."

I think this hits the nail on the head. Complacency it is! And this complacency affects public discussion in America in ways which are good for no one, least of all the conservatives.

I have the temerity to argue that the conservatives in America have become inarticulate to a point where their voice does not do credit to their ideas and often does their cause a positive disservice. I think my analysis is not a partisan one. I confess to a conservative bias, but my concern here is a professional interest in public discussion and debate. In a very real sense, discussion is the essence of the democratic process. Whatever weakens discussion in America, weakens America. A monolithic society is not conducive to vigorous discussion of public questions. We need differing points of view, and we need articulate spokesmen for these points of view.

For the past eight years, I have had charge of the North-western University Reviewing Stand, a national radio forum originating in radio station WGN, Chicago, and carried by the Mutual network. We are on the air each week with discussions of contemporary problems, mainly social, economic, and political questions. Our speakers are members of the University faculty and distinguished guests from business, industry, labor, government, and the press. As moderator of these discussions, I am the recipient of an amazing volume of letters and comments from all over America. One of the most persistent criticisms is the charge that we are radicals, reds, and even Communists. To be sure, we are often labeled radicals and reactionaries on the same program, but the charge of radicalism far outruns any other single criticism.

Why this persistent charge of radicalism? I am sure the answer does not lie in the sponsorship and management of our radio forum. Even our critics express surprise that we should be the ones to commit this indiscretion. What is more, precisely the same charge is directed against the other leading radio forums. The answer must be sought in the discussions themselves.

In the first place, we usually discuss changes in the status quo —questions of public policy. That is an important function of discussion. All kinds of social, economic, and political changes are analyzed in the interest of better understanding. The conservative, by definition, opposes change; he supports the status quo; he usually takes "the traditional position." The very fact that discussion concerns itself with change may suggest that discussion supports such change. Actually, of course, it does not. Properly conceived, discussion is a method for analyzing problems and considering solutions to these problems. It is not even a good vehicle for propaganda.

More important are the persons who take part in these programs. In organizing discussions of controversial questions, we naturally try to secure the most competent spokesmen available for all points of view. We have little trouble getting the advocates of change, the liberals, the radicals. These people invariably accept our invitations with pleasure and alacrity; but not so with the gentlemen on the right, the representatives of business and industry, the conservatives. More often than not, they are too busy, have other commitments, or refuse to appear on the same platform with other speakers we have invited. Sometimes they say quite frankly that they are afraid of give-and-take discussion.

As moderator of these discussions, I frequently find myself wanting to come to the aid of the conservative spokesmen. Often they are nervous and inarticulate. Especially is this true when their basic assumptions are challenged. They lack facility in verbal analysis and synthesis, in give-and-take argument, in rebuttal and refutation. More often than not they are no match for rhetorically seasoned liberals, with long experience on every kind of platform from a cracker barrel to a radio microphone. There are notable exceptions, but my description is faithful to the rule.

I think this is the reason why our radio forum is charged with radicalism—the conservative spokesmen do not come through! It is either this or the less charitable explanation that the conservative position in America today is not tenable in public discussion. Whether or not the conservative position, or any other position, is tenable is precisely what public discussion is designed to test. Given spokesmen of high competence and reasonably equal competence, it provides one of the best tests democracy has been able to devise. Unless these conditions are met, we run the risk of serious distortions in public policy.

If this problem were confined to radio forums, I would not take your time with it. It most emphatically is not so confined. These forums are just a small sample of the kind of discussion that goes on all over America—in homes, schools, churches, places of business, legislative assemblies, and deliberative bodies of all kinds. In this larger arena, we can witness the full measure of the rhetorical bankruptcy of the conservative.

For many years past in America, the conservative has been in the saddle. The industrialists, the banker, the businessman have been the backbone of America—respected, accepted, and looked to for leadership. Whether this reputation was deserved is neither here nor there. It is a fact. But this long, unchallenged tenure has not been an unmixed blessing. The conservative grew soft under it. He came to take his position for granted. He became complacent. And he lost his voice, except for occasional ceremonial chants and cries of distress. In the meantime, the little fellow on the outside grew in strength and lung power, until one day there appeared on the scene a great spokesman for the ill fed, the ill housed, and the ill clothed. Since that time we have lived under New Deals and Fair Deals.

How have the conservatives responded to this rude unseating? Not too well, I fear. The National Association of Manufacturers invited a number of students to attend their annual convention in New York this month. *Time* magazine reports some of the reactions of these young observers:

> Too many of the NAMsters, the students felt, talked in such platitudes and generalities about the drift towards socialism, the welfare state, taxes, that what they had to say lost its effect. What was needed, said one student, was a clear, fresh exposition "to the man in the street in terms of the simple why and wherefore of the price of his bread."
>
> A further student criticism was that, in panel discussions, the NAMsters "were often unqualified to answer our questions."
>
> One student put his finger on NAM's biggest trouble: its failure to capitalize on opportunities to catch the public's ear.

Quite obviously the answer to this problem is not a simple one. Indeed, there may be no answer which the conservatives will like. Whether or not an intransigent liberalism is good for America must be ground out in countless discussions and debates all over America. My hope is that the conservatives will find the means of developing an effective voice in these discussions and debates. I think they are lost unless they do. And I think America stands to lose without their best counsel. I would say exactly the same of the liberals were the situation reversed.

I realize that this thesis comes easily from a teacher of discussion and debate and a moderator of public forums. Some will say the plight of the conservative is dictated by economic, social, and cultural realities in the American scene which have little or nothing to do with "talk" about these realities. I do not propose to assess these realities in this paper, but I do profess to know something about the influence of talk in building attitudes and shaping events. Talk influences men, and men influence events. The case for making good sense and good taste articulate is a familiar one to most teachers of speech. We have substantial experimental data to support this thesis.

In the first place, we know that attitudes toward social problems do change significantly as a result of discussion. In other words, something is accomplished in discussion; people do change their positions on public questions as a result of listening to discussions and participating in them. Secondly, we know that the initial or pre-discussion dispersion of attitudes is significantly reduced as a result of discussion. People get closer together. There is a significant tendency toward consensus. Thirdly, we know that people develop superior attitudes toward public questions through discussion, as measured by the opinions of experts. In other words, discussion has the effect of developing sound positions on social questions. Finally, we know the greatest influence in discussion is exerted by the more competent people, as measured by standard tests of personal competence, such as personality inventories, intelligence tests, social maturity scales, and the like.

I cite these data to make the point that public discussion is a democratic tool which no segment of American society interested in social attitudes can afford to neglect; and by the same token, it is a matter of great importance to American society that all social groups be competently represented in public discussion.

Several suggestions for developing effective spokesmen in deliberative councils are implicit in what I have already said. I should like to spell these out in greater detail.

In the first place, men in executive positions in business and industry must be willing to participate in public discussion. As the President of the United States Rubber Company put it last June:

The eleventh hour is here for business to speak for itself. Now, and from now on, the men who run American business must devote as much —if not more—time and effort to the public relations of their business as they spend on finance, production, and distribution. Unless they do, they will not need to worry about the latter problems. Government will be glad to handle them all.

In the second place, the paid spokesmen of the conservatives, the public relations officers of business and industry, must be selected with careful attention to their qualifications for serious intellectual discussion and vigorous public debate. The main job of such officers is developing relations with the public rather than with their brothers in the bond. This requires social, political, and economic literacy of a high order and top-notch dialectical ability.

Thirdly, the conservatives urgently need to develop greater sensitivity to the changing pattern of communication in America. This pattern is characterized by a growing emphasis on logical values in place of high pressure mumbo-jumbo; by simple, direct statement rather than verbal obfuscation; and by a sense of relativity in language usage in place of arbitrary, dogmatic assertion. These changes are inevitable in a democratic society which is becoming more conscious of the processes of communication and more sophisticated in their use. Any speaker ignores them at his own peril.

Fourthly, the conservatives must rid themselves of some unfortunate stereotypes. In this so-called "era of the common man," the conservative is depicted as the foe of the common man. Unfortunately, this role can easily be given specious plausibility because the conservative does have vested interests in the status quo. In a society in which men are living longer and specialized economic functions tend to draw class lines, it is easy to think of the conservative as an old man who has lost the common touch. Actually, the interests of the common man on any given issue at any given time and place may be just as completely identified with the conservatives as with the liberals. Most certainly it begs the question to assume otherwise. The lines between conservatives and liberals in America need not, and should not, be drawn on the basis of age or class. They should be determined in free and widespread discussion, and the conservatives must learn how to conduct themselves in such discussions in ways which will enlist the sympathy and understanding of common men.

The conservatives have also succeeded in alienating many of the intellectuals in America. Witch hunts in the colleges and universities, journalistic caricatures of the mortar board, and frantic name calling are hardly designed to win the understanding of men who place a high premium on objectivity in discourse. Moreover, there are echelons in the intellectual hierarchy in which there are fashions in ideas just as there are in goods. In some of these quarters, I fear, the conservative position has lost caste for reasons which have very little or nothing to do with its merit.

A minimum program of education and training for the kind of public discussion I am talking about should include: (1) a broad understanding of social, political, and economic issues in American life and culture; (2) clear insight into personal and social values as they affect these issues; and (3) specific training in the philosophy and method of democratic participation.

On this last point may I add with some feeling that such training is not to be secured in classes in after-dinner speaking and polite elocution. What is needed is sound education in discussion, debate, persuasion, and semantics under conditions which provide opportunities for realistic experiences in participation and leadership under the direction of competent teachers.

In conclusion, I wish again to make it clear that I do not present this analysis to plead the cause of the conservative, nor do I mean to question the ability and integrity of the conservative. It is my purpose rather to point out that conservatives generally are not doing their cause justice in public discussion and debate, explain why this is the case, and suggest some of the ways in which this weakness can be corrected. I believe this to be a problem of more than ordinary importance in American public life, and certainly one of great significance to students and teachers of speech.

As Aristotle put it, over two thousand years ago, "Truth and justice are by nature more powerful than their opposites; when decisions are not made as they should be, the speakers with the right on their side have only themselves to thank for the outcome."

THE SCHOLAR AND THE TWENTIETH CENTURY [3]

GEORGE P. RICE, JR. [4]

George P. Rice, Jr., professor of speech at Butler University, Indianapolis, gave this address at the twenty-seventh annual dinner of the honor society, Phi Kappa Phi, at that institution, on May 13, 1949.

Steeped in rhetoric and the humanities, the speaker composed and presented a discourse rich in rhetorical and literary allusion; clear in its recognition of the attributes of a scholar who is also a teacher; comprehensive in its summary of the problems to be solved; constructive in its delineation of the principles by which such solutions can be effected.

The speech is weighted with propositions—syllogistic enthymemes. Some of the representative ideas invite more leisurely analysis, illustration, and explication (for example, the criteria to be used as a measuring rod for the successful solution of the problems) than the thirty-minute address would permit.

Mr. Rice was graduated *cum laude* at the State College, Albany, New York, and there later earned an A.M. degree. At Cornell University he was awarded a doctorate in speech and rhetoric, under the direction of Lane Cooper, Herbert Wichelns, and Frederick G. Marcham. For four years at Albany he was in intercollegiate debate; he was elected to Delta Sigma Rho. He also "coached" the Cornell women. He was a member of the New York State Speakers' Bureau, was chief of the Speakers' Bureau of the Indiana State Mental Hygiene Association, educational director of the National Foundation for Education in American Citizenship. Previous to going to Butler, he taught speech at Pennsylvania State, Cornell, City College of New York, and Columbia University.

Professor Rice states, "The ideal public speaker is a man of intelligence and good will who exercises his powers to lead his fellows to think, to judge, and to act in matters of public concern, that the ends of truth and justice may be served. In America today this means stimulating men to understand their rights and duties under the Constitution and relating these to the newer concepts of 'One World.' " [5]

One of the masterpieces of eloquence of the Golden Age of Greece is a noble panegyric pronounced by Pericles in 431

[3] Text and permission for this printing supplied by the author. See also *Vital Speeches of the Day*, 15:574-6. July 1, 1949.
[4] For biographical note, see Appendix.
[5] Letter to this editor, March 17, 1950.

B.C. upon the civic virtues and valor of Athenians. In it the orator-statesman reminded listeners that great deeds were independent of praise and that he spoke only in obedience to a law which demanded utterance to mark the occasion. It is so with us tonight. Words of approval in this hour can neither add to the magnitude of your accomplishment nor increase the deep satisfaction which accompanies it. However, academicians cherish tradition and ceremony; hence it is altogether appropriate that your society should have called upon a speaker to express those deep sentiments you share and even allow him to suggest certain lines of thought and standards of conduct in keeping with your new privileges and responsibilities. It is a source of singular satisfaction to me that a rhetorician should have the honor of addressing the chapter on its anniversary. The invitation reveals a discerning regard for an ancient discipline whose twenty-five centuries of recorded history merit your respect upon very substantial grounds. Moreover, most men and women who have to do with teaching and learning take pleasure in discussing their way of life in its several aspects with colleagues and friends. I may even claim, like Herodotus, to have a story to tell, and like him, I hope no god or hero will take offense at what I have to say.

This gathering is, of course, no isolated instance of recognition of men and women of superior intellectual abilities. Sister chapters of this society and other groups devoted to similar ideals are meeting during these weeks throughout the United States. We are part of a far-flung brotherhood whose membership stretches across years and miles, for associations which identify and unify the ranks of the fit though few are not modern in origin. The Italian scholar of the Renaissance wore the Ring of Pythagoras as proudly as you now wear the shining symbol which declares your allegiance to intellect. And the Socratic Circle has its modern counterpart in the learned academies of France, England, and the United States. There is a bond which binds this university in unbroken continuity to Oxford, to Paris, to Rome, to Alexandria, and to Athens. We begin, therefore, by offering our homage and admitting our very great debt to the revered band of seekers after Truth in each generation, small in numbers but gigantic in strength, which has drawn and will draw its recruits from the first minds of every age without regard for creed, nation, color, or tongue. Your new status is proof that those who are qualified to judge think you may one day be of this great company. It is at the least a guarantee of your serious interest in the privileges and duties of talented intelligence. It is upon this assumption that I address myself to you upon the thesis of "the scholar and the twentieth century."

I would first define the general attributes of scholars and of scholarship, and then attempt to show the man of learning in relation to some of the pressing problems of our time. Let us begin with definitions. Who is a scholar? What does he do? The word "schole" is Greek and means "leisure." My colleagues at this board would qualify the noun by inserting before it the adjective "industrious," for the scholar is preeminently a gifted person who makes industrious use of his hours for the advancement of the common welfare. By "twentieth century" is intended the present time and the next four or five decades. By "humanism" is meant a mode of thought or action in which the highest aspirations of humanity predominate.

The position of the scholar in any society is exemplified by the Platonic figure of the "body politic." Members of each generation are given special tasks in their community. We may say that to the thinker is assigned the role of eye in this body. His life is one of studious contemplation, and he is the observer and critic of what he sees, the discriminating instrument of the rest. A foremost American Hellenist, Cornell's Lane Cooper, classes the scholar with the poet, the philosopher, the painter, and the composer of music. Those chiefs of state who are wise men secure the future by making suitable provision for colleges and universities and the intellects they house. Emerson thought that "in the ideal state the scholar is man thinking." Such a one devoted his life to gaining and holding new areas on the frontiers of knowledge. He formed hypotheses; he assembled evidence; he judged; and he shared the harvest of his studies. In these and other ways he proved his value to his fellows. But he was and is, as Emerson claimed also, a man of action at need. The Homeric ideal was a "doer of deeds and a speaker of words." This concept is generally approved and admired today. We recall Plato at Syracuse. We celebrate this year the bicentennial of the birth of Johann Wolfgang von Goethe and are reminded of his services to the duchy of Weimar. The dependence of Winston Churchill upon the Oxford professor, Lindemann, is generally known. And there are notable instances in which colleges and universities have turned to diplomacy, professions, business, and even the armed forces for their heads, bringing the combination of doer and thinker to the campus community.

There are certain other qualifications which mark a man of good will who is also intelligent. He knows that true perspective of men and events comes only to him who is happy, because freedom from care brings wisdom in its train through release from many distorting pressures. He cultivates many areas besides the one in which he speaks with the authority of knowledge. He is one who in his early years gives promise and possesses convictions. You will remember the idealism of Thomas Mann who returned a doctorate granted him *in honoris causa* by a great German university because he disapproved strongly its failure to oppose tyranny. He is a philosopher in the true sense of that word, a "lover of wisdom" before he seeks to possess encyclopedia. He is aware of two audiences the immediate which hears his lectures or reads his books or learns his discoveries, and the remote—the as yet unborn judges before the bar of whose opinion he will stand one day through his works. The learned man's progress is marked by indications of his obligation to predecessors and contemporaries, without whose assistance he could not have made his way. Important among his concerns is that of selecting, training, and encouraging gifted young men and women. He examines their ethical and intellectual qualifications with painstaking care. Nor will he assemble large numbers of learners about him. The opinions of Scaliger, Boeckh, Agassiz, and Lang, among many, stress that *only the opportunity for education is democratic and that not all who are eligible can benefit by instruction to the same degree.* Such men know that the state is wisely guided by those who have great natural parts supplemented by artful instruction at the hands of capable teachers. And our scholar is a good teacher. Those who assert it is possible to be an effective teacher without being a good scholar speak hastily. Aristotle tells us that the pleasure of recognition through learning is a basic drive in human conduct. Who shall deny that the best teaching takes place when teacher and learner share the same experience, though on different levels?

Nor is mere transfer of fact and theory from one academic generation to the next the chief function of the scholar. He must inspire his charges to think and to act and to make discoveries for themselves, cultivating independence of action and judgment alike. And he will encourage in them the development to those traits of individuality which so peculiarly distinguish nobility of intellect: the awful patience of the discoverers of radium; the self-denial and persistence which enabled Marie Sklodovska to live in Paris in 1892 on three francs a day while she studied chemistry and physics at the Sorbonne; the capacity for broad vision supported by minute investigation practiced by Schleiermacher and Gaston Paris; the acumen to discern the limits of his powers and to undertake good and useful tasks within them. Thus, George Saintsbury, professor of Rhetoric and English Literature in the University of Edinburgh: "At a very early time of my life it was, as the old phrase goes, borne in upon me that I was not destined to create great literature but that I had perhaps some faculty of appreciation for it, and might even to some extent assist that appreciation in others." That "appreciation in others" was assisted through great numbers of books and numerous articles and addresses over a long span of years; his tasteful industry earned for Saintsbury an enduring measure of fame.

Let us endow our scholar finally with the idealism and high-minded courage of Fichte. Recall his words at Erlangen: "I am a Priest of Truth; I am in her pay; I have bound myself to do all things, to venture all things, to suffer all things for her. If I should be persecuted and hated for her sake, if I should even meet death in her service, what wonderful thing shall I have done?—what but that which I greatly ought to do?"

The modes of thought and action expressed by the qualities I have enumerated are extraordinary and they mark the exceptional man. But it is time that some importance be assigned to the gifted and that a little of the emphasis on the mediocre be lifted. Too much has been said and written to the effect that this is the "century of the common man," another name for the cult of mediocrity. Hear Somerset Maugham on this: "That nation is proudest and noblest and most exalted which has the greatest number of really great men."

The representative scholar is not without a sense of humor. And upon some occasions he goes abroad, a bird of rare and colorful plumage in academic processions, displaying the bright scarlet of theology, the deep green of medicine, the pure white of humanities, moving through all colors of the spectrum, rising finally to the cloth of gold robe for the honorary doctorate of the University of Dublin. I shall tell several tales which stand in contrast to what has been said and show our man in lighter vein.

Among the vast body of fact and apocrypha extant is the story of the great chemist, Chandler, who says of himself "no chemist enjoyed a more oleaginous career." He was brought up on the proceeds of the whale oil industry in New Bedford. In grammar school he was punished with a whale-bone switch. The vessel which carried him to a German university for graduate study bore also a cargo of oil. His first scientific article, rejected for publication on the ground it was too fantastic, dealt with the possibilities of obtaining illuminating oil from the earth. His early career exemplifies the German axiom that "a professor is a man who thinks otherwise." Chandler applied for a position as assistant in chemistry at Union College. He was informed that there was no vacancy, but that a janitor was needed at $500 a year. Chandler took the job, teaching chemistry *gratis*. But in ten years he had a chair in a great university and a national reputation.

And one remembers with amusement an incident involving Columbia's noted professor of dramatic literature, Brander Matthews. He had submitted an article to the *Forum* when that journal was edited by Walter Hines Page. Several weeks went by without word as to the fate of the manuscript, whereupon Matthews, not accustomed to such cavalier treatment, descended upon the *Forum* for purposes of inquiry. He was informed by Page that the article was not acceptable, that material for the *Forum* must be like a rifle shot, whereas Matthews' paper was like a shotgun discharge—smooth spray of no great weight cast in many directions. "You say the *Forum* is like a rifle?" asked Matthews. "Yes," replied Page, "that is how we like to think of it." "Well, then," replied Matthews, "That explains why it has such a smooth bore for an editor."

The same man was an irrepressible wit in faculty meetings and often lightened the somber deliberations of his colleagues by his mirth. Then as now the doctoral candidate in humanities had to pass an oral examination in Latin. This rule could be waived in special cases. Such an instance, it was urged, occurred with an Arab student whose adviser requested the Latin requirement be dropped and Arabic substituted. He remarked at the conclusion of the argument that, in any case, the Arab had recently had all his teeth removed and could hardly pronounce Latin at all. Matthews listened carefully, then rose and said: "Mr. Dean, I move that this man be permitted to substitute gum-Arabic."

There is finally the tale of a piece of literary criticism by Saintsbury on *Twelfth Night*. The line under discussion was, "Then come kiss me, sweet and twenty." "Ideas differ as to the interpretation of this line," said the lecturer. "Some think that both 'sweet' and 'twenty' refer to the lady; others think that only 'sweet' refers to the lady and that 'twenty' refers to the number of kisses. For myself, I prefer to think that both 'sweet' and 'twenty' refer to the lady and that the number of kisses is quite unlimited."

But it is in order now to return to the thesis of this discourse —the relation of the scholar to the main problems of his era. To his usual functions of discovery and dissemination the twentieth century has especially given him the task of applying his own acumen and knowledge to public affairs. Not since the emergence of Europe from the Middle Ages into the bright light of the Renaissance has there been so great a need for his aid in so many directions. The arrival of Atomic Age has stressed these fields of inquiry: the intelligent control of a new and immense source of power; the vital decision of whether conflict or cooperation is to be the pattern of the struggle between capitalism and communism; the subordination of technical to humanistic values in modern society; the maintenance of a proper balance between the interests of management and labor on the one hand and those of the commonwealth on the other; the spiritual and material regeneration of Europe, especially the shattered German state; the practice of the four freedoms by all men; the management of an enormous public debt which bestrides the national economy like a colossus; the eradication of gross political immorality in some of our civic units; and the encouragement of instruments and processes designed to make the present nebulous force we call public opinion an effective and vigorous factor in the control and direction of local and world affairs.

To meet these problems with success we need more groups like the Institute for Advanced Studies at Princeton and a resurgence of the spirit and practice of the old New England town meeting. We need more stress on the value of the spoken word in exchanges of opinion. Remember these words of an Oxford Chancellor addressed to a graduating class of that University a half century ago: "Public address can flourish only where intellectual civilization has made some progress, where the force of reasoning and the connection of sentences can be comprehended, and where the manner of presentation of thought is considered as well as the matter. Further, oratory that is political can occur only in a nation where there are, first, politics to discuss, and in the second, liberty to discuss them; and the opportunities for eloquence of the highest order will be in proportion to the issues at stake. . . . We must find a nation politically free, with high and noble aspirations, endowed with great and widely diffused culture, so that its leading spirits may be able to think lofty thoughts, and its common people may be able to understand and appreciate them; and we must look for a time when the fullest intellectual development coincides with some decisive moment of political life, when the best minds of the country are bent to some issue of the supremest importance. . . . "

The measuring-rod for successful solution of these problems may be found among the following criteria, several of which were suggested by a congregation of scholars at Princeton three years ago.

1. An awareness of the premanence of the Greek tradition in our life.
2. The ultimate mastery of external nature by man through the application of science.
3. The need for a common language to serve as a medium of communication for all men to promote peace, understanding, and good will.
4. The preeminence of truth in human affairs.
5. The primary of divine and human justice under the law.
6. The desire of all men for freedom.
7. The predominance of certain intellectual and emotional sanctions in the oral and written literature of many cultures: the concept of equality; the concern with justice; the subordination of expediency to ethics; a respect for the wisdom and ancestors; reverence for the word of God; the value of reflective thinking of an objective sort; the love of country; an obedience to the laws of logic; and the human tendency to prefer the delightful to the useful.

The scholarly intellect which applies these standards to our common problems will bring to his task a final asset. He will display a love of the language and literature of his native country and an appreciation of those of others. He will extol the power of noble and elevated conceptions powered by the drive of vehement and sustained passion. He will speak and write a clear and appropriate diction and endow his compositions with tasteful forms of support. He will display a good understanding of the architectonics of excellent prose and oral communication. In sum, he will be the possessor of a style which represents truly what he is himself.

The humanist who adopts the historical approach to determine his relation to the present will examine and apply the values in enduring concepts of truth, justice, love, and beauty with the aid of Plato, Virgil, Dante, Shakespeare, Milton, and Goethe. He will appreciate and understand the past—the great ages of Greece, of Rome, of Italy, and England—because they are a part of the greater whole. He knows they form a useful and even indispensable guide to the future, an explanation of the present. The re-creation of a milieu is no easy task. But before one can know and apply the wisdom of the past, be *gemuetlich* with its climate of opinion, he must carefully explore the history of ideas in a long and unbroken continuum. If one understands a culture able to produce an Isocrates, a Cicero, a Peter Abelard, a Lord Chesterfield, an Abraham Lincoln, or a Winston Churchill, he can better appreciate the wisdom of John Donne's *Devotion*, "No man is an island." We have a common humanity. We have common goals and aspirations. This is not the time to insist upon fragmentation of disciplines preserving archaic dichotomies. There is need for a design to provide unity among subject matter, method, and governing philosophy in the humanistic process. To deny this need, I submit, is to be monoptic in an age where clear vision and the widest possible perspective is imperative.

These are distrait and perilous times beyond peradventure, but they are also times of discovery and decision. And it may be the dawn of a new and wonderful epoch. Let us face it with the high courage and optimism John Milton felt in another era of uncertainty and conflict. "Methinks I see in my mind a noble and puissant Nation rousing herself like a strong man after sleep, and shaking her invincible locks. Methinks I see her as an Eagle muing her mighty youth, and kindling her undazzled eyes at the full midday beam, purging and scaling her long abused sight at the fountain itself of heavenly radiance."

Let me finish with the classic peroration recommended by the First Rhetorician: "I have spoken; you have heard; you know the facts; now give your decision."

WHAT SHOULD A COLLEGE PRESIDENT BE? [6]

WILLIAM HAROLD COWLEY [7]

Dr. William Harold Cowley gave this address at the luncheon at the Lubbock Country Club for delegates and honored guests attending the inauguration of Dossie Marion Wiggins as fifth president of Texas Technological College, at Lubbock, on May 10, 1949.

W. P. Clement, Registrar, introduced the speaker as follows:

"In planning for this occasion the committee sought to secure an outstanding leader of higher education in America, and immediately our thoughts turned to the speaker of today, Dr. William H. Cowley of Stanford University. He graciously accepted the invitation to be present and we are signally honored.

"Dr. Cowley is a graduate of Dartmouth College and holds the degree Doctor of Philosophy from the University of Chicago. He has been the recipient of a number of honorary degrees from leading colleges and universities of America. For some time he was President of Hamilton College in New York, but gave up that work to return to his first love, teaching and writing.

"He is today outside the realm of the college presidency by choice, as in 1941 he was elected President of the University of Minnesota and since that time has been approached regarding the presidency of several colleges and universities of the country, but in each instance he has declined in order to give his time to his chosen field. For some time he was editor of a journal of higher education and is at present a member of its editorial board. He is a specialist in student personnel work and an authority on the history and philosophy of higher education. Throughout the modern educational world there are, perhaps, only five or six men who are giving their time exclusively as professors of higher education. Dr. Cowley is one of that group.

"Those of us who have had the privilege of hearing Dr. Cowley on other occasions have been deeply impressed by his insight into the problems of higher education in various areas. Not only is he an authority on the work and problems of a college president, but he is equally at home in discussing the administrative problems of the dean, registrar, and personnel director. The committee, therefore, is delighted to share with you the experience of hearing one of America's outstanding leaders in the realm of higher education. It is, therefore, my honor and privilege

[6] *Bulletin of the Texas Technological College.* 25 no. 4:9-23. August 1949. Permission to reprint granted by Texas Technological College, through the courtesy of Professor W. H. Cowley.
[7] For biographical note, see Appendix.

to present to you Dr. William Harold Cowley, Professor of Higher Education, Leland Stanford University."

This address, as became its luncheon setting, was both thought provoking in its statement of educational philosophy, and highly interesting in its personal reminiscence, anecdote, and congeniality.

Cowley "has an animated delivery, forceful, yet he is fully aware of the audience reaction to his ideas. His appearance is dignified, scholarly, and carries with it an enthusiasm and vitality which one associates with executive ability. The forcefulness of the delivery is related to the strength and vividness of his ideas rather than to the beauty of his language." [8]

Last week I had a letter from an old friend of mine who is the president of a well-known college. Among other things it told of his introduction at a recent banquet by a prominent alumnus:

> In introducing me and reciting some of my multifarious, not to say nefarious, duties and activities, he asked his audience how it is that colleges are still able to persuade people to assume the presidency. For himself, he said that he could only reply that it is something like flagpole sitting: there are just those who go for it.

A few days earlier I had another letter from the president of a leading university commenting on an article I had written, and among other things he wrote:

> When presidents of universities have to deal with questions of high policy, they are forced to call upon others—usually professors—to appraise the issues involved. Isn't there something rather dangerous in the fact that college presidents are so involved in their endless duties that they are not able to do some of these things for themselves?

The title of my talk is "What should a college president be?" Is he really a flagpole sitter? Are his duties so endless and so exacting that he seldom has time to think about the meaning of what he does? The presidents I have quoted imply, if not directly say, these things; and if they are true, then clearly there *is* "something rather wrong" with the position not only for the incumbents but also for their institutions and for society at large. The occasion of the inauguration of a new president seems to provide an appropriate opportunity for taking a critical look at

[8] Letter from David Grant, Stanford University, to this editor, May 1, 1950.

the college president and for suggesting what ideally he ought to be.

May I observe, President Wiggins, that I address myself not only to you but also—and even more pointedly—to your associates on your Board of Directors and on your faculty. In most institutions members of the governing board and of the faculty have only the vaguest of notions about what a college presidency is and what a college president does. My hope is that I may help enlarge the knowledge and understanding of both groups so that you may have their help in conducting your office under better circumstances than most college presidents have yet achieved.

Eleven years ago I sat as you sit today listening to good wishes and advice, and five years ago I resigned after deciding that I didn't like being a college president. Now I am a professor of higher education, and I devote a good part of my time to studying the college presidency. It seems to me to be one of the most important positions in American society, and I discuss today some of the conclusions about it to which I have come during my years in it and my study of it.

Before tackling the question of what a college president should be, we ought first to describe what in general he is now. In my judgment, the answer is that he is one of the most burdened, one of the most harrased, one of the most put-upon people in American life. He is a hewer of wood and a drawer of water, a dray horse, a gallery slave, a bellhop, a hack, and a nursemaid all wrapped up in one. He may seem to be the top brass of an educational institution, but actually he spends most of his time polishing other people's brass—and breaking his back in the process.

He is expected to be an educator, a scholar, an administrator, a businessman, a public speaker, a writer, a money-raiser, a politician, a giver of dinners, a charmer at receptions, a moral force in the community, a commentator on national and international affairs, and popular with students, alumni, faculty, and readers of newspapers. If you think that I'm exaggerating, let me quote a statement made some years ago by President Dodds of Princeton:

I once saw a complete job specification drawn by the trustees of a university in search of a president. Talk about dual personalities! The gifts of a financier, businessman, scholar, preacher, salesman, diplomat, politician, administrator, Y.M.C.A. secretary, were some of the qualifications enumerated in addition to high moral character and a happy marriage to a charming wife.

Obviously no one can meet these specifications, and of course no one does. Yet we go on deluding ourselves that such men are to be found when we ought properly to be deciding what it is possible for a college president to be. Failing to do this, the position becomes more and more impossible, more and more hazardous, more and more subject to criticism.

The criticism began early in this century, and it has been mounting ever since. At first college presidents were accused of being too able, too strong; and groups of professors organized over the country to take power away from them. As one of the most vociferous of these professorial critics put it, "the president is the black beast in the academic jungle." These complaints were directed at that powerful group of presidents who, beginning about 1870 and continuing until about 1910, organized American higher education as we know it today: Eliot of Harvard, Gilman of Johns Hopkins, Harper of Chicago, Low of Columbia, Thomas of Bryn Mawr, and their mighty fellows. The professors largely succeeded in their campaigns to cut down the stature of presidents, and then after the First World War complaints began to be heard that the character and capacity of presidents had deteriorated. One editorial writer in a widely read magazine even went so far as to say that weaklings chiefly held presidential posts and that their small-visioned leadership had led to "the decay of the intellectual life of the nation." In the same vein another non-academic critic last August published this bitter verse in the *American Mercury* entitled "Last words of a college president":

> I walked and sat erect for thirty years,
> A proud merchant of correct ideas,
> Cold gladness and unsullied decorum,
> I fashioned cautious men without souls
> And brittle women with measured passion.
> Behold a traitor
> To his Creator.

This is pushing criticism to its ultimate, but even such unreasonable blasts will almost certainly grow in number until we face the clear fact that college presidents are expected to be and to do too many things. No one has the capacity to be so able, so energetic, and so versatile. We must promptly quit thinking that they should even try to be such paragons, and we must give attention to the question of what they should be in terms of what they *can* be.

What today can a college president reasonably be expected to be? I suggest that he should be three things—three and no more—and that he can be these things only if he is not expected to spread himself thin in other directions. These three things are: first, an organizer; second, a coordinator; and third, an educational philosopher.

I shall discuss each of these abilities in turn, but may I first point out that I have not included an ability which most college presidents and most students of educational administration, as well as most trustees and faculty members, put first, that is, executive ability. Indeed, I am asserting that a college president should *not* be an executive. This is such strange doctrine that I must explain myself.

An executive is a doer, and I am declaring that a college president should not do most of the things that he now does. His doing should be limited to organizing, coordinating, and seeking to understand the place in society of his institution. These responsibilities are so crucially important that he cannot give attention to the myriads of details that now clutter the typical college president's desk and take up most of the hours of his days and his nights.

Let me illustrate what I mean by recalling an experience I had just after I graduated from college a quarter of a century ago. The father of one of my classmates was the president of one of the country's larger corporations, and he invited me to come to his office about a possible position in his organization. By appointment I arrived at nine-thirty on a Monday morning; and I remember how on the way to his office I thought that at the beginning of a busy week such an important businessman would probably be able to give me only two or three minutes of his time. He surprised me, however, by giving me an hour and a half during which not a paper lay upon his desk or crossed it, not a single telephone call came in, and not once did his secretary disturb us. As we talked, I grew more and more interested in what seemed to me to be a strange situation; and when the interview ended, I asked if I might put to him a question that had been developing in my mind while we talked.

The question was this: "How is it, Mr. Du Bois, that at the beginning of a week you have so little to do that you can give me an hour and a half of your time, time which must have cost your company, at your salary, at least a hundred dollars?" I pointed to the fact that his desk had remained totally bare during the entire period, that his phone had not rung once, and that his secretary had not come near him.

My question interested him, and he took another fifteen minutes to answer it. His chief point was this: he considered it his job not to be a doer but rather the organizer, planner, and philosopher of the company. I remember him saying, "You can hire executives or doers by the hundreds, but only the head of the business can see the organization as a whole. Only the president has all the facts necessary to plan for the future. If he wastes his time on routines, he loses his opportunity for rangy understanding of what the company ought to be doing and how it should go about doing it."

He took me over to a case of charts at one side of his office and showed graphs into the future that he spent a good deal of his time working on, and then he opened a drawer of his as-yet-unsullied desk and brought out manuscripts of proposals he was preparing for the discussion of his vice presidents and his board of directors. He ended by suggesting that if ever I became an executive I should never do any routine job that I could get someone else to do, that I should concentrate on thinking through the basic problems of the enterprise and planning for the future.

That incident of twenty-five years ago had not a little to do with my resigning my college presidency twenty years later. I discovered that no one in my institution had any such conception of a college presidency. Everyone expected me to be involved in the details of the institution, to see them whenever they wanted to be seen, to attend innumerable committee meetings, to introduce every visiting speaker, to greet every returning alumnus and, to boot, to entertain all faculty members and their wives at lunch or dinner at least once a year.

Most college presidents continue to live this kind of a harried, routine-full life with the result that they are always hurried, always weary, always short of time to do the crucial business which they alone can do, that is, to organize, to coordinate, and to carry forward the institution to new intellectual and social fronts.

Fortunately, some administrators have been able to persuade their boards and their faculties that they should have personal assistants of high competence, administrative or executive vice presidents, and a full complement of administrative officers to handle routines. These men—and as yet their numbers are few— are able to handle their positions properly and to put their energies where they ought to be put. The rest comment upon their lives as do the two men whose letters I have quoted.

A college president, I am asserting, should not be a routinist; and he can avoid routine only by being the first of the three things that I have listed, to wit, an organizer. You may remark that organizing constitutes a preeminent kind of executive ability, and you would be right. The point that I would stress, however, is that setting up a plan of operations does not involve being engrossed in the detailed functioning of the plan. In general college presidents are expected not only to plan the organizational structure of the institution, but also to be functionaries carrying innumerable routines. These housekeeping duties I would rule out as completely as possible. I would set up the ideal that President Du Bois of the Western Electric Company described to me in that interview in 1924, an ideal, by the way, that I have found honored by most of the higher business executives that I have since come to know.

What does being an organizer mean? Two things preeminently, I suggest: building and perfecting, first, an organizational structure; and second, a system of communications. In other words, an organizer must establish the procedures that make it possible for people to work together in effective cooperation: and he must also establish methods for the exchange of ideas both within the organization and with those associated with the organization.

Let me give an illustration of what a president not overladen with executive responsibilities can do as a planner. Until a few years ago it took the students of a well-known university five or six hours to register at the beginning of each term, and they spent those boresome, line-standing hours sneering at their Alma Mater's inefficiency. A new president decided to put an end to such stupidity and bad blood. He studied the problem carefully, and after experimenting for two or three terms he reduced the time required to fifteen minutes. I submit that if the president in question had allowed himself to get bogged down in details, he would not have been able to achieve the vast saving of student time and tempers that his planning made possible. To be a planner, I repeat, is a major responsibility of a college president, a responsibility which he can neglect only at great risk to the well-being of his institution. Such planning, I shall point out in a few minutes, should not be limited to material considerations, but of that in due course. Here I emphasize planning university administrative machinery.

The other day I had an experience illustrating the importance of the second element of sound organization, that is, a good system of internal communications. I was driving about the campus of a large university with a full professor and with a second-line administrator of the institution. Several new buildings were being erected, but neither of my companions knew anything about them except their names. They had heard some gossip about the new buildings, but they knew nothing authoritatively or of any importance. I commented on their ignorance, and they replied to the effect that the central administration never took the trouble to tell anyone anything, that the president and his immediate associates treated the faculty and most of the administrative staff as mere employees who didn't need to be informed of what was going on. I asked if that didn't mean that the morale of the institution was low, and they replied, "Of course."

This situation isn't unusual in the colleges and universities of the United States. By and large academic administrators haven't yet learned the crucial significance in staff morale of good systems of internal communications, and the result is that antagonisms born of ignorance exist much more frequently in academic communities than in any other social enterprise of which I know. Obviously this ruins cooperation and good will. Many presidents know that it does; but, snowed under with details of administrative mingle-mangle, they neglect their communications. The college president who spends his time fussing with papers on his desk and who neglects to develop his communications gambles with both his own career and with the destinies of his institution.

The second function that I have listed is coordination. Planning is a type of coordination, but here I am discussing the coordination of ideas and of the people who hold them. The proper word for this kind of coordination is politics, but most people think of politics as an underhanded manipulation and double-dealing, and so in the describing of the essential duties of the college president I use the word coordination. But I mean politics, that is getting people to work together, compromising opposing ideas, persuading recalcitrants to come to a middle ground, negotiating differences of opinion; in sum, coordinating the energies of a people.

One of the best definitions of a college president that I know of is this: he is a man who makes compromises—for a living. The writer of the definition made it in derogation, but it's really a high compliment even though those who habitually insist upon having all or nothing sneer at the compromiser. To these men I quote Edmund Burke's statement in his famous speech recommending that the British Crown work out the differences with the colonies rather than seek to discipline them:

All government—indeed, every human benefit and enjoyment, every virtue and every prudent act—is founded on compromise and barter.

If you don't like the word compromise, then employ the euphemism consultation or the euphemism negotiation. All that I am saying is that the well-advised college president gives a good deal of his time to bringing opposing points of view together and that he cannot do this if he is saddled with administrative minutia. Working out compromises requires leisure, that is, plenty of time for turning over in one's mind many courses of action and choosing the one that best fits the situation in hand. Harassed men never make good compromisers. They are too busy to get the illuminations, the hunches, that point roads out of difficulties.

In my judgment the college president needs more time to work on his political problems than any other administrator of whom I can think in American life. This is true because the college president administers an institution permanently peopled by one of the most difficult kinds of human beings extant today. I mean the college professor. The professor is the individualist *par excellence,* perhaps even more individualistic than operatic prima donnas. And the more gifted he is as a scholar or scientist, the more the individualist he is likely to be.

Consider the psychology of the professor. He is the master of a sector of knowledge, and he is not used to being questioned about his field of competence. Yet he is so completely specialized that he seldom sees his specialty in broad perspective. He is too busy digging deep to look very often at the horizon. He has his experiment to finish, his article to publish, his book to write. He lives in an important world, but it is usually a very small and specialized world. He does not have time for educational thinking in the broad, and thus whatever he may be in politics he is usually a conservative in education who doesn't like to be disturbed by new educational ideas. As one commentator put it a few years ago, "every educational improvement in the history of American higher education has been accomplished over the dead bodies of countless professors." And this is not seriously overstating the historical facts. A nineteenth century German philosopher who knew professors well defined a professor as "a man who thinks otherwise." Certainly in educational matters this defines him almost perfectly.

Presidents who have ideas about education are therefore usually highly unpopular with professors, and thus today most presidents avoid educational discussions and stick to administrative routines. Yet I am proposing that through political skill presidents must rise above the limitations that professors would put upon him. And the political skill required here is of the highest order as will become obvious, I think, when I review the campaign waged beginning forty years ago against presidents being educators as well as administrators.

The movement began about 1909 under the leadership of a professor of psychology at Columbia University, the late James McKeen Cattell. Cattell was the editor of several important learned journals including *Science*, and for a number of years he conducted a vigorous and even vicious campaign against college presidents having anything to do with educational policy. He even went so far as to advocate the abolition of the office and also the abolition of boards of trustees. He wanted professors to have all the authority with no check from anyone.

Cattell's father had been President of Lafayette College, and I suppose that the psychoanalysts would explain his antagonism for college presidents by insisting that he must have hated his father. In any event, the story is told that when one day Cattell's young daughter asked him what to call her new rag doll, he proposed the name "President." "Why?" queried his daughter. "Because," responded Cattell, "rag dolls and college presidents have a lot in common. For example, either will lie naturally in any position."

Obviously, a college president cannot negotiate easily with professors who think as Cattell did. Nor can he get on happily with professors like the distinguished University of Chicago scientist who is reported to have walked by President Judson's home "each evening so that he could spit on that gentleman's sidewalk." President Judson's current successor, Robert Maynard Hutchins, has had even worse experiences; and he recently observed that "academic communities, whatever their protestations to the contrary, really prefer anarchy to any form of government." Sometimes it is hard not to agree with him.

Only those presidents can get on with their faculties who either have no educational programs worthy of the name or who are skilled politicians in the sense of being able in counsel and brilliant in compromise. In a recent article in *Life* Professor

Arthur M. Schlesinger of Harvard reported that every one of the six presidents of the nation considered by historians to be the greatest in our history were men with positive ideas about the directions the country should take, but they were also and paramountly skilled political negotiators or compromisers.

Professor Schlesinger first emphasizes the point that I have been stressing about the relative unimportance of presidents being good executives, and he writes that "as administrators, the six great presidents did not distinguish themselves." Then he goes on to describe their skill in compromising:

> They had to work experimentally within the framework of the democratic tradition. . . . Political considerations permitted them to be idealists if they liked, but not doctrinaires. "What is practical must often control what is pure theory," wrote Jefferson, the political theorist. As James Russell Lowell put it in his essay on Lincoln, the ultimate test of statesmanship is not a "conscientious persistency in what is impractical" but rather, "loyalty to ends, even though forced to combine the small and opposing methods of selfish men to accomplish them."

In other words, the president with an educational program must be a master in negotiations, a skilled compromiser, a brilliant politician in the best sense of that abused word. He must also be able to take abundant criticisms without serious psychic damage; and the more positive his program, the more numerous and bitter will be the criticism from those whose comfortable arrangements he upsets. On this score Professor Schlesinger has also written pointedly:

> Strong leaders arouse strong opposition. . . . Even the comparatively sacrosanct Washington was not immune. As he remarked, he was assailed "in such exaggerated and indecent terms as could scarcely be applied to a Nero, a notorious defaulter or even to a common pickpocket." When he retired an opposition paper rejoiced that "the man who is the source of all the misfortunes of our country . . . is no longer possessed of power to multiply evils upon the U.S."

Your efforts as a compromiser, President Wiggins, will of course not be limited to the faculty. You will also need to use your political abilities with the alumni and also with your Board of Directors. You will often be impatient with them both, and you will perhaps sometimes find comfort in the knowledge that other presidents have had their troubles with both groups. If you are inclined, now and then, to recall General Goethals' remark that "all boards are long, narrow, and wooden," take comfort in the thought that board members and alumni aren't around very often.

We come now to the final and most important of the functions of a college president—being an educational philosopher. By this I do not of course mean theoretical dreaming. Rather I mean formulating and defining institutional purposes, and I would recall again my interview with the President of the Western Electric Company and his statement that he considered his chief responsibility to be philosophizing, that is, seeing the work of his company as a whole and plotting the course to be followed into the future. This, and not a dreamer, is what I mean by a philosopher; and I suggest that if business needs such philosophers, education needs them even more.

A business corporation produces goods and services for the well-being of society, but a college has considerably more important work. It exists for the discovery of new knowledge, for the interpretation of that knowledge in the lives of peoples, and for forming the minds and the moral standards of the rising generation. If business corporations need philosophers at their helms, then colleges and universities need them infinitely more.

Being an educational philosopher means working on *educational* problems. These are the core questions of colleges and universities; and even at the risk of faculty disapproval and opposition, college presidents must wrestle with educational questions. Organizational structures, systems of communication, political negotiations are only means to the end of education. Hence college presidents must be educators primarily; to be an educator means to be an educational philosopher.

Unfortunately most college presidents seem to have forgotten this; and if they haven't forgotten it, they have allowed themselves to be frightened away from their main jobs by opposition or to become so burdened with routines and machinery that they have little if any time to think about what the routines and the machinery are for. Thus while colleges and universities grow in the numbers of their students, in the sizes of their budgets, and in the grandeur of their plants, most of them lack direction.

They recall the cartoon, described by President Hopkins of Dartmouth at my inaugural luncheon, of two motorcyclists speeding down a road. One turned to the other and said, "I think we've lost the way." "Never mind," said the other, "we're making such good time, let's keep right on."

President Wiggins, I am declaring to you that beyond doubt the cardinal, the paramount, the most insistent part of your job is being an educational philosopher, that is, the man who should be continuously interpreting the educational directions of this institution. If Texas Technological College is to have a large social aim, then you must discover and state it. You alone will be seeing the institution as a whole. Professors are specialists who see only their small though important sectors, and the same is true of second-line administrators. Your board of directors will have ideas, but they are busy men in other walks of life. Only you will see the complete institution. Only you will have all the facts necessary for developing the pattern of the college.

To drive home this point, let me quote from a little book that President A. Lawrence Lowell of Harvard wrote a few years after he retired from the presidency of Harvard in 1933. It is entitled, *What a University President Has Learned*, and I recommend, President Wiggins, that you own it and read it periodically. The passage I would have you think about now reads as follows:

> For distinguishing the essential elements of a plan from accessories, for perceiving the differences between the whole of a part and a part of the whole, the benefit of a pattern . . . is great. Such a pattern is by no means rigid; the final objective is perfectly definite, but the details are fluid and must be kept so throughout. . . . With a pattern of this kind it is comparatively easy to discern quickly the value of any proposal made; for one has not to consider it by itself as a distinct thing on its own merits alone, but in its relations to the whole, whether it fits or can be made to fit into the pattern.

The pattern that President Lowell has written about is not a pattern of buildings and administration machinery. It is a pattern of *education*. It is a pattern which defines the purposes of education first, and only after the purposes of education have been defined does it move on to the means necessary for the accomplishment of those purposes.

It must be obvious to you that by a philosopher I do not mean a man of theory living in an ivory tower. Instead I mean a very practical man living in the midst of buzzing activity who seeks to make directions clear. Such a practical philosopher above all things needs leisure: leisure to talk with many people, leisure to read the thoughts of our best minds living and dead, leisure to think calmly and deeply.

College presidents are called the leaders of their institutions, and undoubtedly during these ceremonies President Wiggins will frequently be referred to as the leader of Texas Technological College. May it be so, but it cannot be so unless he develops a pattern, an educational philosophy. A leader is a man who is going somewhere and who had the ability to persuade people to follow him. Not to have a pattern, a plan, or philosophy is to be lost on a stormy sea without a chart or a rudder.

President Wiggins, I have been attempting to answer the question, "What should a college president be?" and I have suggested that he should be three things preeminently: an organizer, a coordinator of men and their ideas, and chiefly an educational philosopher. To be these things, I have urged, he must not permit himself to be a routinist swamped in executive trivia. These he must assign to others and give his energies to the large and long-range development of his institution. Today you enter officially upon the presidency of a very young but potentially great institution. You begin in troublous times, in times of great world-wide perplexity and fear. Each of us must make his contributions to the making of a better world; and you are in a strategic position, in a strategic state, and in a strategic nation. You have a tremendous opportunity, and when in some distant year you lay down the burdens of office, may it be said of you: "Wiggins was no flagpole sitter. Not he. He dreamed dreams, and he had the ability to make them into realities because he knew how to organize the work of the college and to deal happily with people. He knew what a college president should be and he turned his knowledge into brilliant fact." Power to you, President Wiggins!

UNIVERSITY ASSEMBLY [9]

HAROLD W. STOKE [10]

President Harold W. Stoke, of the State University of Louisiana, gave this address at a University Assembly Meeting, at the Agricultural Auditorium, at 4:15 P.M. on Monday, September 19, 1949.

The speech is a sort of "state of the Union" applied to the Louisiana campus. In the beginning the President reports on the physical state of the campus and refers to faculty changes. He, for example, introduces the new deans—Dean C. G. Taylor of the College of Liberal Arts, Henry George McMahon of the Law School, and Dr. William W. Frye of the Medical School. The speech throughout is personal, interesting, and intellectually stimulating.

Concerning his speech experiences and methods of preparation, he states, "I did some debating in college, but suspect that such public speaking as I am capable of doing was learned for the most part as teacher, talking to large lecture sections of classes in government.

"In preparing speeches, I generally try to decide as clearly as possible just what it is I am trying to say. I then try to make it as simple as possible, keeping in mind the fact that an audience usually has no intrinsic interest in what I am about to say unless I can create that interest in them." [11]

I am told that one of the fascinations of golf is the opportunity it gives to begin anew at every tee, that no matter how dissatisfied we were with our last score, the next hole will surely be made in par. This is no less true in opening a new school year. We now stand at the tee.

Many of you have continued to work steadily through the summer and to you I extend deep sympathy. Some others have been fortunate enough to have had vacations, study, travel or other interesting variations. A larger number than usual are completing sabbatical leaves of absence. We have missed you while you were gone and we are very happy to welcome you back. We shall all profit vicariously from your experiences. . . .

The operation of a university, especially of a state university

---

[9] Text and permission for this reprint furnished through the courtesy of President Harold W. Stoke.
[10] For biographical note, see Appendix.
[11] Letter to this editor, April 21, 1950.

is conditioned very largely by the atmosphere prevailing in the society in which it exists. It shares in the prevailing prosperity or stringency. Even more, it shares in the prevailing climate of ideas, of preoccupations. If a nation is at war, its universities are at war. If a nation is unhappy, if it is suffering some disillusionment and uncertainty, its universities will reflect that fact. I do not mean to say that as a university we have no independence of life and mind but that the life and mind we have will be powerfully shaped by the dominant interests of our society.

Perhaps the most difficult period for a university is when there *is* no strong and dominant force to give it direction and to shape its activities. When the prevailing interests of a society are patriotic, religious, scientific, or revolutionary, the universities have missions that are clear and convincing, resolving our doubts and channeling our energies. But what happens when we do not have such compulsions, when we must rely upon our own philosophies and resources to give meaning and value to our work?

This is currently our situation. The clear and present compulsions of war under which we have worked so long have passed. The bustling excitements of postwar accommodations, with their subtle flattery as to our usefulness and indispensability, have passed their peak. Our ship is entering quieter waters. As a crew we have become conditioned to storms. Have we lost our skill in more precise navigation?

This year our enrollment is less than that of a year ago. Our opportunity to examine our work, to redirect our time and energy, to reach decisions as to the value of some of our activities is something we have looked forward to. Next year our entering class will again be large. Our chance to achieve perspective this year is unique.

A few years ago, on a visit to London, I was invited to tea by Mr. Charles Galton, the long-time secretary of the Fabian Society. He told me many amusing stories of the early Fabian days, of Graham Wallas, George Bernard Shaw, the Webbs and many others. Among these stories was one of H. G. Wells. When Wells first started his journalistic career, he became very much interested in the achievements of a certain headmaster of

one of England's most famous public schools. Beatrice and Sidney
Webb had become interested in young Wells and decided to
help him with his career by inviting him to their home, a center
where many great and near-great gathered. They asked Wells
whom they might invite who might be of interest to him. He
had become very much interested in the achievements of a certain
headmaster in one of England's most famous public schools, and
he promptly named this great schoolmaster. The evening came
and so did the educator, but the results were sad. The schoolmaster seized the floor and held it. He pontificated and solio-
quized. He was opinionated and stuffy. Wells' hero-worship
visibly evaporated.

"Wells wrote many books after that," Galton chuckled, "and
in them he turned to the engineer, the statesman, the scientist
and even the military as the future hope of society. But never
in all of his later works could he bring himself to turn again to
the schools as the source of social salvation."

I have pondered that story many times searching for solid
ground for refuting or affirming Wells' opinion. Whether justified or not, more millions are turning to the schools as the future
hope of society than have ever turned to them before. In the
words of Robert Hutchins, words with the solemn overtones of
a Jeremiah, "Education may not save us, but it is the only hope
we have."

These are portentous words. It is more than a little appalling
if the world has no hope save education and we are the trustees
of that hope. Our society looks upon the universities now as
something more than mere places of formal teaching and learning. We are that, yes, but we are more. We are now part of a
social system, a part of a method by which that system solves
its problem of unemployment, rewards its warriors, improves its
technological development, bolsters up the pillars of national
sentiment and is even an important factor in redistributing the
national income. Never have the schools played the role in
national life which they are playing today, and their part in the
future will be greater if we play it well.

Our students, too, are at the stage in their own lives where
they need us most. If we have asked ourselves at what period

of human life are aspirations highest and beliefs most idealistic, I think we should say it is at the college age. It is then that the unrealism of childhood has been corrected, but the discouragements and disillusionments which come from the revelations of self-limitations and from the discovery of the depths of social resistence are not yet dominant. It is a period in which energy needs channels, ambition needs worthy objectives, idealism needs faith. These things it is our opportunity and obligation as teachers to provide. I am convinced that our students will respond to far more exacting challenges than we have yet asked them to meet.

Nor does our intellectual responsibility as a university stop with what we can do for our students. Did you ever stop to think that each of us today can no longer be adequately described by the term "teacher." Rather we are called historians, psychologists, chemists, political scientists, biologists and by these very designations the world is informed that we are not only teachers but trustees for important bodies of knowledge upon which our society depends. Where shall our hungry, yearning society turn if not to us for its answers? Where, more logically, than to the universities, operating in atmospheres of thoughtfulness and detachment, shall the world look for the formulation of the satisfying ethical principles it needs so badly, for fresh insight into human nature, for its new canons of social justice, for its knowledge of nature and of art? The burden of expectation which each of us bears upon his shoulders today is enormous. I hope that by the end of the year each of us may honestly say that we have met, at least in part, that expectation. I am sure I can wish for each of you nothing more satisfying.

APPENDIX

BIOGRAPHICAL NOTES [1]

ACHESON, DEAN G. (1893-   ). Born in Middleton, Connecticut; B.A., Yale, 1915; LL.B., Harvard, 1918; honorary M.A., Yale, 1936; honorary LL.D., Wesleyan, 1947; private secretary to Louis D. Brandeis, 1919-21; practiced law, 1921-33; Under Secretary of Treasury (resigned), 1933; practiced law, 1934-41; Assistant Secretary of State, 1941-45; Under Secretary of State, 1945-47; practiced law, 1947-48; Secretary of State since January 1949; Ensign, U.S. Navy, World War I; member, Delta Kappa Epsilon, Scroll and Key. (See also *Current Biography: 1949.*)

BRADLEY, OMAR NELSON (1893-   ). Born, Clark, Missouri; B.S., United States Military Academy, 1915; Command and General Staff School, 1929; Army War College, 1934; honorary LL.D., University of Missouri, Drury College, Harvard, Dartmouth, Princeton, and many other colleges and universities; commander, 2nd lieutenant, infantry, U.S. Army, 1915, advanced through the grades to general, 1945; in Tunis, Sicily, Normandy, France, Germany campaigns, 1944-45; administrator, veteran's affairs, 1945-47; chief of staff of U.S. Army, 1948-49; chairman, Army-Navy-Air Force Joint Chiefs of Staff since August 1949; awarded many military honors and decorations. (See also *Current Biography: 1943.*)

BUNCHE, RALPH JOHNSON (1904-   ). Born in Detroit, Michigan; A.B., University of California, 1927; A.M., Harvard University, 1928, Ph.D., 1934; post-doctoral studies in anthropology and colonial policy, Northwestern University, London School of Economics, and University of Capetown, South Africa,

---

[1] The chief sources of these notes are *Who's Who in America, Current Biography, Religious Leaders in America, Who's Who in American Education, Directory of American Scholars,* and the *Congressional Directory.*

1936-37; Rosenwald Fellowship, Europe and Africa, 1931-32; Social Science Research Council Fellowship, 1936-38; on Carnegie Corporation's Survey of Negro in America, Southern United States, 1939; assistant, political science department, University of California, 1925-27; teacher of political science, Howard University, since 1928 (head of department since 1929); senior social science analyst in charge of research on Africa and other colonial areas, Office of Strategic Services, 1941-44; territorial specialist, division of territorial studies, Department of State, 1944-45; adviser, United States delegation Dunbarton Oaks, 1944; adviser, other United States Delegations connected with the United Nations; director, Department of Trusteeship, United Nations, since 1946; on United Nations Palestine Commission, 1948; personal representative of Secretary General with the United Nations mediator on Palestine, 1948; acting United Nations Mediator on Palestine since 1948. (See also *Current Biography: 1948.*)

COWLEY, WILLIAM HAROLD (1899-   ). Born at Petersburg, Virginia; A.B., Dartmouth College, 1924; Ph.D., University of Chicago, 1930; honorary degrees, including LL.D., Hamilton, 1938, L.H.D., Hobart, 1939, Litt.D., Union College, 1940; with New York business corporations, 1913-18; Bell Telephone Laboratories, 1924-25; University of Chicago, 1927-29; research associate and assistant professor of psychology, Bureau of Educational Research, Ohio State University, 1929-34; associate professor, 1934-35; professor, 1935-38; president of Hamilton College, 1938-44; professor of higher education, Stanford University since 1945; member, Phi Beta Kappa; contributor of articles to magazines and journals.

DENNY, GEORGE VERNON, JR. (1899-   ). Born in Washington, North Carolina; B.S., University of North Carolina, 1922; LL.D., Temple University, 1940; instructor in dramatic production, University of North Carolina, 1924-26; actor, 1926-27; manager of W. B. Feakins, Inc., 1927-28; director, Institute of Arts and Sciences, Columbia University, 1928-30; associate director, League of Political Education, 1931-37; founder and director, America's Town Meeting of the Air; president of

Town Hall, Inc., since 1937; treasurer, Economic Club of New York; member of executive board, American Association for Adult Education; served Students' Army Training Corps, 1918. (See also *Current Biogaphy: 1940*.)

DEWEY, THOMAS EDMUND (1902-   ). Born in Owosso, Michigan; A.B., University of Michigan, 1923, LL.M., 1937; LL.B., Columbia University, 1925; honorary degrees at Tufts, Dartmouth, and other institutions; admitted to New York bar, 1926; chief assistant, United States Attorney, 1931-33; special prosecutor, Investigation of Organized Crime, New York City, 1935-37; elected District Attorney, New York County, 1937; Republican Governor of New York since 1942; defeated as candidate for the presidency, Republican ticket, November 1944 and 1948; author, *The Case Against the New Deal*, 1940. (See also *Current Biography: 1944*.)

DULLES, JOHN FOSTER (1888-   ). Born in Washington, D.C.; B.A., Princeton, 1908, LL.D., 1946; Sorbonne, Paris, 1908-09; LL.B., George Washington University, 1911; LL.D., Tufts, Wagner, Northwestern and other colleges; began law practice, New York City, 1911; director, Bank of New York; trustee, Rockefeller Foundation; chairman, Carnegie Endowment for International Peace; chairman, Federal Council of Churches Commission on a Just and Durable Peace; secretary, The Hague Peace Conference, 1907; captain and major, United States Army, 1917-18; counsel, American Commission to Negotiate Peace, 1918-19; member, Reparations Commission and Supreme Economic Council, 1919; member, United States delegation, San Francisco Conference on World Organization, 1945; Council of Foreign Ministers, London, 1945; General Assembly, United Nations, 1946; Meeting of Council of Foreign Ministers, Moscow, 1947; London meeting of "Big Four," 1947; United States Senator from New York, appointed July 1949 (to complete term of Senator Wagner); defeated by Herbert Lehman, November 1949, for election as United States Senator; appointed counsellor, Department of State, April 1950; Phi Beta Kappa; writer and speaker on international affairs. (See also *Current Biography: 1944*.)

EINSTEIN, ALBERT (1879-   ). Born at Donau, Germany; educated at Luitpold Gymnasium (Munich), Aarauer Kantons-schule (Switzerland); Technische Hochschule (Zurich); Doctor, *honoris causa*, Geneva, Oxford, Cambridge, Paris, Princeton, Harvard, London, Brussels, and elsewhere; Professor at Universitat Zurich, Preuss. Akademie d. Wissenschaft (Berlin); came to United States in 1933, became citizen, 1940; appointed life member of Institute for Advanced Study, Princeton, N.J., 1933; discoverer and exponent of the theory of relativity; Nobel Prize, 1922; author, *Meaning of Relativity*, 1923; (with others) *Living Philosophies*, 1931; *On the Method of Theoretical Physics*, 1933; *The World As I See It*, 1934; also other books, brochures and magazine articles. (See also *Current Biography: 1941.*)

EISENHOWER, DWIGHT DAVID (1890-   ). Born in Denison, Texas; B.S., United States Military Academy, 1915; Army Tank School, 1921; graduate, War College, 1929; 2nd Lieutenant, U. S. Army, 1915; Lt. Colonel, Tank Corps, World War I; advanced through grades to General of the Army, December 1944; Chief of Operations Division, Office of Chief of Staff, 1942; Commanding General, European Theatre of Operations, June 1942; Allied Commander in Chief, North Africa, November 1942; Supreme Commander of Allied land, sea, and air forces in Western Europe, November 1943; Chief of Staff, United States Army, 1945-48; elected President of Columbia University, 1948; author of *Eisenhower Speaks*, 1948; *Crusade in Europe*, 1948. (See also *Current Biography: 1948.*)

FAIRLESS, BENJAMIN F. (1890-   ). Born at Pigeon Run, Ohio; student, Wooster College; graduated in civil engineering, Ohio Northern University, 1913; honorary D.Sc., Kent State University, University of Pittsburgh; D.Eng., Ohio Northern, Stevens Institute; civil engineer, Wheeling and Lake Erie Railroad, 1913; with Central Steel Company, successively civil engineer, mill superintendent, general superintendent, vice president in charge of operations, 1913-26; vice president and general manager, United Alloy Steel, 1926-28; president and general manager, 1928-30; executive vice president, Republic Steel Corporation, 1930-35; president Carnegie Illinois Steel Corporation, 1935-37; president and director, United States Steel Corporation since 1938.

JOHNSON, LOUIS ARTHUR (1891-   ). Born in Roanoke, Virginia; LL.B., University of Virginia, 1912; LL.D., Salem College, 1938, Kenyon College, 1939; began practice of law, Clarksburg, West Virginia, 1912; director, various banks, Consolidated Vultee Aircraft Corporation, and other corporations; Secretary of Defense, Washington, D.C., since March 1949; member, Federal Advisory Council, United States Employment Service; Assistant Secretary of War, 1937-40; Captain, infantry overseas, First World War; decorated Commander, Legion of Honor (France); National Commander, American Legion, 1932-33; Chairman, National Finance Committee, Democratic National Committee; member Delta Chi, Delta Sigma Rho, Tau Kappa Alpha. (See also *Current Biography: 1949*.)

KALTENBORN, HANS V. (1878-   ). Born in Milwaukee, Wisconsin; A.B., cum laude, Harvard, 1909; reporter, Brooklyn *Eagle*, 1902-05, dramatic editor, editorial writer, assistant managing editor, associate editor, 1910-30; radio news analyst since 1922; news editor of the Columbia Broadcasting System, 1929-40; with the National Broadcasting Company since 1940; radio reporter, Republican and Democratic Conventions, summer, 1932, London Economic Conference, summer, 1933, League of Nations, Geneva, 1935; author of *We Look at the World*, 1930, *I Broadcast the Crisis*, 1938. (See also *Current Biography: 1940*.)

KLINE, ALLAN BLAIR (1895-   ). Born at Waterbury, Nebraska; A.B., Morningside College, Iowa, 1915; B.S., Iowa State College, 1936; farm operator, Iowa, 1920-44; president, Iowa Life Insurance Company, (1945-47), Iowa Farm Mutual Insurance Company (1944), Iowa Farm Serum Company (1944-47), Iowa Plant Food Company (1945-47), Benton County Farm Bureau (1928-37), Iowa Farm Bureau (1944-47); president, American Farm Bureau, since 1947; director, Federal Reserve Bank of Chicago; sergeant, medical corps, World War I;

member, National Planning Board and various other economic and agricultural councils or commissions. (See also *Current Biography: 1948.*)

McBURNEY, JAMES HOWARD (1905-   ). Born in Tyndall, South Dakota; Yankton College, 1925; A.M., University of South Dakota, 1929; Ph.D., University of Michigan, 1935; student, Columbia, 1935-36; instructor in speech, Norfolk (Nebraska) High School, 1925-26, Fremont, Nebraska, 1926-27, East High, Sioux City, Iowa, 1927-28; University of South Dakota, 1928-29, University of Michigan, 1929-35; assistant professor, Columbia, 1936; associate professor of speech, Northwestern University, 1936-41, professor, 1941-42, professor and dean of school of speech since 1942; moderator, Northwestern University Reviewing Stand, Mutual Broadcasting System; president, Speech Association of America, 1949; member of Phi Beta Kappa, Delta Sigma Rho; author, *The Working Principles of Argument* (with J. M. O'Neill), 1932; *The Principles and Methods of Discussion* (with K. G. Hance), 1938; *Foundations of Speech* (with others), 1941; *Speech: A High School Course* (with Lew Sarett and W. T. Foster), 1943; *Discussion in Human Affairs* (with K. G. Hance), 1950.

McMAHON, BRIEN (1903-   ). Born in Norwalk, Connecticut; A.B., Fordham University, 1924; LL.D., 1946; LL.B., Yale, 1927; practiced law, Norwalk, Connecticut, since 1927; Assistant United States Attorney General, in charge of Criminal Division, 1936; elected U. S. Senator from Connecticut, November 1944 for term expiring January 1951; author, *McMahon Act for Control of Atomic Energy*; chairman, Special Committee on Atomic Energy, U. S. Senate, 1945-47; chairman, Joint Congressional Committee on Atomic Energy, since 1948. (See also *Current Biography: 1945.*)

MEDINA, HAROLD R. (1888-   ). Born in Brooklyn, New York; A.B., Princeton University, 1909; LL.B., Columbia University, 1912; honorary LL.D., St. Johns, 1947; with Davies, Auerbach, and Cornell law firm, 1912-18; senior member of law firm, Medina and Sherpick, 1918-47; lecturer in law, Columbia

University, 1915-17, associate in law, 1917-25, associate professor of law, 1925-47; Judge, U. S. District Court, Southern District of New York, since July 1, 1947; presided in New York City over trial of eleven Communists, January-October, 1949; served on many legal commissions and committees; Phi Beta Kappa; author, *Pleading and Practice Under New Civil Practice Act*, 1922; (with Carr and Finn) *Civil Practice Manual*, 1936-42; and other legal books; contributor to legal reviews. (See also *Current Biography: 1949*.)

MURRAY, PHILIP (1886-   ). Born in Blantyre, Scotland; came to the United States, 1902, naturalized, 1911; member, International Board of United Mine Workers of America, 1912, international vice president, 1926-42; president of Congress of Industrial Organizations since 1940; president of United Steel workers since 1942; member of numerous governmental commissions related to labor problems. (See also *Current Biography: 1949*.)

POWELL, ADAM CLAYTON, JR. (1908-   ). Born in New Haven, Connecticut; A.B., Colgate, 1930; M.A., Columbia, 1932; LL.D., Virginia Union University, 1947; Minister, Abyssinian Baptist Church, New York City, since 1937; first Negro elected to City Council of New York, 1941; elected to Congress, November 1945; member of 79th-80th-81st Congress (1945-51), 22nd New York District; chairman board of directors, Powell-Buchanan Publishing Corporation; author: *Is This a White Man's War?* 1942; *Stage Door Canteen*, 1944; *Marching Blacks*, 1945. (See also *Current Biography: 1942*.)

REUTHER, WALTER PHILIP (1907-   ). Born in Wheeling, West Virginia; apprentice tool and diemaker, Wheeling; employee, Briggs Manufacturing Company, Ford Motor Company (a foreman), Detroit; attended Wayne University for three years; traveler, by bicycle, through Germany, Russia, China, Japan; student of auto plants and machine shops, 1933-35; organized auto workers in Detroit, 1935; member of the executive board, International Union of Automobile Workers, 1936-46; vice president of the International Union, United Automobile, Aircraft and

Agricultural Workers of America of the Congress of Industrial Organizations, 1942-46, president, since March 1946; led General Motors strike, 1945-46; severely wounded by assailant, 1948. (See also *Current Biography: 1949*.)

RICE, GEORGE P., JR. (1911-   ). Born in Albany, New York; B.Sc., cum laude, State College, Albany, 1932, M.A., 1936; Ph.D., Cornell University, 1944; student at Cornell under Lane Cooper, Herbert Wichelns and Frederick G. Marcham; teacher of speech successively at Pennsylvania State, Cornell University, City College of New York, Columbia University, and professor of speech at Butler University, Indianapolis; educational director, National Foundation for Education in American Citizenship; contributor to *Quarterly Journal of Speech, Classical Journal, School and Society*, and other professional publications.

ROOSEVELT, JAMES (1907-   ). Born in New York; graduate of Groton School, 1926; A.B., Harvard, 1930; with Roosevelt and Sargent, Inc., Boston, insurance broker, 1930-38; removed to Los Angeles, California, and entered the motion picture industry, 1938-40; west coast representative of Roosevelt and Sargent after 1946; captain (later colonel) U. S. Marines, 1941-45; decorated, Navy Cross, Silver Star; candidate for Governor of California, 1950.

SIMS, HUGO SHERIDAN, JR. (1921-   ). Born, Orangeburg, South Carolina; A.B., Wofford College, South Carolina, 1941; LL.B., University of South Carolina, 1947; Editor, *The Times and Democrat*, Orangeburg, 1941-42; Columnist, *Editor's Copy*, newspaper syndicate, 1941-42; admitted to South Carolina State Bar, 1947; House of Representatives, State of South Carolina, 1947-48; member 81st Congress, 2nd District of South Carolina, 1949-51; entered Army, 1942, advanced from private to captain; Commander Company A, 501st Parachute Infantry, 101st Airborne Division overseas, 1944-45, awarded D.S.C., Silver star and citations from France, Belgium, and Netherlands; war service recorded in "The Incredible Patrol," *Life Magazine*, January 15, 1945. (See also *Current Biography: 1949*.)

STOKE, HAROLD W. (1903-   ). Born at Bosworth, Missouri; A.B., Marion (Indiana) College, 1924; M.A., University of Southern California, 1925; Ph.D., Johns Hopkins, 1930; associate professor of history and political science, Berea College, 1926-28; assistant, associate, and professor of political science, University of Nebraska, 1930-37; principal supervisor of training in public administration, Tennessee Valley Authority, lecturer in political science, University of Pennsylvania, 1937-39; dean of graduate school, University of Nebraska, 1939-40; professor of political science, University of Wisconsin, 1940-43; president, University of New Hampshire, 1944-47; president, Louisiana University since September 1947; consultant on military training, office of Provost Marshal General, 1943-44; member, Classification Committee Association of American Universities, 1940-44; author, *The Foreign Relations of the Federal State*, 1931; *The Background of European Governments* (with Norman L. Hill), 1935.

SYMINGTON, WILLIAM STUART (1901-   ). Born, Amherst, Massachusetts; served in United States army, 1918; at Yale, 1919-23; International Correspondence School; with Symington Companies, Rochester, N. Y., 1923-35; Rustless Iron and Steel Company, Baltimore, Md., 1935-37, President, Emerson Electric Manufacturing Company, St. Louis, Mo., 1938-45; surplus property administrator, Washington, 1945-46; Assistant Secretary of War for Air, 1946-47; Secretary of Air Force, National Defense 1947-50; chairman, National Security Resources Board, 1950. (See also *Current Biography: 1945*.)

TAFT, ROBERT ALPHONSO (1889-   ). Born in Cincinnati, Ohio; attended public schools of Cincinnati and the Taft School, Watertown, Connecticut; A.B., Yale University, 1910; LL.B., Harvard University, 1913; admitted to the bar, 1913; assistant counsel for the United States Food Administration, 1917-19; counsel for the American Relief Administration, 1919; Republican member of the Ohio House of Representatives, 1921-26, speaker, 1926; Ohio State Senate, 1931-32; United States Senate, since 1939; candidate for presidential nomination on Republican ticket, 1948. (See also *Current Biography: 1940, 1948*.)

TRUMAN, HARRY S. (1894-   ). Born in Lamar, Missouri; student, Kansas City School of Law, 1923-25; captain, Field Artillery, World War I; judge, Jackson County Court, 1922-24; presiding judge, 1926-34; United States Senator from Missouri, 1935-41, reelected for the term 1941-47; elected Vice President of the United States on the Democratic ticket, November 1944; sworn in as President on the death of President Roosevelt, April 1945; elected President in 1948. (See also *Current Biography: 1945*.)

UREY, HAROLD CLAYTON (1893-   ). Born, Walkerton, Indiana; B.S., University of Montana, 1917; Ph.D., University of California, 1923; at University of Copenhagen, 1923-24; D.Sc., Montana, Princeton, and other universities; chemist, Barret Chemical Company, Philadelphia, 1917-19; instructor in chemistry, University of Montana, 1919-21; associate in chemistry, Johns Hopkins, 1924-29; associate professor, chemistry, Columbia, 1929-34, professor, 1934-45; professor of chemistry, University of Chicago, since 1945; prominent in development of atomic bomb, World War II; member of many learned societies; author (with A. E. Ruark) of *Atoms, Molecules and Quanta*, 1930; editor, *Journal of Chemical Physics*, 1933-40; contributor to scientific journals; specialized in structure of atoms and molecules; discoverer of hydrogen atom of atomic weight two; awarded the Nobel prize in chemistry, 1934. (See also *Current Biography, 1941*.)

CUMULATED AUTHOR INDEX

An author index to the volumes of *Representative American Speeches* for the years 1937-1938 through 1949-1950. The date following the title of each speech indicates the volume in which it appears.

641

20702